William Chatterton Couplant

Philosophy of the Unconscious

Vol. III.

William Chatterton Couplant

Philosophy of the Unconscious
Vol. III.

ISBN/EAN: 9783337078126

Printed in Europe, USA, Canada, Australia, Japan

Cover: Foto ©Thomas Meinert / pixelio.de

More available books at **www.hansebooks.com**

PHILOSOPHY

OF

THE UNCONSCIOUS.

BY

EDUARD VON HARTMANN.

SPECULATIVE RESULTS ACCORDING TO THE INDUCTIVE METHOD OF PHYSICAL SCIENCE.

Authorised Translation

BY

WILLIAM CHATTERTON COUPLAND, M.A. B.Sc.

IN THREE VOLUMES.

VOL. III.

LONDON:
TRÜBNER & CO., LUDGATE HILL.
1884.

Ballantyne Press
BALLANTYNE, HANSON AND CO.
EDINBURGH AND LONDON

CONTENTS OF VOL. III.

METAPHYSIC OF THE UNCONSCIOUS—(*continued*).

APPENDIX.

PHILOSOPHY OF THE UNCONSCIOUS.

METAPHYSIC OF THE UNCONSCIOUS—Continued.

XIII.

THE IRRATIONALITY OF VOLITION AND THE MISERY OF EXISTENCE.

NATURE OF THE PROBLEM.

THE object of this chapter is to inquire whether the *being* or the *non-being* of this present world deserves the preference. And here, more than at any other stage of our inquiry, must we crave the reader's indulgence, since a tolerably exhaustive treatment of the subject would require a book to itself. In this place our exposition must be rather of the nature of an episode, both on external grounds and more particularly because the result of this inquiry, although important for the clearing up of the ultimate principles of Philosophy, has no direct bearing on the main theme of the work as proclaimed in its title, "The Unconscious." Nevertheless, in a short examination, presenting many new points of view, I hope to afford suggestions even to the opponents of the opinions here advanced, which may to a certain extent compensate them for the perusal of this digression.

If we glance at the judgments of the greatest minds of

all ages, we find those, who have at all found occasion to express their opinion on the subject, pronouncing the condemnation of life in very decided terms.

Plato says in the "Apology": "Now, if death is without all sensation, a dreamless sleep, as it were, it would be indeed a wonderful *gain*. For I think if any one selected a night in which he had slept so soundly as to have had no dream, and then compared this night with the other nights and days of his life, and after serious consideration declared how many days and nights he had spent better and more pleasantly than this one, that not merely an ordinary mortal, but the great king of Persia himself, would find these but few in number as compared with all his other days and nights." More clearly and picturesquely it would hardly be possible to state the advantage which, on the average, non-being possesses over being.

Kant says (Werke, vii. p. 381): "One must indeed make an ill reckoning of the worth of the journey (of life) if one can still wish that it should last longer than it actually does, for that would only be a prolongation *of a perpetual contest with sheer hardships*." Page 393, he calls life "a trial-time, wherein most succumb, and in which even the best *does not rejoice in his life*."

Fichte declares the natural world to be the very worst that can be, and is himself only consoled by the belief in the possibility of a preferment to the blessedness of a supersensible world through the medium of pure thought. He says (Werke, v. pp. 408–409): "Courageously men betake themselves to the chase after felicity, heartily appropriating and fondly devoting themselves to the first best object that pleases them and that promises to repay their efforts. But as soon as they withdraw into themselves and ask themselves, 'Am I now happy?' the reply comes distinctly from the depth of their soul, 'Oh, no; thou art still just as empty and destitute as before!' Convinced that this is a true deliverance, they imagine that they have failed only in the choice of their object, and throw themselves upon another. This, too, will just as little content them as the first; *no object beneath the sun and moon will satisfy them.* . . . Thus they pine and fret their life through; in every situation in which they find themselves, thinking if it were only *different* how much *better* their lot would be, and yet, after it has changed, finding themselves no better off than before; at every spot at which they stand, supposing if they could only reach yon height their uneasiness would cease, yet finding again, even on the height, their old woe. . . . Perhaps they even resign the hope of satisfaction in this earthly life, but accept in compensation a certain traditional doctrine concerning a blessedness beyond the grave. In what a deplorable illusion are they caught! Quite certainly, indeed, lies blessedness also beyond the grave for him for whom it has already begun on this side; through the mere interment, however, one does not enter into blessedness; and they will in the future life, and in the infinite series of all future lives, just as vainly seek blessedness as they have sought it in the present life, if they seek it in anything else than in that which already encircles them so closely here that it can never be brought nearer to them in endless time, in the Eternal.—Thus, then, errs the poor offspring of eternity, thrust out of his paternal abode, always surrounded by his celestial heritage, which his timid hand fears only to touch, inconstant, and roaming in the waste, endeavouring in vain to settle; fortunately, through the speedy ruin of all his habitations, reminded that he will nowhere find rest but in his father's house."

Schelling says (Werke, i. 7, p. 399): "Hence the veil of sadness that is spread over all Nature, the deep indestructible melancholy of all life." He has, moreover (Werke, i. 10, pp. 266–268), a very beautiful passage which should be read in its entirety; here I can only quote a few fragments: "Certainly it is a painful way the Being which lives in Nature traverses in his passage through it; to that the line of sorrow, traced on the countenance of all

Nature, on the face of the animal world testifies. . . . But this *misfortune of existence* is hereby annulled that it is accepted and felt as non-existence, in that man seeks to bear up in the greatest possible freedom from it. . . . Who will trouble himself about the common and ordinary mischances of a transitory life that has apprehended *the pain of universal existence* and the great fate of the whole?" "Anguish is the fundamental feeling of every living creature" (i. 8, 322). "Pain is something universal and necessary in all life. . . . All pain only comes from being" (i. 8, 335). "The unrest of unceasing willing and desiring, by which every creature is goaded, is in itself unblessedness" (ii. 1, 473; comp. also i. 8, 235–236; ii. 1, 556, 557, 560).

I shall content myself with these citations; a few more will be found in Schopenhauer's "World as Will and Idea," ii. chap. 46.

But what do such subjective expressions of opinion without annexed reasons prove? Must we not rather mistrust them *because* they proceed from eminent intelligences, affected by that melancholy sadness which is the inheritance of almost all genius, because they do not feel at home in the world of their inferiors? (Comp. Aristotle, Prob. 30, 1.) Certainly the worth of the world must be measured by its own standard, not by that of the genius. Let us look, therefore, further.

Imagine some one who is no genius, but a man with the best general culture of his time, endowed with all the other good things of an enviable lot, in the most vigorous years of manhood, who is fully conscious of the advantage which he enjoys over the lower orders in the uncivilised nations and over his fellows of ruder ages, and who by no means envies those above him, who are tormented by all sorts of discomforts spared to himself—a man who is neither exhausted and rendered *blasé* by immoderate pleasure, nor has ever been crushed by exceptional strokes of fate.

Let us imagine Death to draw nigh this man and say, "Thy life-period is run out, and at this hour thou art on the brink of annihilation; but it depends on thy present voluntary decision, once again, precisely in the same way, to go through thy now closed life with complete oblivion of all that has passed. Now choose!"

I question whether the man would prefer the repetition of the past performance to non-existence, if his mind be free from fear, and calm, and if he has not altogether lived so thoughtlessly, without all self-reflection, that, in his inability to offer a summary criticism of the experiences of his life, he does but give expression in his answer merely to the instinct of the desire of living at all cost, or allows his judgment to be thereby too much biassed. How much more, however, now must this man prefer non-being to a re-entrance into life, which offers him not the favourable conditions his past life offered, but, on the contrary, leaves it perfectly to chance into what new life-conditions he enters, which thus offers him, with a possibility bordering on certainty, worse conditions than those which he first disdained!

In the situation of this man, however, the Unconscious would find itself at every moment of a new birth, if it really possessed an option.

But in this example, likewise, the reproach attached to the opinions of genius is not to be avoided, that we have interrogated an intelligence far above the average, but that, as each single phenomenon must be judged by its own standard, the world as a whole can only be judged with approximate correctness if the judgment is passed according to the *average standard* of all the several phenomena. The above example, however, if it is correct in itself, proves that *this* stage of intelligence already condemns the phenomenon by which it is supported, of which it is indisputably the sole competent tribunal, whilst, on the contrary, the error only consists in this, that it regards itself as competent to condemn *also what is below it*, whilst this likewise must be measured by its own standard.

This error is, however, not to be wondered at, for it also quite universally occurs where the intelligence does not stand so high as to condemn the appearance by which *it* is supported. Let any one, *e.g.*, ask a woodcutter, or a Hottentot, or an orang-outang whether he would prefer annihilation or new birth in a rhinoceros or a louse. They would probably all prefer annihilation, but, nevertheless, prefer the repetition of their own life to annihilation, precisely as the rhinoceros and the louse would prefer a repetition of their life to annihilation.

This error arises, however, from this, that the interrogated at the moment of decision projects himself with *his present* intelligence into the life of the lower phase, when he of course must find it unendurable, and forgets that then at the lower stage also only the intelligence of this lower stage would be at his command for judging.

There remains, then, in fact, nothing for it but to judge every phenomenal stage of the Unconscious by its own standard, and then to draw from all these special judgments the algebraic sum, which then at the same time represents a real unconscious unity, namely, the totality of all the subjective determinations of feeling posited in the All-one Being. Every judgment from an alien standpoint yields unavailable results; for every being is just as happy as it feels itself to be, not as *I should* feel in its place with *my* intelligence, since this is an unreal supposition.

Pain and pleasure *are* only so far as they are *felt*; they have thus no reality at all except *in the sentient subject*; consequently an objective reality does not *directly* appertain to them, but only in virtue of the objective reality of the subject in which they exist, *i.e.*, their reality is immediately a *subjective* one, and only *so far as* they have a subjective reality have they *indirectly* also an objective one. It follows from this that there is no other direct measure of the reality of sensation than the subjective, and accordingly that an illusion or untruth of *feeling as such* is impossible.

But undoubtedly feeling may be untrue *so far* as the *ideas* are untrue by which it is aroused, but then the delusion indeed always lies in the idea of the object, but the feeling itself, *no matter* whether it *rests* on a real basis or on an *illusion*, is always *equally true* and *equally entitled* to be taken account of in the sum total.

If, now, the difference in the sentence which the intelligence of the louse would pass on its life and that which my intelligence passes on my life depends solely on this, that the louse is entangled in illusions which I do not share, and that these illusions afford it an excess of felt, thus real felicity, which causes it to prefer its life to non-existence, manifestly the louse would be right and I wrong. The decision, however, is not so simple; for beside this source of error on my side there remain further sources of error in the answer of the louse, which corrupt its judgment, as the former mine — to wit, although undoubtedly the life-value of every being can only be considered according to its own subjective standard—and here illusion is as good as truth—yet it is by no means asserted that every being draws the *correct* algebraic sum from all the affections of its life, or, in other words, that *its collective judgment* on its own life is a correct one in respect of its subjective experience. Quite apart from the degree of intelligence necessary for the pronunciation of such a summary judgment, there remains, in the first place, the possibility of errors of memory and combination; and secondly, of a *bias of the judgment by the will and unconscious feeling.*

If we may assume that the former errors might be got rid of in the judgment of a large number of individuals, the latter source of error, on the contrary, weighs so much the heavier. Whoever knows how powerful is the unconscious bias of thought and judgment by the will, by instincts and feelings, will immediately allow the great importance of the errors thereby rendered possible. Let any one reflect how easily unpleasant impressions are blotted out of the mind and how pleasant ones remain, so that even an event or adventure disagreeable enough in reality appears in memory in the most charming light (*juvat meminisse malorum*); in consequence of this the recapitulating memory must attain to a far more favourable summing up of the pleasure-content of personal life than a review of the pleasure and pain actually felt in the course of life undistorted by the glasses of memory would yield. What memory is unable to accomplish in the way of hushing up really felt pain, the instinct of hope most certainly accomplishes for future feeling (comp. below No. 12), and the balance of the past will be involuntarily falsified by all younger persons by the introduction of the idea of a future which is purged by hope of the main causes of past pain without the causes of pain hereafter to be added being taken into account. Thus it is not the true life as it *actually* was and will be, but as it is exhibited to the uncritical eye in the embellishing mirror of memory and in the deceptive roseate hue of hope that is used for drawing the balance between the sum of pleasure and the sum of pain; and hence it is no wonder if a result appears to be yielded which little enough agrees with reality.

Let one consider, further, that the foolish vanity of man goes so far as to prefer to seem rather than to be not merely well but also happy, so that every one carefully hides where the shoe pinches, and tries to make a show of opulence, contentment, and happiness which he does not at all possess. This source of error falsifies the sentence that one passes on others according to what they express and reveal of the balance of pleasure and pain of their life, just as the two just-named sources of error the judgment on their own part. If one, however, judges according to what other people are wont to declare concerning the sum of happiness of their whole life, it is clear that we have here to deal with the *product* of the two mentioned errors. One already sees from this with what caution we must accept the judgment of mankind on their own felicity.

Lastly, when we consider, as is *a priori* to be expected, that the same unconscious will which has created beings with these instincts and passions will also through these instincts and passions influence conscious thinking in the direction of the same life-impulse, we should rather only wonder how the instinctive love of life should come to be able in consciousness to condemn this same life; for the same Unconscious which wills life, and, moreover, for its quite special ends wills just *this* life in spite of its wretchedness, will certainly not omit to fit out the creatures of life with just as many illusions as they need, in order not merely to make life supportable, but also to leave over enough love of life, elasticity, and freshness for the life-tasks to be accomplished by them and claiming all their energy, and thus to cozen them concerning the misery of their existence.

In this sense Jean Paul well says: "We do not love life because it is beautiful, but because we must love it; and hence it happens that we often draw the inverted conclusion: since we love life, it must be beautiful." What is here called love to life is nothing else but the instinctive impulse of self-preservation, the *conditio sine qua non* of individuation, the negative expression of which is the avoidance and warding off of disturbances, and in the highest degree the fear of death, of which mention has been made at the beginning of Sect. B. Chap. i. Death in itself is no evil at all, for the *pain* connected with it falls indeed still into *life*, and would not be *more* feared than the same pain in sickness, *if* the cessation of individual existence were *not* bound up with it, which is *not* felt, thus cannot be any evil at all. As little then as the fear of death can be understood otherwise than from the blind instinct of self-preservation, so little the love of life. As is the case in general with the fear of death and the love of life, so in particular in many phases of life, which instinctive impulse spurs us to retain and eagerly to experience, in consequence of which our judgment on the algebraic sum of the enjoyments and pains special to this phase is corrupted and the impression of the experience just made glossed over by the new deceitful hope. This is the case with all the properly impelling passions, hunger, love, honour, avarice, &c.

It must now be inquired here, in respect of the different impulses and aims of life, how far instinct and passion themselves cause a corruption of the judgment with regard to the total enjoyment or pain endured through the particular aim; but this would be a very difficult problem, because the assent of every reader would depend on this, that in judging of his previous judgment he perfectly emancipate himself in each of these directions from the corrupting influence of impulse and passion, which is hardly to be expected; for a conscientious life-long self-observation is scarcely able to effect that. Apart from the small prospect of success which this effort by its very nature would offer, there would be also an external inconvenience connected with it. This consideration, namely, would by no means dispense us from the task of afterwards subjecting all those feelings to a criticism which, in spite of their complete reality, rest on illusions, and *which therefore are destroyed along with the destruction of these illusions with advancing conscious intelligence.*

This inquiry we cannot be spared, because all progress has in view the increase of conscious intelligence.

The lower animals and plants, since the commencement of organic life, have been more and more displaced by higher ones—the higher animals by man,—and humanity will in time attain, on the average, a pitch of intelligence and cosmic intuition which at present only a cultured few have reached.

The question how far the feelings rest on illusions is thus of the highest importance for the decision of our problem, since what *will become* of the world, whither it is tending, is manifestly of far greater importance for the estimation of its value than the provisional stage of development at which it may accidentally happen to be.

We should thus, then, have to consider the same impulses and phases of life once more under this second point of view, and it is evident that here many repetitions must occur, partly not to disturb the understanding, partly because in the concrete case the two points of view are so intimately connected that it often appears hardly possible strictly to separate them. I therefore prefer to pursue the consideration from both points of view simultaneously.

In many cases where the reader might be disinclined to admit that the ordinary theoretical *assumption* of a preponderating enjoyment rests on an *error*, *i.e.*, on a corruption of the *judgment* by impulse or by other sources of error, he would hardly refuse to allow that the preponderating *enjoyment itself* supposed by him, *if* it really exists, still depends on an *illusion*, and is accordingly rendered questionable by the thorough destruction of the illusion. Both, however, come, for the object of our inquiry, almost to the same thing; for if it is true that with the progressive intelligence of the world the illusions of existence also must be more and more undermined, until finally all is recognised as "vanity of vanities," the condition of the world would become ever more unhappy the more it approaches the goal of its evolution, whence we should conclude that it would have been more rational to prevent the development of the world the earlier the better, best of all to suppress its arising at the moment of its origin.

Before all things, however, I beg the reader, in the following inquiries, to keep continually in view that the above-stated sources of error (pp. 7–9) in the estimate of life constantly tend to preoccupy and mislead his judgment in favour of an over-estimate of pleasure and under-estimate of displeasure, and that the views and opinions on life which he brings with him to this philosophical inquiry are already themselves results that are thoroughly saturated by the influence of the sources of error named, and thus, as imported prejudices, oppose the unprejudiced consideration of the actual facts.

First Stage of the Illusion.

Happiness is considered as having been actually attained at the present stage of the world's development, accordingly attainable by the individual of to-day in his earthly life.

1. *Criticism of Schopenhauer's Theory of the Negative Character of Pleasure.*—I must in this inquiry presuppose an acquaintance with the so-called Pessimism of Schopenhauer (see "World as Will and Idea," vol. i. §§ 56–59, vol. ii. chap. xlvi.; "Parerga," 2d ed., vol. i. pp. 430–439, and vol. ii. chaps. xi. and xii.), and entreat the perusal of the sections indicated in the above order,—a request for which the reader hitherto unacquainted with Schopenhauer's piquant style will certainly be obliged to me. How far I differ from the views there expounded will be sufficiently evident from what has been previously said. The attempted proof ("Welt als Wille und Vorstellung," 3 Aufl. Bd. ii. S. 667–688) that this world is the worst of all possible ones is a manifest sophism; everywhere else Schopenhauer himself tries to maintain and prove nothing further than that the existence of this world is worse than its non-existence, and this assertion I hold to be correct. The word Pessimism is thus an *inappropriate* imitation of the word Optimism.—Further, futile as I must regard the attempts of Leibniz to demonstrate out of existence the misery of the world in order to save the Supreme Wisdom and the best of all possible worlds, as little can I approve that Schopenhauer overlooks so much the wisdom of the world's arrangements in dwelling on its misery, and, although he cannot quite deny it, that he leaves it as far as possible unnoticed and makes light of it.—Then I keep clear of the notion of guilt which Schopenhauer imports into the

creation. I have frequently expressed myself against a transcendent use of ethical conceptions, because these have a meaning only for conscious individuals in their intercourse with one another. Only this can I conclude with Schopenhauer from the misery of existence, that the creation owes its first origin to an *irrational* act, *i.e.*, to such an one in which reason has had no part, therefore to the *mere groundless will*.—Lastly, however, I have still to signalise Schopenhauer's wrong use of the concept of Negation. As Leibniz endeavours to attribute to pain an exclusively negative character, so Schopenhauer to pleasure; not, indeed, altogether in the privative sense of Leibniz, but in such a way that pain alone is said to arise *directly*, but pleasure *only* to become possible *indirectly*, through abolition or diminution of pain. Now I do not in the least intend to dispute that every removal or diminution of a pain is a pleasure, but not every pleasure is a removal or diminution of pain, and, conversely, it just as much holds good that the removal or diminution of pleasure is a displeasure.

Undoubtedly a reservation must be made which tells in favour of pain—to wit, both pleasure and pain attack the nervous system, and thereby produce a kind of fatigue, which, with the highest degree of pleasure, may become fatal atony. Hence results a need increasing with the duration and the degree of feeling, *i.e.*, a conscious or unconscious will, to cause the cessation or remission of feeling to occur. With displeasure this need, springing from the attack on the nerves, *co-operates* with the direct aversion to the endurance of a pain; with pleasure, on the contrary, it *opposes* the direct desire for the retention of pleasure, and always diminishes the same; nay, it can finally overcome it. (Think of exhaustion in sexual gratification.) Pain is (apart from complete blunting of the nerves by great pain) the more painful, pleasure the more indifferent and cloying, the longer it lasts.

Here lurks already the first reason why, with a perfectly

fair balance for the measurement of direct pleasure and displeasure in the world, the scale would turn in favour of pain through the additional nervous affection. But further, while through this additional need of remission in respect of every enduring feeling, the indirect pleasure, *i.e.*, that arising through cessation of a pleasure, relatively diminishes, it appears even *a priori* that a proportionately much larger part of pleasure than of pain in the world points to an *indirect* origin from the remission of its contrary. But now, since, as will appear from this whole inquiry, it is true that, on the whole, there is far more pain than pleasure in the world, it is no wonder that, in point of fact, through the remission of this pain, by far the largest part of all the pleasure which one meets with in the world finds it sufficient explanation, and but little pleasure remains whose origin is immediate.

Accordingly for *practical purposes* it comes pretty much to what Schopenhauer asserts, namely, that pleasure has an indirect origin, and pain a direct. This can, however, not affect the *principle* of the matter, for it is and remains indisputable that there is also pleasure which does *not* arise through remission of a pain, but is positively raised above the indifference-point of sensation. Let any one think of the enjoyments of agreeable taste and of those of art and science, which latter, since they did not fit into his theory of the negative character of pleasure, Schopenhauer prudently rejected and treated as painless delight of the intellect liberated from the will, as if the intellect liberated from the will could still *enjoy*, or as if there could be a *pleasurable sensation* without a *will* in whose satisfaction it consists! If we cannot avoid claiming relish, the sexual pleasures taken as purely physical and apart from their metaphysical relations, and the enjoyments of art and science as *pleasurable sensations;* if we must grant that these, without a previous pain, without previously sinking below the indifference-point or zero-point of sensation, could positively rise above it; lastly, if we keep firm hold of our principle that pleasure only consists in the satisfaction of a desire, Schopenhauer's assertion must necessarily be false that pleasure is *only* a remission or cessation of pain.

But now he says, in proof of his theory, the will is, as long as it exists, unsatisfied, for otherwise it would exist no longer; the unsatisfied will, however, is want, need, displeasure. If now it is satisfied, this displeasure is abolished, and therein consists the satisfaction or pleasure; another there is not. This argument appears irrefutable, and yet its consequence is, as shown, in contradiction with experience. The conciliation easily results when one more closely regards the enjoyment of agreeable taste or an art-pleasure, and asks oneself where then the will lurks that, as long as it is unsatisfied, is displeasure. There is neither a displeasure nor an unsatisfied existing will to be found. There remains nothing for it then but to assume that the will is only evoked at the same moment at which it is also satisfied, so that there exists no time for its unsatisfied existence. It is in accordance with this that it is indeed one and the same thing what influences (excites) the will and what satisfies it, as one may directly convince oneself when one comes upon a disagreeable morsel among pleasant tastes, or when faulty dissonances occur in a piece of music; then, namely, the will is indeed set in motion (stimulated), but it is not satisfied, and now at once the displeasure is there. Here, in the case of the will, which, on arising, immediately meets with the satisfaction again annihilating it, it is clear that the pleasure of satisfaction is certainly something positive, not issuing directly and alone from the lessening of pain, that rather even the *indirect pleasure*, presenting itself on the diminution of the pain, must be understood as direct satisfaction *of the* will to get rid of the pain. Had Schopenhauer not brought with him to this inquiry the preconceived opinion of the enjoyment of the intellect independently of will, he would doubtless have perceived these relations, and would not have stopped at his conception of the negative character of pleasure.

All that, however, would perhaps not have sufficed to establish this conviction in him, if there had not been one thing more in his excuse. We have seen (Sect. C. Chap. iii. vol. ii. pp. 94–96) that the non-satisfaction of the will must indeed by its nature always be conscious; satisfaction, however, by no means directly, but *only then*, when the conscious understanding attains consciousness by the *comparison of opposite experiences;* that satisfaction also is *dependent on external circumstances*, and is anything but a direct and infallible consequence of the will. I beg that the examples there quoted may be read through once more in order to save repetition at this place.

It deserves particular notice that in the whole vegetable kingdom and the lower stages of the animal kingdom we cannot suppose the degree of consciousness requisite for the comparison of experiences and recognition of their dependence on external causes, that accordingly we must not deem these organisms capable of any apperception of will-satisfaction, thus of any sensation of pleasure, whilst pain and displeasure thrust themselves even on the dullest consciousness with pitiless necessity. But even higher animals must in general be capable of far fewer satisfactions of will than one is usually inclined to assume according to the analogy of man. As concerns man himself, even in him, since of course not every man at every moment of a petty satisfaction of will is compelled to draw comparisons with opposite experiences, in general only such satisfactions of will become conscious, *i.e.*, felt as pleasure, whose accompanying circumstances direct the man, without his assistance, to the contrast of opposite experiences, *e.g.*, unusual, rare satisfactions, either in kind or degree, or such as, through the association of ideas, recall opposite experiences, whether of others or of one's self.

All satisfactions of will that have become habit and rule become ever less felt as such, *i.e.*, as pleasure, the less they permit the memory of opposite experiences to arise. It is clear that by far the larger part (not intensively but numerically) of the satisfactions of the will is thereby lost to consciousness, whilst the non-satisfactions are felt uncurtailed. Wherefore Schopenhauer says, quite correctly ("Welt als Wille und Vorstellung," 3 Aufl. Bd. ii. S. 657): "We feel the wish as we feel hunger and thirst; as soon, however, as it is fulfilled, it is with it as with the enjoyed morsel, that ceases to be for our feeling at the moment that it is swallowed. Pleasures and joys we miss painfully as soon as they cease; but pains, even when they disappear after long presence, are not immediately missed, but their absence has to be brought home to us by means of reflection. In the degree in which enjoyments increase, the receptivity for them diminishes; the accustomed is no longer felt as enjoyment. For that reason, however, the receptivity for suffering increases; *for the omission of the customary is painfully felt.*"—(Parerga, 2 Aufl. Bd. ii. S. 312): "As we *do not feel* the health of our whole body, but only the little part where the shoe pinches us, so also we do not think of all our perfectly satisfactory affairs, but of some insignificant trifle that vexes us." Untrue, however, is it when he adds: "On this depends the negative character, often emphasised by me, of well-being and happiness, in contrast to the positive character of pain." Undoubtedly there exists in the apperception of pleasure and pain a certain justification of these conceptions, so far as pain becomes conscious by itself alone, but pleasure only in contrast to the idea of pain. Undoubtedly the effects are frequently the same *as if* the theory of Schopenhauer of the negative character of pleasure were correct, but yet there is between both a world-wide difference, and the principle remains untouched that pleasure and pain are in general distinguished as the mathematical positive and negative, *i.e.*, that it is indifferent which sign one gives to the one, which to the other.

It has, again, been very clearly shown how infinitely

more fruitful than mere criticism is reflection on the reasons by which great men have been led to frame false hypotheses. While, namely, we found the hypothesis of the negative character of pleasure just as incorrect as that of Leibniz on the negativity of evil, we have at the same time apprehended three moments, each of which falls into one scale in favour of pain, and which in combination practically yield almost the same result as the theory of Schopenhauer. They are—(1.) the stimulation and fatigue of the nerves, and the need thence arising of the cessation of enjoyment, as of pain; (2.) the necessity of regarding all pleasure as *indirect* which only arises through cessation or remission of a displeasure, but not through instantaneous satisfaction of a will at the moment of the excitation of the same; (3.) the difficulties which oppose the apperception of the satisfaction of will, whilst displeasure *eo ipso* produces consciousness;—we may add: (4) the brief duration of the satisfaction, which is little more than a passing moment, whilst the non-satisfaction lasts as long as the actual will, thus, as there is hardly an instant when an actual will was not present, is, so to speak, eternal, and only always limited by the satisfaction which hope affords.

The first point depends on the nature of organic life, in particular of the nervous functions, as foundation of consciousness; the last three points follow immediately from the nature of the will itself. The latter undoubtedly hold good, therefore, not merely for our world, but for every world that is at all possible as objective form of the will. But the first point will also hold good wherever there is question of a balance between pleasure and displeasure; for since pleasure can only be obtained through the contrast with displeasure in a consciousness already highly developed, but a consciousness again presupposes individuation with the help of matter or its analogue, so also in every other world conceivable as objectified will the law of fatigue and the hebetation of pleasure thence arising will hold good in this analogue of matter. We may accordingly regard *all four* points as necessary consequences of the nature of the will in respect to pleasure and pain, and have to see in them the eternal barriers which the Unconscious must encounter in every attempt at creation, and which render it *a priori* impossible to fashion a world in which pain should be outweighed by pleasure. But these four points have also the further value of being able to serve in the progress of our *a posteriori* inquiries in every special subject of consideration as an objective corrective of instinctive prejudice, just as the former statement of the most important subjective sources of error (pp. 7–8) serves as a subjective corrective. I beg the reader, therefore, to keep the one as the other constantly in view.

We must still pay some attention to the second of the four points. If we look for examples of such pleasure-sensations as only consist in a cessation or remission of pain, we must carefully beware lest we do not introduce at the same time cases in which pleasure is enhanced by an additional satisfaction of will, as, *e.g.*, the relish of food and the cooling refreshment of drink add to the satisfaction of hunger and thirst, the physical sexual enjoyment to the stilling of the longings of love. Pure examples in the sensuous sphere are a subsiding toothache; in the intellectual, the recovery of a friend from a dangerous illness. When we consider such pure examples, no one will any longer doubt that the pleasure arising through cessation of pain is very much *less* than was that pain, just as conversely pain arising through the cessation of a pleasure is far less than that pleasure.

This phenomenon might at the first blush surprise us, since we regard the intensity of feeling as dependent only on the degree of change, but not on the relation of the beginning or end of the change to the indifference-point of the sensation. However, in my opinion, it is explained in the case of the ceasing displeasure by the subsequent vexation, detracting from the pleasure, that one has had so long to endure the pain; one feels less bound to return thanks, as it were, to one's fate for the liberation from the pain than entitled to grumble and demand satisfaction for the infliction of the pain, because the whole movement took place below the point of indifference, whereas in the ceasing pleasure the blunting effect of fatigue, renders more indifferent to the termination of the enjoyment. According to this explanation, that lessening of the pleasure in proportion to the pain, in whose cessation it consists, only occurs if the circumstance that the whole movement has taken place below the zero of sensation also actually falls into consciousness. The less the consciousness of the interested person places the movement below the zero-point of sensation, the more as a matter of fact does the pleasure become equal in degree to the displeasure in the cessation of which it consists. This is least possible with sensuous pain; hence nobody would consent to be stretched on the rack in order to enjoy the pleasure of the cessation of the pain. In the intellectual sphere, however, the contest with distress and the rejoicing over every attained victory securing the immediate future is the proof of it. As soon as mankind makes clear to itself that this delight is similarly related to the preceding uneasiness as the remission of pains to the tortures of the rack, and that this movement, equally with that, falls wholly below the zero-point of sensation, so soon will it too enjoy those victories over want as little as the racked enjoy the relaxation of the cords.

What now-a-days is called the spectre of the poverty of the masses is nothing but this dawning consciousness that the struggle with want, care and its alleviation lies entirely on the negative (pain) side of the zero-point of sensation, whilst formerly, when the poverty of the masses was ten times greater, this consciousness was wanting, and the people endured their poverty as sent from God. Another proof how progressive intelligence makes man unhappy.

This contest of man with want is, however, only one example; if we look round at the possible joys of the world, we shall very soon become aware that, with the exception of the physically sensuous, the æsthetic and the scientific enjoyments, there is hardly a happiness to be perceived which did not depend on the liberation from a preceding displeasure. Quite specially, however, does this hold for great and vivid joys. Voltaire says, "Il n'est de vrais plaisirs qu'avec de vrais besoins."

Closely connected with this is the interesting question whether in general pleasure can be a countervailing equivalent for pain, and what *coefficient* or exponent must be assigned to a degree of pleasure to counterbalance for consciousness an equal degree of pain. Schopenhauer, citing the verse of Petrarch, "Mille piacer' non vagliono un tormento (a thousand pleasures are not worth one pain,)" makes the eccentric assertion that altogether a pain can never be balanced by any degree of pleasure; that therefore a world in which pain can occur at all is, under all circumstances, with ever so much preponderating happiness, worse than none. This view could hardly be supported; whether, however, there do not lie in it a core of truth so far as the co-efficient necessary for equivalence does not at all need to be = 1, as is usually assumed, that were well worthy of consideration.

If I have the choice either of not at all hearing, or of hearing first for five minutes discords and then for five minutes a fine piece of music; if I have the choice either not to smell at all, or to smell first a stench and then a perfume; if I have the choice either not to taste, or to taste first something disagreeable and then something agreeable, I shall in all the cases decide for the non-hearing, non-smelling, and non-tasting, even if the successive homogeneous painful and pleasurable sensations appear to me to be equal in degree, although it would certainly be very difficult to ascertain the equality of the degree.

Hence I conclude that the pleasure must be *perceptibly*

greater in degree than a pain of like kind, if they are to be equivalent in consciousness, so that one determines their combination as equal to the zero of sensation and prefers it to the latter on a small enhancement of the pleasure or lowering of the pain. For the rest, this coefficient probably fluctuates with different individuals within certain limits, and only its *mean* amount should be greater than 1.

On the causes underlying this remarkable phenomenon I venture to make no supposition. This much is certain, that, if the fact is correct, this circumstance also tells against a preponderance of happiness in the world, for suppose the case that even the sum of pleasure and pain objectively taken were equal, yet their combination subjectively would stand *below* the zero-point, as the combination of a stench and a fragrance is below zero. The world accordingly resembles a money-lottery: the appointed pains one must pay in in full, but the gains one receives only with a deduction, which answers to the difference between the constant coefficient of the pleasure-and-pain equation and 1. Were this remarkable inequality in value of pleasure and pain, which seems to me highly probable, confirmed on other sides, it should be added to the above four points as a fifth. In this sense Schopenhauer says (Parerga, ii. 313): "It is in harmony with this that we commonly find joys far below, pains far above our expectation." (P. 321): "Deserving of envy is no one, of commiseration numberless." (W. a. W. u. V., ii. 658): "Before one declares with such confidence that life is a desirable or thankworthy good, let any one calmly compare the sum of possible delight which a human being may enjoy in his life with the sum of possible suffering which may afflict him in his life. I believe the balance will not be difficult to strike."

It is now our task to inquire whether in the life of the *individual* the sum of pleasure or pain preponderates, and whether in the individual as such the conditions are given for attaining, under the most favourable circumstances conceivable in one's life, an excess of pleasure over pain. As the field to be viewed is too vast for a simultaneous survey, a solution will be facilitated by considering separately the sum of pleasure and pain according to the main directions of life. But during the future considerations the reader must always keep in mind these premised general observations, since the circumstances mentioned are continually acting as essentially limiting co-efficients of pleasure, whilst, on the contrary, they either leave the pain unaffected or even increase it.

2. *Health, Youth, Freedom, and a Competence as Conditions of the Zero-point of Feeling, and Contentment.*—The states mentioned are mostly claimed as the highest goods of life, and not without reason; nevertheless they fail to afford positive pleasure, save when they have just arisen by transition from the opposite states of pain. During their undisturbed continuance, however, they represent only the zero-mark of sensation, and by no means a positive elevation above it; the building-ground on which the expected enjoyments of life are to be erected. It is in accordance with this that the persistence of the states awakes as little a feeling of pleasure as of pain, since at the zero-point in general there is nothing to be felt, but that every fall from this level into sickness, old age, bondage, and distress is painfully felt. These goods have thus, in fact, the purely privative character that Leibniz would ascribe to evil: they are the privation of age, sickness, servitude, and distress, and are intrinsically incapable of being raised above the zero-point of sensation on the side of pleasure, thus incapable of producing a pleasure, unless by remission of an antecedent pain, even if it consist only of an imaginary fear or care.

In health all this is quite self-evident; nobody feels a limb except when he is ill; only the nervous feels that he has nerves; only he who has diseased eyes that he has those organs: the healthy, however, perceives only by sight and touch that he has a body. With freedom it is just the same. Nobody feels if he himself determines his actions, for this is the self-evident natural condition, but undoubtedly he feels painfully all external constraint, every invasion of his self-determination, as it were, as an injury of the first and most original law of Nature, that he shares with every animal, with every atomic force.

Youth is, in the first place, the time of life in which alone perfect health and an unimpeded use of the body and mind is found, whilst with age its infirmities also make their appearance, which are felt painfully enough. But, in the second place, youth alone, a direct consequence of the unimpeded use of the body and mind, possesses *the full capacity of enjoyment*, whilst in age undoubtedly all the burdens, inconveniences, vexation, disagreeables, and torments make themselves doubly sensible, but the faculty for enjoyment diminishes more and more. This capacity for enjoyment has, however, still only the value of the level; it is only *capacity, i.e., possibility* (not reality) of enjoyment. What is the good, however, of the best teeth, if one has nothing to bite with them?

Finally, also, the competency or assurance against want and privation cannot be regarded as a positive gain or enjoyment, but only as the *conditio sine qua non* of bare life, which has to wait for its enjoyable fulfilment. To endure hunger, thirst, frost, heat, or damp is painful; protection from these evils by needful dwelling, clothing, and food cannot be called positive good (enjoyment in eating does not belong to this category). Were, namely, the bare life assured in its conditions of existence already a positive good, mere existence in itself must fill and satisfy us. The contrary is the case: the assured existence is a torment, unless a filling up of the same is added. This torment, which is expressed in ennui, may be so insupportable that even pains and ills are welcome to escape it.

The most usual filling of life is *work*. There can be no doubt that work for him who must work is an evil, be it in its consequences for himself, as for humanity and the advancing evolution, ever so rich in blessing; for nobody works who is not compelled, *i.e.*, who does not take work upon himself as the less of two evils—whether the greater evil be want, the torment of ambition, or even mere ennui—or who had not the intention through undertaking this evil to purchase for himself greater positive good (*e.g.*, the satisfaction in rendering life more pleasant for himself and those dear to him, or for the value of the performances produced *by means of* work). All that can be said on the value of work reduces itself either to economical advantages (with which we shall deal later on), or to the avoidance of greater evils (idleness is the beginning of all vices); and the utmost that man can attain to is, "that he should rejoice in his own works, for that is his portion," *i.e.*, that he should become habituated to bear the inevitable as well as possible, as the cart-horse at last draws the cart with tolerable good-humour. At work man consoles himself with the prospect of leisure, and in leisure we have to console ourselves with the thought of work. Thus the alternate play of leisure and work comes to this, that the sick turns himself in his bed to get out of his uncomfortable position, but soon finds the new position just as uncomfortable, and so turns back again.

As a rule, work is the price for a secure existence. It is not enough, therefore, that the assured existence represent in itself no positive good, but only the zero-point of sensation; this purely privative good must *still be purchased by pain*, in contrast to health and youth, which one only obtains as gifts. And how great is often the pain which is inflicted on the poor by work! I am not thinking of the labour of slaves, but of the labour of the operatives of our large towns. "At the age of five to enter a cotton-mill or other factory, and from that time onward to be fixed there and perform the same mechanical work for ten, twelve, and finally fourteen hours, is to purchase dearly the pleasure of breathing" (W. a. W. u. V., ii. 661).

No less considerable sacrifices than the earning of a maintenance does the conquest of a relative freedom demand, for *complete* freedom is never obtained. On the other side, the assurance of existence and the attainable degree of freedom have the advantage that one can in general conquer them by one's own energy, whereas we are altogether passively receptive with regard to youth and health.

If now one actually possesses these four privative goods, the external conditions of *contentment* are given; if then the requisite internal condition, *resignation, acquiescence* in the inevitable, be added, contentment will dwell in the mind so long as no considerable misfortunes and pains afflict it. Contentment *craves* no positive happiness; it is just the *forgoing* of such. It only desires freedom from considerable evils and pains, thus about the zero-point of feeling. Positive goods and positive happiness *can add nothing* to contentment, but undoubtedly they can endanger it; for the greater the positive goods and good fortune, the greater is the probability of suffering by their loss great pains, which temporarily destroy contentment. Contentment can thus be so little regarded as a sign of positive happiness, that rather the poorest and those with fewest wants can most easily obtain permanent possession of it. If, nevertheless, contentment is so frequently lauded as a happy state, nay, as the supreme attainable felicity (Aristot., Eth. Eud., vii. 2: *ἡ εὐδαιμονία τῶν αὐτάρκων ἐστι*, Happiness is the possession of the self-sufficient; Spinoza, Eth., part. 4, Prop. 52, Obs.: Self-contentment is truly the utmost that we can hope), this can *only* be true if the state of *painlessness* and voluntary *resignation* of all *positive* felicity deserves the *preference* before the essentially transient *possession of positive happiness*. Altogether, if, as I believe, it is justifiable to call health, youth, liberty, and an easy existence the highest goods, and contentment the supreme happiness, it follows at once from that how doubtful must the case stand with all positive goods and positive happiness that one can justly place before them the privative goods, those consisting in mere *freedom from pain.* But what, then, does freedom from pain offer? Truly nothing more than non-existence! If, then, a "but" is still connected with positive goods and happiness, which places them, on the whole, still below contentment, *i.e.*, still below the zero-point of sensation, at which non-existence permanently stands, it is thereby declared that they also rank below non-existence. *Equal* in value to non-existence would only rank the *absolutely* contented life, if there were such: there is none, however, for even the most contented is not always perfectly and in all respects contented, consequently *all* life ranks in value below the absolutely contented, consequently below non-existence.

3. *Hunger and Love.*

> "Until this paragon of spheres
> By philosophic thought coheres,
> The vast machine will be controlled
> By love and hunger, as of old,"

says Schiller very rightly. They are both, not only for progress and development in the animal kingdom, but also for the commencing development of humanity and the ruder states which characterise the same, almost the sole springs of action. If the value of *these* two factors for the individual must be pronounced to be small, there is little prospect of showing the value of individual life for its own sake in other ways.

Hunger is painful in the extreme, which certainly he alone knows who has felt it; its satisfaction, the gratification of satiety, is for the brain the mere removal of pain, whilst for the subordinate centres it undoubtedly may entail a positive elevation above the zero-point of sensation in the comfortable feeling of digestion. This will, however, for the common feeling or total well-being of the individual, have less weight the more the subordinate centres recede relatively to the brain, which receives only feeble traces of the comfortable feeling of digestion, but feels so much the more depressed in its mental tone and working power through the satiation. Whoever finds himself in the fortunate situation of being able, whenever the commencement of hunger is announced, instantly to satisfy the same, and whoever is not inconvenienced by the lowering of the power of the brain through satiety, may certainly receive through hunger a certain excess of pleasure by the pleasure of digestion; but how few are in this doubly enviable position! Most of the 1300 millions of the earth's inhabitants have either a scanty nourishment, unsatisfying and prolonging life with difficulty, or they live for a time in superfluity, from which they derive no preponderating enjoyment, and must for another period actually starve and suffer want, when they must accordingly endure the pains of hunger for long periods, whilst the pleasure of satiety, with perfect stilling of hunger, only occupies a few hours of the day. But now let any one compare the dull delight of satiety and digestion with the distinct gnawing of hunger or the hell-torments of thirst to which animals in deserts, steppes, and such regions, that in the hot season are perfectly dry, are not seldom exposed. How much more, however, must among many species of animals the pain of hunger exceed the pleasure of satiety in the course of life, which at certain seasons *die* of hunger from want of food, often in considerable numbers, or for weeks and months just on the brink of starvation, prolong their existence in slightly more favourable conditions of life! This happens both with graminivorous birds and birds in the winter of the polar and temperate zones and in the arid tropics, as also with carnivora and beasts of prey, which often for weeks wander about vainly in search of booty until they perish of inanition. It is not so long since in Europe one calculated on a famine every seven years, and if this has been changed by our present means of communication into mere dearth, *i.e.*, into famine merely for the poorest classes, this or a similar state of things certainly continues to exist in by far the largest part of the earth.

But even in our large towns we read ever and anon of cases of literal dying of hunger. Can the gluttony of a thousand gourmands outweigh the torments of one starving human being?

And yet extreme starvation is with us the rarer and lesser evil produced by hunger; far more fearful is the bodily and mental wasting away of the race, the dying off of children, and the peculiar diseases engendered by it. One has only to read the accounts of the weaving districts of Silesia or of the dens of misery of London. The less, however, a check is given to the progressive increase of humanity by devastating wars, the more the hosts of epidemics disappear by increasing cleanliness and their spread is hindered by precautionary measures, the more must the ability to procure sustenance prove the *sole* natural limit to increase, since the proportion of births remains tolerably the same; and the hypothesis of Carey that hereafter the ability of the human race to procreate and increase will diminish is altogether arbitrary, and justified by no historical analogies.

However great may be the progress of agriculture and chemistry, still at last a point must be reached beyond which the production of the means of subsistence cannot go. The increase of the number of human beings by generation has, however, no limit save that which is assigned by the impossibility of obtaining subsistence; this has always formed the main source of restriction, and will become so more exclusively. This limit, however, is not abrupt and well defined, but it passes from a sufficiency to impossibility of existence through infinitely numerous life-stages, of which each succeeding one is more hungry and wretched. To deceive instinct the stomach is often filled with substances that are neither agreeable in taste nor nutritious; thus in China, *e.g.*, the poorest class, that cannot purchase rice, eat a kind of sea-tangle, which contains scarcely any nutritive matter. If one thinks of the masses which live on tasteless or insipid aliment (rice, potatoes), one will no longer be able to assert that, for the great excess of pain which hunger produces in the world, the relish connected with eating could offer a certain makeweight.

The result in respect of hunger is then this, that the individual, by the simple stilling of his hunger, never experiences a positive rise above the zero-point of sensation; that under specially favourable circumstances he can certainly gain a positive excess of pleasure by the relish and pleasure of digestion connected with hunger; but that in the animal kingdom and human kingdom, on the whole, the torment and pain produced by hunger and its consequences far outweigh, and always will outweigh, the pleasure connected with its satisfaction. Considered in itself, therefore, the need of food is an *evil;* only the progress of development, to which it acts as a spring through the struggle for food, *not* its own value, can teleologically justify this evil.

I cannot refrain from quoting here the words of Schopenhauer (Parerga, ii. 313): "Whoever wishes to put to a brief trial the assertion that in the world enjoyment outweighs pain, or at least is in equipoise with it, should compare the sensation of the animal which devours another with that of this other."——

As for the other spring of Nature, *Love*, I must in regard to its theory refer to Chap. ii. B. In the animal kingdom one can hardly speak of an active sexual selection on the part of the male, even among the highest birds and mammals; of a passive selection through the struggle of the males in which the strongest remains victor, only among a small part of the higher animals.

For the rest, the sexual impulse is not individual, but is purely general. But now in the infinitely larger part of the animal kingdom there do not exist organs of sexual pleasure acting as stimulants to coition; without such accordingly coition is an office indifferent to the egoism of the individual which is carried on by the impelling constraint of instinct, as the spinning of the web of the spider or the building of the bird's nest for the eggs hereafter to be laid. To the absence of enjoyment in the office of fecundation in the case of most animals also the frequently indirect form of this function deviating from direct copulation points. When in the vertebrates a personal physical enjoyment appears to occur, it is at first certainly as flat and insignificant as possible; but soon there is also added the contest of the males for the female, which in many species of animals is waged with the greatest bitterness, and has for its consequence often painful injuries, not seldom also the killing of one of the rivals. Add to that, among those animals which at the time of rut form herds led by the victorious male, the involuntary continence of the younger members, whether they separate into smaller detachments or remain with the main herd, when an invasion of the rights of the head of the family is punished in the cruellest fashion. This involuntary continence of the largest part of the males, and the pains and vexation caused the defeated by the contests, seem to me a hundredfold to exceed the pleasures accruing to the prosperous males from the sexual pleasure. As for the females, in the first place, among most animals they far more rarely couple than the privileged males; and, secondly, the pains of child-bearing in their case far outweigh the pleasure derived from copulation.

With man, especially the cultivated, birth is more painful and more difficult than for any other animal, and mostly entails even a longer sick-bed. I need not hesitate, therefore, to declare the total sufferings of child-bearing for the woman greater than the total physical pleasures of coition. We should not be misled by the circumstance that impulse causes the woman to pronounce the contrary decision, practically, and perhaps also theoretically. Here we have a glaring case where impulse blinds the judgment. One has only to think of that woman who could not be deterred from sexual intercourse by the repetition of the Cæsarean operation, and one will estimate the value of such judgment more truly. The man seems to be better off in this respect; but he only seems so.

Kant says in his "Anthropology" (Werke, vii. Abth. 2, S. 266): "In the former (the epoch of natural development), in the state of nature, at any rate, he is in his fifteenth year impelled by the sexual instinct and capable of reproducing and maintaining his kind. In the second (the epoch of civic development) he can (on the average) hardly venture it before the twentieth year. For although the youth has early enough the power to satisfy his own and his wife's inclination as citizen of the world, he is far from possessing the power to maintain his wife and child as subject of a state.—He must learn a trade, obtain customers, before commencing housekeeping with his wife, when, in the more polished classes, the five-and-twentieth year may well pass before he is ripe for his destination. How now does he fill up the interval of a compelled and unnatural continence? Hardly otherwise than with vices."

These vices, however, soil the æsthetic sense, blunt the delicacy of the mind, and not seldom lead to immoral actions. Lastly, through their inherent immoderation, and for other reasons, they unsettle the health, and only too often sow the seeds of ruin for the following generation.

But whoever actually and exceptionally keeps free from all the vices filling up the provisional period, and by an effort of reason overcomes the torments of aroused sensibility in ever-renewed struggle, has in the interval between puberty and marriage, the interval, if not of most endurance, yet of the most flaming sensibility, to endure such an amount of pain, that the subsequent total of sexual pleasure can never make amends for it. The age of marriage for men is, however, constantly rising with advancing civilisation; the provisional period thus becomes continually longer, and is longest precisely in the classes where the nervous sensibility and irritability, thus also the torment of privation, is greatest.

But now in Man the purely physical side of sexual love is subordinate, far more important is the individualised sexual instinct, which promises an extravagant felicity of never-ending duration from the possession of a particular individual.

Let us first consider the consequences of love in general. One side generally loves more ardently than the other; the less loving is usually the first to draw back, and the other feels faithlessly abandoned and betrayed. Whoever could see and weigh the pain of deceived hearts on account of broken vows, as much of it as is in the world at any moment, would find that it alone exceeds all the happiness derived from love existing at the same time in the world, for the simple reason that the pain of disillusion and the bitterness of betrayal lasts much longer than the blissful illusion. Still more cruel becomes the pain for the woman who has sacrificed everything for her lover from genuine deep love, only to live in close contact with him as a clinging plant. If such an one be torn from her stay and cast adrift, she stands truly fallen, *i.e.*, without support in the world; deprived of her strength, robbed of the protection of love, she must, a detached flower, wither and fade,—or shamelessly plunge into the current of base life in order to attain forgetfulness.

How much married and domestic peace is not destroyed by clandestine love! What colossal sacrifices of paternal happiness and well-being in other respects does not the unblessed sexual impulse demand! Father's curse and expulsion from the family circle, even from the social circle in which one has become rooted; such is the price paid by man or maiden in order merely to be united to the beloved one. The poor seamstress or servant-girl who consumes her joyless existence in the sweat of her brow, she, too, falls one evening a prey to the irresistible impulse; for the sake of rare brief joys she becomes a mother, and has the choice either of committing infanticide or of spending the largest part of her earnings, scarcely sufficient even for herself, on the maintenance of the child. Thus for long years she must bear care and want with threefold severity, if she will not throw herself into the arms of a life of vice, which secures her for the years of youth a less toilsome livelihood, only to be followed by an age of the more frightful misery; and all this for the little bit of love!

It is a pity that there are no tables of statistics showing what percentage of all love-affairs in every rank of life lead to marriage. One would be horrified at the small percentage. Leaving out of sight old bachelors and maids, even among married couples one will find the number by no means large of those who have not behind them a little broken-off affair; many, however, who could tell of several. Of the concluded marriages, again, only a very small part are concluded from love, the rest from other considerations: one may gather from that how small a part of all love-affairs terminate in the haven of marriage. Of this small part, however, again, very few attain a so-called happy marriage, for happy marriages are altogether much rarer than one might think, in consequence of the make-believe in order to keep up the appearance of happiness; but, in fact, the happy marriages are least of all to be found among those concluded from love, so that of the small part of the amours terminating in the haven of marriage, the majority again comes worse off than if they had ended in marriage. Those few, lastly, which lead to the happy marriage attain this *not through love itself*, but only by this, that the characters and persons happen so to fit that conflicts are avoided and love passes into friendship.

Those rare cases in which the happiness of love gently and imperceptibly glides into that of friendship, and all bitter disillusion is spared it, are so rare that they are even balanced by those bad marriages, which are concluded from love. Of all love-affairs not terminating in marriage, however, the larger part does not attain its goal at all, and the smaller part, which does attain it, makes the people, at least the female part, still more unhappy than if they had not attained it.

After these general considerations we cannot be doubtful that love prepares for the individuals concerned far more pain than pleasure. Hardly anywhere will instinct so much oppose this result as here, and perhaps few will grant it but those in whom instinct has lost its power through age.

Let us, however, consider the process in satisfied love in detail, in order to see that even here pleasure rests substantially on illusion. Undoubtedly, in general, the quantity of the pleasure is proportional to the strength of the satisfied will, provided that the satisfaction falls in its full extent into consciousness,—a supposition which, in perfect strictness, is so much the less admissible the more obscure is the will and the more its contents extend from the region of unconsciousness into that of consciousness.

But let us leave this on one side, and grant that a very strong will, no matter how arisen, to possess the beloved object is consciously present; then undoubtedly must the satisfaction of this will be felt as intense pleasure, and that the more the more clearly the person concerned becomes conscious of the fulfilment of his wish as of a fact dependent on external circumstances; the greater therefore is the contrast of the fulfilment with a preceding recognition of difficulties and obstacles. A caliph, on the other hand, who is conscious that he has only to issue his commands in order to possess any woman that pleases him, will hardly be at all conscious of the satisfaction of his will, however strong it may be in any particular case.

Hence it follows, however, that the pleasure of satisfaction is only purchased by preceding pain at the supposed impossibility of attaining possession; for difficulties whose conquest one foresees as certain are already no longer difficulties.

But, according to our previous general considerations, the preceding pain through the certainty or probability of non-success will be greater than the corresponding pleasure in fulfilment. But now, as certainly as the final enjoyment on fulfilment is a real one because it depends on the satisfaction of an actually existing will, so certainly is the idea on which the enjoyment depends an illusion. Consciousness, namely, finds in itself a violent longing for the possession of the beloved object, which surpasses in intensity and passionateness every phenomenon of will else known to it. Since, however, at the same time, it does not suspect the unconscious goal of this will (which lies in the nature of the child to be created), it supposes a prospective extravagant enjoyment to be the goal of that extravagant longing; and instinct supports this illusion, since the man, if he should mark that there is a cheating of his egoism for the sake of alien ends, would soon seek to suppress the instinct of passionate love. Thus comes to pass the illusion with which the lover proceeds to the sexual act, and which may be experimentally proved to be such by this, that the satisfaction of the will on the possession of the loved one remains just the same if a counterfeit, from whom his will would recoil with disdain and abhorrence, be successfully imposed on the lover without his knowledge.

Nevertheless the pleasure in the satisfaction of the accomplished will is quite real,—but *this* pleasure was indeed not in the mind of the lover, but rather that extravagant bliss *by which* he thinks the violent will for possession set in motion!

Of such a bliss or pleasure there exists, however, nothing at all, since the enjoyment is purely compounded of the satisfaction of that violent will for possession to be first set in motion, and of the common physical sexual enjoyment. When the violence of the impulse allows consciousness to a certain extent to breathe again and to attain some clearness, it becomes aware of the disillusion of its expectation. Every disillusion as regards an expected enjoyment is, however, a pain, and indeed a so much greater pain the greater was the expected enjoyment, and the more certainly it was expected. Here, then, when an extravagant bliss, expected with absolute certainty, turns out to be pure illusion (for the two real moments of the enjoyment were indeed as a matter of course expected besides this blessedness), the pain of disenchantment must reach a high degree; so high a degree that it perfectly counterbalances, when it does not outweigh, the really existing enjoyment. Certainly the impulse, not annihilated at a stroke, but continually renewed for some time, although with generally decreasing strength, prevents this disillusion from being apprehended immediately and in full extent by consciousness; the renewed pining after satisfaction perverts the judgment, and obstinately keeps up the illusion of the contrary experience for the future.

But this duping of the conscious judgment by impulse does not last for ever. The attained possession soon becomes customary property. The idea of the contrast with the difficulties of the attainment disappears more and more; the will for possession becomes latent, as no disturbance of possession is threatened, and the satisfaction of this will becomes ever less felt as pleasure. Now the disenchantment finds for itself a way more and more into consciousness.

But *this* disillusion is not the only one that attains to consciousness, but there are many others. The lover had fancied he was entering on a new era, to be transported by possession, as it were, from earth to heaven, and he finds in his new state all the old surroundings and daily drudgeries. He had thought to gain in the beloved one an angel, and finds now, when the impulse no longer distorts his judgment, a human being with all the human faults and weaknesses. He had imagined that the state of extravagant felicity would be eternal, and he now begins to doubt whether he has not been very much deceived as regards the expected bliss of possession. In short, he finds that everything is as before, but that he was a great fool in his expectations. The only real enjoyment in the first time after acquiring possession, the satisfaction of the accomplished will, has disappeared, but on the ecstasy supposed to be eternal has supervened sorry disenchantment yielding a lasting pain, which is only very slowly extinguished by the accustomed devotion to the common daily round.

Undoubtedly very rarely on the conclusion of a marriage, at least on one side, are there not sacrifices made, were it only of liberty; these sacrifices now emerge into consciousness, and increase the displeasure at the disillusion. If elsewhere only vanity succeeds in hiding pain and misfortune and vaunts a non-existing happiness and pleasure, here also shame co-operates to the same end, since one would hardly ascribe the disenchantment to one's own stupidity. The erewhile lovers seek to hide the pain of disenchantment not only from the world and one another, but if possible also from themselves, which again contributes to enhance the discomfort of the situation.

Thus then the real enjoyment in the union of lovers must not only be paid for in advance by fears, anxiety, and doubt, nay, often temporary despair, but subsequently again with the pain of disenchantment—that enjoyment, the perception of whose illusory character at the moment of enjoyment itself can only be averted by the violence of the impulse suspending, or indeed corrupting, the judgment.

But now we have so far paid little attention to the state before the union of the lovers, and yet it is just here where the tenderest, most blissful sensations are found, as, in particular, those in the first flush of the dawn of the newly opened heaven. On what does that unquestionably real pleasure depend? On *hope*, on nothing but hope, which only anticipates a future good, and only imagines that that will be ecstatic bliss; on a hope which is hardly conscious of itself as hope, but with every moment is revealed in a truer light. The greatest difficulties opposing union cannot destroy this hope and its felicity; but that it is really nothing but hope is proved by this, that the lovers despair, and even destroy themselves, when the impossibility of their union has become certainty. If, now, this love-happiness preceding union is only hope of the happiness to be expected after union, it becomes illusory when that is seen to be illusory.

This is the reason why only first love can be true love; in the second and after loves the impulse meets with too great resistance from the consciousness, which now more or less clearly perceives the illusory nature of the first love. Thus Goethe says in "Truth and Fiction," speaking of "Werther": "Nothing, however, gives more occasion to this weariness (this loathing of life) than a return of love. . . . The thought of the Eternal and the Infinite, which peculiarly elevates and supports it, has vanished; it appears transient, like all that recurs."

Whoever has once understood the illusory nature of successful love after union, and therewith also of that before union, whoever has come to see the pain outweighing the pleasure in all love, for that man the phenomenon of love has no more health, because his consciousness offers resistance to the imposition of means to ends that are not *his* ends; the pleasure of love has been for him undermined and corroded, only its smart remains to him unrelieved. But although such an one will not be able entirely to resist the impulse, this will yet be the endeavour of his reason, and he will be, at any rate, successful in any particular case in moderating the fervour of love into which he fell as ingenuous youth, and in reducing accordingly also the degree of pain and the excess of pain over pleasure which would otherwise have fallen to his lot. He will, however, at the same time be *conscious* that he is entangled against his will in a passion that causes him more pain than pleasure, and with this perception *from the standpoint of individualism* the doom of love has been pronounced (comp. i. 231–233).

These last reflections refer only to that love which is so fortunate as to attain its end; but if we include all cases, this account of the worth of love wears a very unfavourable aspect. Illusory pleasure and predominant pain, even in the most successful case; generally thwarting of the will without attaining of the goal, accompanied by grief and despair; annihilation of the future of so many women by loss of chastity, their sole social support,—these are the results we have found.

It could not admit of doubt that reason would counsel entire *continence*, were it not that the torment of the ineradicable impulse which thirsts for fulfilment is a *far greater* evil than a temperate indulgence in love (comp. i. 240). One must therefore pronounce the sentence of Anakreon to be wholly true, which runs—

> *χαλεπὸν τὸ μὴ φιλῆσαι,* Not to love is hard,
> *χαλεπὸν δὲ καὶ φιλῆσαι,* But also hard to love.

If love is once recognised as evil, and yet must be chosen as the *less* of two evils as long as the impulse persists, reason necessarily demands a third, namely, *eradication of the impulse, i.e.*, emasculation, if thereby an eradication of the impulse be attainable. (Comp. Matt. xix. 11–12, "All men cannot receive this saying, save they to whom it is given. For there are some eunuchs which were so born from their mother's womb; and there are some eunuchs which were made eunuchs of men; and there be eunuchs *which have made themselves eunuchs for the kingdom of heaven's sake*. He that is able to receive it, let him receive it!")

From the point of view of the eudæmonology of the

individual, this is in my opinion the sole possible result. If anything cogent is to be advanced to the contrary, it can only be such considerations as require of the individual a stepping out of the sphere of his egoism. The result as regards love is thus the same as regards hunger, that it is *in itself* and *for the individual* an *evil*, and its justification can only be sought in this, that it conduces to the progress of development in the manner shown in Chap. ii. B.

4. *Compassion, Friendship, and Domestic Felicity.*—Compassion, on which, according to Aristotle, mainly the pleasure in the tragical (comp. my "Aphorismen über das Drama"), and, according to Schopenhauer, all morality depends, is, as every one knows, a feeling composed of pain and pleasure. The reason of the pain is clear; it is simply the fellow-feeling with the obvious pain of another, which may be so severe as to allow no trace of pleasure to survive in the compassion, but converts it wholly into heart-rending woe, whose awfulness impels to avert the gaze. Think of the spectacle of a battlefield after the fight, or a man lying in uncontrollable convulsions.

But whence the pleasurable feeling found in moderate compassion comes is more difficult to understand. Of the satisfaction caused by the possible affording of assistance, there is here, of course, no question, for this comes after the commiseration. The mischievous joy of malignity is the only pleasurable feeling which the sight of another's suffering is able directly to arouse, but this any one can very well distinguish from the mild pleasure of compassion.

I see no other possibility of comprehending the pleasure in compassion, and have also nowhere found the slightest attempt at any other explanation than this, that the contrast of foreign suffering with one's own freedom from this suffering at once *excites* and *removes* the latent aversion to the endurance of such suffering, and causes the removal to be *distinctly realised*. Hereby, certainly, the pleasure in compassion is declared to be purely egoistic, yet I fail to see how this can detract from the dignity or the noble consequences of compassion. It is in perfect harmony with this that, for very finely strung, self-renouncing natures, compassion is a highly unpleasant stimulant, a true torment, which they seek in every way to avoid, whilst man indulges his compassion with greater ease the ruder he is, and that, further, at the spectacle of very great suffering even the coarser mind can so far forget itself in others' well-being, that the same effect arises as when more finely-feeling souls view a smaller misery, so that compassion is still only pain. If the coarse multitude revels in alien suffering, one must not forget that it also possesses sufficient bestiality to unite with the compassion more or less the delight in cruelty, which takes pleasure in alien misery as such; one must, therefore, exercise caution in citing the instance of the coarse multitude to decide the question whether pleasure or pain predominates in compassion as such. According to my subjective judgment the latter is decidedly the case; but whether the judgment of others tallies with my own or not, it is undoubted that the emotional crudeness of mankind on the average is steadily decreasing, and that with decreasing crudeness the pain in compassion is more and more gaining the upper-hand over the pleasure.

But now the case turns out still more unfavourably for pleasure when we take into account the immediate *consequences* of compassion in the mind. Compassion, namely, at once excites the desire to assuage others' woe, and this is also the end of this instinct. This desire finds, however, only in very rare cases a partial, still more rarely a total satisfaction; it will, therefore, far more frequently excite pain than pleasure.

If, then, the title of the less of two evils cannot be denied to the instinct of compassion as a corrective and restricter of egoism, and of the injustice springing from the latter, yet in itself regarded it is still always an evil, for it brings to the sufferer more pain than pleasure. Comp.

Spinoza, Eth., part iv. Prop. 50: "Compassion is for a man who does not live according to the guidance of reason in itself bad and useless. Proof: For compassion is (according to Def. 18) pain, thus (according to Prop. 48) in itself bad. The good, however, that follows from it . . . we seek to do according to the mere command of reason," &c.

Of *sociality* and *friendship* the same cannot be said, although it has often been asserted, and for certain dispositions also rightly. Thus, *e.g.*, La Bruyère says, "Tout notre mal vient de ne pouvoir être seul." (We may compare also Schopenhauer, "Parerga," i. 444-458.)

But certainly it may be maintained that the sociable instinct is an instinctive need arising from the weakness and impotence of the individual whose satisfaction, like health and freedom, just places man at the level where he is able to pile up certain positive enjoyments, and that only a small part of true friendship—which, moreover, is so rare—represents a value positively exceeding the zero-point of feeling.

As there are herding animals, so is Man a social animal. Impotent, unprotected against the forces of Nature, and at the mercy of every foe, his instinct directs him to cultivate the society of his fellows. Here it is really the felt want that begets the need, and the pleasure of *this* sociality is only the removal of that want or need.

In addition to warding off distress and hostile attacks, in the second place, the social community has the advantage over solitary effort in facilitating the production of positive achievements, *e.g.*, domestic works, economic or artistic production, the increase of culture or knowledge through exchange of thought, the collection of interesting novelties; all this a society renders more possible, but does not as such effect; it is only the foundation, which may remain unutilised or utilised in the most varied fashion. It is thus in this point only the potentiality of pleasure, but not pleasure itself; this belongs rather to the structures to be reared on this foundation, and must be sought in these, not in sociality. Nay, even the positive pleasure which may be built up on its basis may for the most part be attained in like or little-altered fashion even in solitude.

That, on the other hand, sociality, through the regard for others, and the constraint which it imposes upon the individual, is attended by very real inconveniences, and occasionally with hopeless misery, our "societies" prove.

From social life springs a greater mutual interest, *i.e.*, an increased sympathy. If in each individual the sum of pleasure should outweigh the sum of pain, then also as regards each individual the sum of joy in common would outweigh the sum of sorrow in common, did not the weakening of sympathetic joy prevent this through the envy which is unavoidable even in respect of the dearest friend. But since in the life of the individual the sum of pain exceeds the sum of pleasure, so sympathy for the same likewise must consist of predominant pain, and this can in no case be balanced by the circumstance that one is sure of sympathy for one's own sorrows and joys in the breasts of friends. Certainly we pine for consolation, but when one well considers it, what sort of consolation can it afford that one with one's own disagreeables and vexations spoils the fair humour also of one's friend?

Nevertheless, the solitary endurance of grief or vexation is so tormenting, that we feel ourselves relatively happy in being able to pour it out, although in recompense the vexation of our friend will *vice versa* be poured out on ourselves. Here, too, it turns out that the enhancement of mutual sympathy in friendship is the less of two evils, of which the other only appears the greater on account of one's own weakness.

When, therefore, the highly landed bliss of friendship is subjected to a true estimation, it is found to depend partly on man's feebleness in enduring suffering, since, in fact, very strong characters are least in need of friendship, partly however in pursuing a common end; in a word, on similarity of interests, whence also the apparently more inseparable friendships are loosened or expire when on one side the dominant interests change, so that they now no longer correspond to those of the other. The pleasures attained through mutually pursued interests can, however, also only be put down to the account of these interests, not directly to that of friendship. The firmest community of interests exists in *marriage;* the community of goods, of earnings, of sexual intercourse, and of the education of children are strong bonds, which, in alliance with the polar completion of the spiritual qualities of both sexes, certainly suffice to found a strong and lasting friendship, which also perfectly suffices without the aid of love in the narrower sense to explain the beautiful and sublime phenomena of readiness for self-sacrifice in married life. Add to that the powerful force of habit. As the dog maintains the sublimest and most touching friendship and fidelity for his master, to whom not his own choice but chance and custom have bound him, so also the relation of spouses is essentially an alliance of habit; wherefore both *mariage des convenance* and love-matches after a series of years exhibit on the average the same physiognomy.

Dühring, who in his "Worth of Life" pleads the cause of love, and asserts that it does not disappear in marriage, comes (pp. 113–114) himself to the following conclusion:—"The love of married couples may, therefore, in powerfulness of its effects, perhaps not lag behind passionate love. The feeling is only *latent*, as it were, emerges, however, in all its force when a hostile fate has to be encountered. The forces which once maintained a living play of sensation now in the matured relation are in equipoise, to become again *perceptible* for feeling on any disturbance of the equilibrium." If the feeling is latent, it does not exist for consciousness; and if it emerges into consciousness merely on some disturbance, it is only felt as pain; hence, in either case, makes nothing *for* the value of life, which is here alone under discussion. The magnitude of its effects may, however, be just as well derived from friendship and the attachment of habit.

In any case, there is in most marriages so much discord and vexation, that when one looks with unprejudiced eye, and is not deceived by the vain attempts at dissimulation, one hardly finds one in a hundred that is to be envied. This is simply due to the imprudence of men and women, who also do not endeavour in little things to accommodate themselves to mutual weaknesses; to the accidental way in which characters are assorted in marriage; to the equal insistance on rights where indulgence and friendship should compromise; to the convenience of discharging all displeasure, vexation, and ill-humour on the nearest person, who must listen; to the mutual irritability and embitterment which is increased by every fresh case of a supposed infringement of rights; to the sorry consciousness of being chained to one another, the absence of which would prevent a host of inconsideratenesses and disharmonies through fear of consequences. Thus we get that matrimonial cross, which can so little be regarded as exceptional, that Lessing is not so far wrong when he says—

> "No more than one bad wife has ever yet been known;
> The pity only is, each holds her for his own."

This does not at all contradict the fact that the power of habit at once asserts its right and sets itself in violent opposition when a disturbance or solution of the marriage is threatened from without. In both cases it is always only the painful side of the relation which imposes itself on consciousness. The rending of the worst marriage, which furnished a genuine hell for the partners, always causes so much pain to the survivor, that I have heard an experienced man say, "If a marriage is ever to be broken, then the earlier the better; the more prolonged and closer the ties of habit, the more enduring the pain of separation." One has only to draw from this perfectly correct judgment the logical consequence, then is separation best before union.

Sensible people, whose judgment is not biassed by impulse, are also usually quite clear respecting this, that, from the rational standpoint of *individual* well-being, non-marriage is better than marriage. If no love and no external ends (rank, wealth) impel to the marriage contract, there is, in fact, only one reason for choosing marriage as the supposed *lesser* of two evils; thus, for a girl to evade the terrors of old-maidhood, for a man to avoid the inconveniences of bachelorhood, for both to escape the torments of the unsatisfied instinct or the consequences of illicit gratification.

Commonly, however, they make the experience that they have been bitterly deceived concerning the greater of the two evils, and only shame and considerate tenderness forbids them to confess it. How uncomfortable also the unsatisfied instinct to found a household and family may become for old bachelors and spinsters has been already mentioned (Chap. i. B.)——

When, now, the parties are married, they begin to long for children—another instinct, for the understanding can hardly possess this longing. The instinct goes so far as to urge to the adoption of others' children, and to the education of them as if they were one's own.

That the latter also is no act of reflection is already evident from the instinct of monkeys, cats, and many other mammals and birds that do exactly the same. Moreover, by this procedure an already existing child is merely put into a better situation of life than would else have fallen to its lot. It would be different if a child still to be created, to be fashioned say in a retort by a chemical process, were to be adopted in default of one's own.

"Let one only imagine," says Schopenhauer ("Parerga," ii. pp. 321–322), "that the generative act was neither a want nor accompanied by extreme pleasure, but an affair of pure rational reflection: could then the human race continue to exist? Would not rather every one have so much compassion for the coming generation as to prefer to spare it the burden of existence, or at least *be unwilling to take on itself* (the responsibility) of imposing such burden in cold blood?"

Besides the direct instinct to rear children, the desire for children with people in easy circumstances or increasing in wealth has yet another ground. These, namely, at a certain stage of life begin to perceive that they themselves have no enjoyment of their surplus wealth; if, however, they were in consequence to forego the cares of business, their interest in life would be gone, and they would fall a prey to the dreariest emptiness of existence and ennui.

To escape this evil they desire the lesser evil, possession of children, in order by this expanded egoism to have a motive for the continuance of their business activity.

But if one objectively compares on the one hand the joys, and on the other the sorrow, chagrin, vexation, and cares which children bring their parents, the predominance of pain can hardly be doubtful, although the judgment biassed by instinct strenuously opposes it, especially in women, with whom the instinct to rear children is far stronger.

Let one first of all compare the sum of satisfaction which is produced by the birth, and the sum of pain and sorrow which is called forth by the death of a child in the hearts of all concerned. Only after calculating the resulting excess of pain can one proceed to the contemplation of their life itself. To this end I recommend the chapter entitled "Mother's Frenzy" in Bogumil Goltz's "Zur Charakteristik und Naturgeschichte der Frauen."

In the first period predominates the very considerable discomfort and trouble of nursing and of vexation with careless servants, then the difficulties with neighbours and the anxiety of sickness; later on, the care of marrying the daughters and the worry over the follies and debts of sons; add to all this the anxiety in procuring the necessary means, which with the poor is greatest in the first, among the educated classes in the later periods. And with all the moiling and toiling, all the worry and care, and the constant fear of losing them, what is the real happiness that children bring him who possesses them? Apart from the diversion which they afford as playthings, and the occasional gratification of vanity owing to the hypocritical flattery of amiable gossips—hope, only the *hope of the future.*

And when the time comes to fulfil these hopes, and the children are still alive and unspoilt, they quit the parental home, go their own way, usually into the wide world, and write even only when in want of funds. So far then as that hope is *egoistic*, it is *always* deceptive; so far, however, as the hope is merely *for* the child, not *in* the child, what then?

In old age, as we shall see, human beings lose all illusions, save the one illusion of the sole instinct remaining to them, in that they cherish for their children the realisation of their hopes from the same miserable existence, whose vanity they have in all respects perceived in their own case. If they grow old enough to see their children also old people, they certainly lose that too; but then they hope for their grandchildren and great-grandchildren. Man is never too old to learn.

5. *Vanity, Sense of Honour, Ambition, Lust of Fame and Power.*—Love, honour, and the acquisitive instinct are in the mental sphere probably the three most powerful moving springs. We shall here consider the second of these. Honour may be divided into an objective and subjective honour. A man's *objective* honour is in general terms others' estimation of him.

We may divide objective honour into—

Positive Honour.

A. *Outward* Honour:
- *a.* Repute of Possession.
- *b.* „ „ Position.
- *c.* „ „ Rank.
- *d.* „ „ Beauty.

B. *Inward* Honour:
- *a.* Reputation for Industry.
- *b.* „ „ Intelligence and Culture.
- *c.* Moral Reputation.
  - (α) For Charity.

Negative Honour.

  - (β) For Justice.
- *d.* Civil Honour.
- *e.* Female (Sexual) Honour.

Negative honour each one inherently possesses until he loses it; positive honour must be acquired by circumstances (birth, actions, achievements). The former denotes only the zero-point of worth; the latter positively exceeds the same. The repute of possession depends on power; that of position on power and performance; easily ossifies, however, in forms coming down from earlier times. The reputation of rank is, so far as it exceeds the reputation of the power and labour connected with rank, an artificial creation of the state, to enable it to pay low salaries. The repute of beauty must not be looked for among ourselves, but among peoples that have the sense for the beautiful (ancient Greeks). The repute of industry is proportional to the economic value of the work; that of intelligence and culture especially forms a substitute for labour, when mental work is not regarded as work (respect of peasants for scholarship). Moral honour is positive only in active love; that of justice is merely negative; likewise will and sexual honour, which latter only applies to woman.

Subjective honour is twofold: the *direct* subjective honour of a man is his estimation of himself; *indirect* is his estimate of the estimate of himself by others, or his estimate of objective honour.

The former is called self-estimation, self-respect, self-esteem, pride; if the estimate remains *below* the true value: modesty, humility; if it *surpasses* the true value: over-estimate of self, conceit, arrogance; the latter, on the contrary, is called vanity. Although men may refuse to allow this word in the case of noble efforts, essentially it is the same, whether a girl is vain of the report of her beauty or a poet of the fame of his works. Both parts together, thus pride and vanity, make up subjective honour, which now, according to the object of the estimation, admits of the same division as objective honour. As regards the negative part, it is called sense of honour; as regards the positive, ambition. The direct and indirect part of subjective honour may stand to one another in very different relations of intensity; commonly, however, the latter will preponderate; indeed so far preponderate that one often meets with the view, as if subjective honour *only* consisted in this evaluation of the valuation of others; whereas, on the contrary, this is vanity *pur et simple* to assign any value to the judgment of others concerning one's own worth, whilst one at the same time denies all value to oneself, thus regarding the judgment of others as false.

Pride, the high estimate of oneself, is an enviable quality, no matter whether the estimate is true or false, if one only regards it as correct. Certainly an inflexible pride is rare; mostly it has to sustain alternating struggles with doubt, or even despair, which cause more pain than pride itself pleasure. Pride also increases the sensitiveness to external opinion, and is on its part compelled to adopt the hypocritical mask of modesty, if it will steer clear of unpleasantnesses. All this may be considered pretty well to balance the pleasure of extreme self-esteem. But now, as for that sense of honour and ambition which rests for the most part or exclusively on vanity, although they may for our present stage of development be valuable practical instincts, yet one cannot deny that in the first place they are vain, *i.e.*, rest on illusions, and, secondly, that they procure for him who is possessed by them a thousand times more pain than pleasure.

Female chastity alone protects social relations from complete disorder. The citizen sense of honour restrains the as yet blameless from trespasses or crimes, from which neither the fear of temporal nor of eternal punishment could deter. Scholarly ambition spurs on the boy and youth in their arduous acquisition of the material of culture demanded by our age. The ambition to achieve something great, which, in regard of rare and considerable performances and deeds, is called lust of fame, sustains the starving artist or scholar, whose creative force would be paralysed if the impossibility of ever in the least particular satisfying his ambition or love of fame could be demonstrated to him. Thus the sense of honour prevents greater evils and ambition furthers the evolution of humanity; but apart from the circumstance that, with the higher development and power of reason, subjective honour may very well be dispensed with, and its good effect otherwise produced (one may recall the difference between the French bravery from *point d'honneur* and the German from sense of duty), yet at all events the individual, the instrument of the impulse, must suffer therefrom.

The possession of negative honour can afford no pleasure, save when it has been recovered after apparent loss (*e.g.*, through calumny); in itself it answers only to the zero-point of sensation, as it represents only the zero-point of worth. It is thus, as all similar moments, a fertile source of pain, but no source of pleasure, except through the quite special and rarely occurring interruption of displeasure.

Ambition, however, is certainly a positive impulse, and indeed one of those "which, like salt water, makes one the more thirsty the more one drinks."

Wherever one listens one hears the stereotype lamentations of Government functionaries and officers at neglect and tardy promotion, the wailings of artists and scholars at suppression by envy and cabals, everywhere vexation at the undeserved favouring of others. For a hundred mortifications of ambition there is hardly one satisfaction; the former are bitterly felt, the latter received as long-deserved tribute of justice, if not with the repining, that they did not come earlier. The general over-estimate of self causes every individual to raise extravagant claims; the universal mutual envy and disparagement of merit causes the refusal of even just claims. Every satisfaction of ambition only serves to screw up one's claims more highly, and in consequence it must be a triumph outdoing all former ones that can produce a fresh satisfaction, whilst each of the former ones does not obtain equal recognition on account of this deficit of pain.

Take the case of a young public singer; she rises step by step to a certain elevation in the favour of the public; the triumphs connected with this rise of favour she claims as her right; life in them is to her as the air which she breathes; she is amazed if ever they are wanting. But a younger rival comes at last, and thrusts her into the second rank, as she her predecessors; and the fall from her height is a thousand times more painful to her than its converse was pleasurable, whilst she hardly felt as happiness the actual tenure of the same.

As in this instance, so with all ambition and lust of fame: even when the achievements or works remain, they do not always maintain the same interest for the public.

But now, in addition to all this, ambition is *vain*, *i.e.*, rests on illusion. Even the estimate of worth, as it obtains in objective honour, depends in part on illusion. I need only mention the artificially inflated honour of rank and nobility derived from the Middle Ages, but among us already almost extinct in its old significance. And even where the value that objective honour prizes is no illusory one, yet its estimate is far too often false. The *vox populi vox dei* only holds in questions that are vital questions for the development of the people, and where, in consequence, the Unconscious instinctively guides the judgment of the masses. In all other things the *vox populi* is so blind, dazzled by outward show, misled by claquers, given over to commonplace, and without understanding for the good, true, and beautiful, that one rather may be almost sure it is on a wrong tack. (Comp. Schopenhauer, "Parerga," ii. chap. xx.) In all cases that are not vital questions of development or finally settled by science, one may be confident, *a priori*, that the majority are wrong and the minority right; nay, a joint judgment is even so difficult, that, when a number of clever people agree, they almost certainly perpetrate some folly.

To such a judgment that man surrenders his life-happiness who makes ambition his guiding star. Even in small matters certainly no one would continue to concern himself about the opinions of mankind, before whom could be laid all the calumnies and adverse judgments uttered by friends and acquaintances behind his back. And now as to the ambition which fishes for orders, dignities, and titles! Every one knows that they are not apportioned to merit, but in the best case to him who is favoured by fortune, or to length of service; to those who happen to have influential relatives or advocates, to the cringer and flatterer, or even as reward for services not of the cleanest; and yet—incredible to relate—the world is greedy for them!

But now suppose the object of objective honour *had* a value, and the judgment of those in whose judgment objective honour consists *were* correct, *still* ambition would be empty; for what sort of value can it have for a man what others think and judge of him? None whatever, except so far as the character of their action towards him is at the same time determined by their judgment on him. In this, however, the opinion, as such, is quite indifferent, and is only regarded as means of thereby attaining a particular kind of action. This is, therefore, no ambition in the ordinary sense, as little as we call him covetous who strives to get money, but who also spends all that he gets; it is the assigning a value to objective honour *as such* that makes ambition and the sense of honour, and the circumstance that with the objective honour *partially* also the conduct of men towards the honoured one becomes different and more advantageous to him, is only a gladly accepted accidental consequence.

For the most part, indeed, the modification of action will be limited to this, that the *behaviour* becomes *more deferential*, thus to an expression of adjudgment of objective honour, which, to a sensible man, must be just as indifferent as the opinion itself. True utility hardly flows at all from positive objective honour, only harm from injured subjective honour, so that finally all the significance of objective honour consists in this, that one has to guard against harm through injury to negative honour. All the subjective value of an objective honour as such rests, however, manifestly on imagination, for the theatre of my joys and sorrows is still *my* head and not the head *of others*; thus it can neither add to nor take away from my weal and woe what other people think of me, therefore their opinion as such can have no effective value for me, consequently ambition is vain. The sense of honour which, according to our explanation, relates to negative honour, is indeed abstractedly just as insignificant; but this much can, at any rate, be said for it, that if one once lives among men, one must at least act as if one had some regard for objective honour, because otherwise the world would fall on one as the crows on the owl in daylight.

If herewith I declare the sense of honour and ambition to be empty and illusory, by no means is any judgment pronounced on the value of the *objects* of honour; I have even to a certain extent the greatest regard for the same, *e.g.*, for morality. But *if* such objects have a value, they have it not because they are objects of honour, as the wrong-headed might think, but because they are directly felicific. Most distinctly is this so with posthumous fame;

Spinoza can indeed not be the better for it that Collegian X. says, "That was a clever fellow;" but that he was able to think such thoughts, therein lay his satisfaction. Undoubtedly what renders me happy may lie in this, that I am conscious of doing or accomplishing something for the good of others; but that is still always the sympathetic joy in a real happiness, whereas, on the contrary, the *recognition* of the value of my deeds or performances procures these others by no means pleasure, but rather displeasure. The difference is the same as when I bestow something on a beggar; do I rejoice that through my gift his distress is momentarily relieved, my joy has a real object; do I watch for his "Thank you, sir," or "God bless you," in order to relish the recognition, I am a vain, foolish man.

Thus has also the desire of honour appeared to be, if a useful, yet also an illusory instinct, causing more pain than pleasure. (Comp. Schopenhauer, "Parerga," i.; "Aphorisms on Worldly Wisdom," chaps. i., ii., and especially iv.)

With the lust of power it is just the same. So far as it is a mere endeavour after freedom, it is not yet a positive impulse; so far as the power of ruling is only sought to procure for one's self more enjoyments by its help is it mere means to alien ends, and must be measured by the value of those enjoyments. There is, however, also a passion for commanding and ruling as such. It is clear that this is possible only at the expense of infringing the same impulse, and, moreover, the impulse for liberty in the ruled. Further, however, the same holds good of it as of ambition and loss of fame: the more one drinks of it, the thirstier one becomes. The *accustomed* power is no longer enjoyed, but without doubt all resistance to the same most painfully felt, and the greatest additional sacrifices made for its removal. On the whole, and with regard to the consequences for others, then, the love of power is a far more pernicious passion than ambition.

6. *Religious Edification.*—Already in Chap. ix. B. we mentioned that the exaltation of religious feeling in devotion and edification, which is always more or less of a mystical nature, is able to afford so great a bliss that it carries its subject above all earthly sorrows. But in the first place, these high degrees of exaltation are rare, for as they are essentially of a mystical nature, they cannot be acquired by industry and trouble, but presuppose a disposition, a peculiar talent, as much as art-enjoyment; and, secondly, they are, like all pleasure, not to be had without a characteristic displeasure.

One comes to see this best when one considers the life of penitents and saints. The highest degrees of religious exaltation are hardly conceivable without a prolonged mortification of the "flesh," *i.e.*, not only of sensual appetites, but of all secular pleasures. Rarely is this renunciation supported by the consciousness of the illusory nature of earthly pleasure and the predominance of the pain simultaneously arising from earthly longings, for that requires philosophy, but for the most part the foregoing of earthly felicity is felt as a *true* sacrifice, whereby the higher mystical religious felicity is to be *purchased*, so that the subject of it properly speaking never frees himself from the lamentation on the loss of earthly happiness itself. But however that be, the long-suppressed natural impulses surge up from time to time only the more mightily, and the violence of the struggles which the renouncers, certainly in ever rarer but ever more powerful relapses, have to sustain testifies to the magnitude of the torments experienced by them for the sake of the heavenly kingdom, until at last habit and bodily infirmity gradually induce a more equable state.—Of the bodily pains and privations of Asceticism itself I shall be silent, since it is, if decidedly a very effective, yet not indispensable means to the attainment of the religious mystical exaltation.

When we pass to the lower stages of edification which come into contact with secular life, an item of pain not mentioned above becomes especially important: fear of one's own unworthiness, doubt of the divine grace, anxiety concerning the future judgment, the fear of the burden of past sins, however small the latter may appear in the eyes of others. Taken all in all, pleasure and pain will weigh tolerably equally even in religious feeling; but should really an excess of pleasure be the result, the possibility of which I should more readily admit in this sphere than in any other (with the exception of art and science), the other consideration must also be taken into account, that this pleasure also is illusory. We have already laid bare this illusion in Chap. ix. B.; it briefly consists in this, that the endeavour immediately to grasp and to enjoy in conscious feeling the identity of the one Unconscious with the conscious subject, which exists in reality and may easily be comprehended by the understanding as rational truth, must in its nature of necessity remain without result, since consciousness cannot possibly transgress its own limits, thus cannot apprehend the Unconscious as such, therefore, also, not the unity of the Unconscious and the conscious individual.

If the awakening and delivering from illusion is with the progressive evolution of humanity inevitable in any sphere, it is in the religious. One cannot say that the present time of unbelief is just as transitional as, *e.g.*, that of the cultured ancient world at the birth of Christ; although more religious periods than the present may recur, yet a similar era of faith to that of the Catholic Middle Ages has been for ever rendered impossible by the universal modern mental culture. Even the Middle Ages were only possible because classical culture had been buried beneath ruins, and this we have now no more to fear. The more nations cultivate their rational tendencies, the more they come to stand and advance on their own feet, *i.e.*, on their consciousness, the more they lose their mystical talent; this is the provisional talent of youth, the maturity of conscious understanding attends the manhood of nations. We may analogically conclude from the gradual destruction of religious illusions that also the destruction of other illusions will assuredly be in time accomplished, as soon as they are no longer needed as springs of progress, whether they be superseded by other powerful impulses (reason), or the goal be attained in the direction of their special efficiency. So far as the delight of religion consists in the hope of transcendent felicity after death, it will be dealt with later on.

7. *Immorality.*—Immoral action or wrong-doing proceeds from the egoism inevitably attending individualism, and consists originally in this, that in order to procure a gratification or to avoid a pain, I inflict on one or several other individuals a greater pain. All other forms of wrong-doing are derived from this original one. It is therefore clear that the essence of wrong or the immoral consists in this, to alter the proportion of pleasure and pain in the world unfavourably to pleasure, since the pain of suffering wrong is greater than the pleasure (or the spared pain) of doing wrong. It follows from this, the greater the immorality the greater the sufferings of the world. (To apply the idea of justice to this proportion is, as has been shown above, altogether inadmissible.) Suppose, then, pleasure and pain were perfectly balanced in the world (which case truly, as one among infinitely many possible proportions, has *a priori* an infinitely small probability), the existence of immorality would immediately induce the preponderance of pain. In an intrinsically evil world, however, it will cause the cup of misery to overflow the more, as no harm imposed by Fate pains so acutely as that which one's fellow-beings have inflicted. As regards the vileness, worthlessness, malice, and meanness of mankind, Schopenhauer indulges in vivid descriptions, which can hardly be pronounced overdrawn, and the repetition of which I must here dispense with. Only one thing I will here add, namely, that

the imprudence of man often produces the same effect as malignity, in that it is often the cause of the bitterest torments to one's neighbours, without bringing any advantage or enjoyment, as wickedness manifestly does.

If, however, wrong-doing increases the suffering of the world, on the other hand, right-doing is by no means able to diminish the same, for it is, indeed, nothing else but the maintenance of the *status quo* before the first wrong, thus no positive elevation above the level line. No one in possession of his clear sight will have any enjoyment therefrom, unless when the fear of wrong is taken away from him. He, however, who gives every one his due can have no motive for pleasure at all, for he has curbed his individual will, and yet has done no more than his duty. A genuine joy only the exercise of positive morality, of active charity, can afford; yet it will always be conjoined for the doer with the pain of sacrifice, for the receiver with the pain of shame at benefits received. This augmentation of the pleasure of the world through active charity is of no account in comparison with the mass of immorality. At all events, the positive morality of active charity is also only to be regarded as a *necessary evil*, which may serve to alleviate a still *greater one*. It is far worse that there are alms-receivers than it is good that there are alms-givers, and only the Talmud finds distress and poverty in order that the rich may have occasion to show their good works. Accordingly, all works of charity only soothe the greater or lesser woes springing from human necessity. Were man free from suffering, self-sufficient, and without needs, like a god, what would he want with works of charity?

8. *Scientific and Art-Enjoyment.*—As feels the wearied traveller, when, after long wandering in the desert, he at last espies an oasis, so do we feel when, on approaching Art and Science, at last a gleam of light appears in the night of struggle and suffering. When Schopenhauer himself in

the "Parerga" (2 Aufl. ii. 448) insisted that the mental condition in artistic or scientific reception or production is mere painlessness, one might think that he had never known the state of ecstasy or rapture into which one may fall over a work of art or a newly opening sphere of science. But if he had seen the positive nature of such a state of supreme enjoyment, he could no longer have been able to assert that it was involuntary and unmotived, but he would have seen that it is the condition of supreme and perfect positive *satisfaction*, and satisfaction *of what*, if not of a will? Certainly not of the vulgar practical interest or will, but of the endeavour after knowledge, or after that harmony, after that unconscious logic under the veil of sensuous form; in short, after that somewhat in which beauty consists, no matter wherein it consists. That ecstatic rapture (*e.g.*, over a performance of music, over a picture, a poem, a philosophical treatise) is certainly something extremely rare; even the capacity for it is only the endowment of favoured natures, and even these will not be able to boast of too many such moments in their life. This is as it were a compensation which falls to the lot of such sensitive natures for the pains of life, which they must feel far more strongly than other men, whose obtuseness makes much easier to them.

Whether at the same time the latter do not on the whole fare better is hardly doubtful; for since pain so much preponderates in life, a blunter feeling for it would not be too highly paid by the deprivation of a pleasure never missed though great in itself, and in every case confined to a few moments of life. This is confirmed by the fact that men on the average think so much less of the value of life, the finer their feelings and the more intellectual they are. What holds good of the extreme case holds, however, just as well of the intermediate stages, which fill up the interval between the capacity for the highest ecstasy and insensibility to all and every art. From the circumstance that every one is indifferent to this or that art one can certainly not conclude in general to the obtuseness of his feelings, but certainly when anybody is indifferent to art in general.

Now let any one ask himself what percentage of the earth's inhabitants altogether are, in any degree worth mentioning, susceptible to artistic and scientific enjoyment, and one will cease to rate the importance of art and science for the world's happiness in general too highly. Let one consider further how small a percentage of the recipients, again, are able to procure for themselves the enjoyment of personal creation, of artistic or scientific production, which considerably exceeds that of reception.

In estimating this reception of the common people, one should, however, not forget to eliminate the causes of interest independent of art itself; thus, *e.g.*, curiosity or pleasure in the horrible or gruesome, the interest in national singers or story-tellers, the delight in dancing stimulated by popular music, the regard for practical utility in the interest in scientific communications, &c. But among the educated classes many affect an interest, and consequently a capacity of enjoyment, in regard to art and science which they do not possess. One has only to remember how many are tempted to become artists and scholars by the prospect of a career which perhaps pleases them better on account of its freedom, without having any vocation for the same. If one rejected all the uncalled and untalented, the ranks of scholars and artists would sensibly melt away. The prospect of future position and the facilities of entrance (scholarships, &c.) tempt to the scholar's career; the freedom of the vocation and the nature of the work, which appears more like sport, often, however, the mere hope of profit, entice to the artist's life. Think of the unhappy girls who prepare themselves for becoming music-mistresses. Further, let one take into account everything that is not produced by pure love of art and science, but by ambition and vanity. Let once the artist or savant attain the certainty that no one will ever know the authorship of his works, although hereby ambition is by no means entirely disappointed, since a man's name is something accidental and indifferent, especially for the future, yet more than the half of the pleasure in his performances will be taken away. Were there, however, a means of really at the same time depriving all artists and scholars of all ambition and vanity, assuredly production would almost cease, if it were not compelled to be mechanically continued for the sake of bread.

But now the troop of dilettanti! How little sense and love for the subject, how terrible the want of all understanding, how dependent on fashion and pretentious show,—and yet this dilettante crowding of the arts and sciences! The riddle may thus be read: not for their own sake are the arts sought, but as showy tinsel to adorn one's own dear self. The equally unintelligent critics are enraptured at the dress if the *person* pleases them, and despise it if they have no other ground for flattering the person; they then contemn the dilettante performance the more profoundly the more genuine value it possesses, because they think themselves bound to abash with fitting scorn the audacious assumption that any object may possess intrinsic merit. Of course, under such circumstances, the aim becomes to produce startling effects in as many directions as possible, in order to dazzle every blockhead in the easiest way.

This is the principle of modern education, especially of girls; a couple of drawing-room pieces on the piano, a few songs, a little foliage-drawing and flower-painting, to chatter in a few modern languages and to read the literary scribble of the day, then they are "finished." What else is it than systematic instruction in vanity, in every acceptation of the term? And with this juggling can one believe in delight in art? In aversion for art, rather, which reveals itself from the moment of marriage, when vanity no longer gets the better of love of ease. With boys it is not much better. They too must play the part of dilettanti for the sake of their parents' vanity. And then in music, as universal instrument, the unlucky, encyclopaedic, soulless piano! In science, likewise, ambition and vanity must aid. Only ambitious boys are able to go willingly to school; considering the subjects taught and our scholastic methods, ambition apart, learning is scarcely conceivable without extreme aversion.

Add to this that in science, quite otherwise than in art, the enjoyment of reception is extremely small compared with that of production, because the ardent longing fails for that knowledge of whose sure and easy attainment one is beforehand convinced. Who to-day is still able to have a tithe of the enjoyment from the knowledge of photography or the electric telegraph that the inventors had, or even as those who at the time of invention watched each new advance with eagerness?

If now we deduct all the receptivity and enjoyment in art and science which depend on mere appearances or affectation, whether they are affected from ambition and vanity or for the sake of gain, or because such a career has once been adopted for other reasons, of the seeming enjoyment of art and science existing in the world a very considerable, I believe by far the larger part, will fall away. The remainder, however, does not exist, without being purchased by a certain displeasure, although I shall by no means dispute that the pleasure of enjoyment predominates. This is clearest in the pleasure of producing. As is well known, no master ever yet fell from heaven, and the study which is requisite before one is ripe for a remunerative productivity is disagreeable and toilsome and mostly brings little pleasure, unless through overcome difficulties and hope of the future. In every art the technique must first be acquired, and in science one has first to attain the height of the special department if production is not to lag behind what already exists. What wearisome books has one not to read only to conscientiously convince oneself that there is nothing valuable in them, and others, again, to pick a grain of gold out of a heap of sand! Truly these are no small sacrifices. When one at last has advanced so far in one's preparations and preliminary studies as to be able to produce, the really sweet moments are still only those of conception, succeeded by long periods of mechanical elaboration. And not always is one disposed for production. If it were not for the urgent wish to complete the work in a definite space of time; if ambition or love of fame did not act as an incentive, or outward circumstances compel execution; lastly, did not the gaping spectre of ennui lurk behind idleness, very frequently the pleasure to be expected from production would not conquer the love of ease; nay, in spite of all, one is tempted only too often to cease labouring at the precious work.

The musician and scientific teacher, moreover, easily become disgusted with their calling through the monotony of their compulsory professional duties. The dilettante is still worse off with his production. His taste and understanding are usually in advance of his facility of performance, and hence his performances do not satisfy him, unless he be very vain and conceited.—Relatively less are the feelings of pain accompanying receptive enjoyment. In Science, however, they are far greater than in Art; *e.g.*, the reading of a strictly scientific book is in itself a labour, the undergoing of which always costs a certain amount of effort—an effort which most people would never make for the sake of a possible enjoyment.

Least fatiguing is the receptive enjoyment of *Art*, and I shall almost appear to trifle if I mention the disagreeables connected therewith; yet they are important, since with increasing love of ease (*e.g.*, in age) they are, in fact, able to deter most receptive minds from obtaining the enjoyment of art. They are the visiting of the galleries, the heat and closeness of the theatres and concert-rooms, the risk of catching cold, the fatigue of seeing and hearing which is wont to be so severe, because payment has to be made for viewing the whole gallery or hearing the entire concert, whilst half of the entertainment were sufficient. Of the enjoyment of amateur performances and the subsequent debt of compliments I would rather be silent, as my readers may perhaps be amateurs themselves.

The result then is, that of the few inhabitants of the earth who *seem* called to enjoy science or art, very few *are* really called, and most affect the call from ambition, vanity, the desire of gain, or other reasons; that those to whose lot such enjoyments really fall must yet pay for them with all kinds of less or greater sacrifice of pleasure; that thus, on the whole, the excess of pleasure which is produced by science and art as such in the world is exceedingly small compared with the sum of existing misery; and that this excess of pleasure is, moreover, distributed to those individuals who feel the pain of existence more profoundly than others—so much more profoundly than others that the pleasure they obtain is far from being a compensation. Lastly, it must be added that this species of enjoyment more than any other spiritual pleasure is limited to the present, whilst others usually are enjoyed in anticipation. This is connected with the peculiar circumstance previously discussed at length, that the same sense-perception which affords satisfaction also evokes the will which is satisfied.

9. *Sleep and Dreams.*—So far as sleep is dreamless, it is a complete inactivity of the brain and brain-consciousness, for as soon as the brain becomes at all active, it begins to sport with images. Such an unconscious state renders also all pleasurable or painful feeling impossible; but if a nervous stimulation occur which must excite pleasure or pain, it also interrupts the inactive state of the brain. Unconscious sleep, therefore, as regards the properly human or brain-consciousness, must be considered as equal to the zero-point of sensation. This does

not preclude other nerve-centres, like the spinal cord and ganglia, from continuing to be conscious; this is even necessary for the continuance of respiration, digestion, blood-circulation, &c.; but this is still merely a profoundly animal consciousness, occupying somewhat the level of an inferior fish or worm, which can have only very slight importance in the account of *human* happiness. But also in this animal consciousness of the lower nerve-centres alternate pleasure and pain; in the normal and undisturbed exercise of the vegetative functions a pleasure can only be felt in case that animal consciousness suffices for the perception of this pleasure. Every disturbance, however, is immediately felt as pain, and pain always procures for itself the degree of consciousness that is necessary for its perception.

There is one source of error which may lead to our assuming a clearer satisfaction in unconscious sleep than can in fact exist; this is the comfortable feeling that one often detects on falling to sleep or awaking, *i.e.*, in passing from the dormant to the waking state and conversely. But here the cerebral consciousness is still actual, and that satisfaction manifestly a perception of the cerebral consciousness; one therefore forgets that just this cerebral perception of satisfaction disappears in dreamless sleep. Of the satisfaction, however, which my lower nerve-centres feel I can form no conception, because *I* am simply and only my brain-consciousness. Yet, notwithstanding, unconscious sleep is the relatively happiest condition, because it is the only *painless* one known to us in normal life.

As for dreams, all the troubles of the waking state are prolonged into the dormant condition, but not the one thing which may in a measure reconcile the cultivated with life—the pleasures of Science and Art. Add to that that a joy cannot well be otherwise expressed in dreams than as a pleasant, cheerful *mood*, *e.g.*, the feeling of being disembodied, of floating, flying, and the like, whilst displeasure is expressed not only as mental mood, but also in all sorts of definite inconveniences, vexation, chagrin, quarrelling, and conflict, inability to accomplish one's desires, or other cross purposes and disappointments. On the average, therefore, the verdict with regard to the worth of dreams will be in accordance with that on the real life, but, on certain sides, will be far more unfavourable.

Falling to sleep is, if one can fall quickly to sleep, a pleasure, but yet only because fatigue had made waking a torment, and falling to sleep frees me from this torment. Awakening is also said by many people to be pleasurable. I have, however, never found it so, and fancy that this assertion rests on a confusion with the pleasure which consists in not being obliged to rise when actually weary, but in being able to go on slumbering with semi-consciousness. But how few people are in a position to enjoy this pleasure! That an awakening quickly passing into a state of complete vigilance should be a pleasure to anybody I cannot believe; I regard it rather as a pain, since one has once more to exchange the ease of rest and sleep for the drudgery of the day. That on being wide-awake, and after a sufficient period of sleep, the fatigue of the past evening has disappeared and the *status quo* of capacity for work and enjoyment is restored, cannot possibly pass for positive pleasure, since only the level of sensation has been again attained. But it certainly is a decided pain when one rises fatigued, not having had one's fill of sleep. In this position, inability to spare sufficient time for sleep before work, we find, however, a large part of the poorer classes of all nations. Even of Westphalian peasants I have heard that the whole family, after the field-work of the day, is compelled to spin for some hours into the night, although this labour is worth little more than a farthing an hour.

10. *The Acquisitive Instinct and Comfort.*—Under the acquisitive instinct I here mean especially the effort to possess beyond what is absolutely necessary, *i.e.*, beyond

dwelling, food, and clothing for self and family. I need hardly set myself to prove the small percentage of the population, even in civilised communities, for whom a satisfaction of this impulse is possible, as modern statistics speak both loudly and terribly. If we ask, however, what advantage a possession beyond the necessary can afford, it is especially this, that as a capital sum, and still more through its permanent investment, it protects from distress and removes the fear of future distress. But this utility is no positive one, it only secures from future and wards off present pain (fear and anxiety). In the second place, property gives the power of attaining positive gratifications; it begets the repute of possession; it confers power and influence over those who expect advantages from my possessions; it purchases the pleasures of the palate, and even the delights of love; in short, property, or its symbol, money, is the enchanter's wand, which procures access to all the enjoyments of life. But now we already know that all these enjoyments not only rest on illusions, but even the endeavour after them on the whole always brings more pain than pleasure; that thus all endeavour after them is *doubly foolish*. The pleasures of the palate and the enjoyments of science and art are the only exceptions. The former, however, have again the disadvantage that their privation, when they are withdrawn by change of circumstances, is felt far more painfully than their possession was before found agreeable. To procure the gratifications of science and art, money is undoubtedly convenient, yet one cannot say that much is required. But as for the purchase of love, one should remember the two following points: first, what Goethe says—

> "In vain thy mistress' heart to bend,
> The gold into her lap dost throw;
> Love must for nought her raptures lend,
> If thou love's joys wilt truly know."

And then, what holds good of the purchased possession of women far more than of spontaneous surrender, that hereby, and in its consequences for her whole life, the woman experiences far more of pain than the purchasing man can ever obtain of pleasure. So far, then, as riches lead to the desire for women, and increase ambition and love of domination, they are absolutely detrimental to life-happiness. Still more pernicious, however, does the acquisitive instinct become if it forgets that property is only an intrinsically worthless means to further ends, and regarding it as end in itself, turns into covetousness and avarice. Then, indeed, just as ambition and love themselves, it rests only on illusion, and becomes through the insatiableness of the instinct, whose thirst is extinguished by no satisfaction, whose least non-satisfaction, however, causes pain, a true torment.

If nothing could be added to the foregoing, the real importance of the acquisitive instinct for the happiness of life would be exhausted with protection from future want and with the procuring of the pleasures of science and art together with the gratifications of the palate; in that case we should have to ascribe to this impulse rather an economic value as an instinct careful for the evolution of humanity, than of direct importance for the welfare of those concerned; but we have not yet mentioned its most important function in the latter respect, to wit, the *making life comfortable*. The keeping of servants, equipages, comfortable dwellings in town and country, of majordomos and stewards, what is the object of it all except to make life comfortable? For the value of luxury as such is always wholly illusory.

But is comfort a positive pleasure, or does its agreeableness not rather consist in the removal of discomfort and reduction of the same to the threshold of sensation? Active motion, exercise, effort, and labour are disagreeable; passive motion and repose, on the contrary, are comfortable; but although one may understand how effort and motion may produce pain by means of the invasion of bodily health caused by the expenditure of force, yet it is absolutely unintelligible how repose, unchanged persistence, is to produce a positive pleasure; it can manifestly only represent the zero-point of sensation.

We accordingly come, strange to say, in the case of that which excites the greatest envy, wealth, to the same negative result as in the case of the bare prolongation of existence wherewith we began. This is certainly significant and characteristic for the worth of life.

It is beyond a doubt that the acquisitive impulse can always only be means to further ends, and its value must be measured by their value; but that in no case can it lay claim to intrinsic worth, and that, when it does so, it immediately falls into the rank of illusory impulses that produce an excess of pain. Compare on this Luke xii. 15: "Take heed, and beware of covetousness: for a man's life consisteth not in the abundance of the things which he possesseth;" and Matt. vi. 19–21 and 24–34.

11. *Envy, Jealousy, Chagrin, Pain and Lamentation for the Past, Repentance, Hatred, Vindictiveness, Anger, Sensitiveness*, and other qualities and passions of which common sense sees that they bring more pain than pleasure (comp. vol. ii. pp. 36–37), I need not specifically notice, especially as there is reason to hope that, as time goes on, they will be more and more suppressed by the reason. In estimating the present state of the world they still, however, weigh heavily in the balance.

12. *Hope.*

> "And, however hard the burden,
> That he faint not by the way,
> Hope with dreams of bliss enduring
> Feeds him till his dying day!"

However ill it goes with man, so long as a spark of vital force glows within him, he clings to hope of future happiness. Were there no hope in the world, despair would be the order of the day, and notwithstanding the instinct of self-preservation and the fear of death, we should have to record innumerable suicides.

Thus hope is the necessary auxiliary instinct of the self-preserving impulse; it is that which alone renders possible for us poor fools the love of life in defiance of our understanding.

Hope is a *trait of character.* There are people who from natural disposition always see the future black, others who always regard it of rosy hue (Dyskoly and Eukoly). Eukoly springs from a certain elasticity of the mind, an abundance of energy and vitality, which is not diminished by the most palpable experiences, and after the heaviest strokes of fate raises its head with the old spirit. No quality of character is so dependent on the general bodily constitution and the influences of the blood-circulation on the nerves and brain as this tendency to look hopefully upon the future. No quality of character, however, is so important in respect to the subjective influence of thought in considering the question of the worth or worthlessness of life. As now manifestly, even with the greatest worthlessness of life, hope is a *useful* instinct (whilst, on the other hand, if life really possessed a value, one could not see what would be the utility of a gloomy view as a mental characteristic), we must be extremely on our guard against a corruption and perversion of our judgment by the former instinct.

Without doubt hope is a *very real pleasure.* But what, then, does one hope? Unquestionably to catch and retain pleasure. But if happiness is not to be had, because, as long as one lives, pain always preponderates over pleasure, it follows that hope is *a contradiction and worthless;* that it is indeed the *illusion* κατ' ἐξοχήν; that its function is just to *dupe* us, *i.e.*, to make fools of us, in order only that we may endure to perform our yet uncomprehended task. But he who has once acquired the conviction that hope itself is as worthless and illusory as its object, must very soon find his instinct of hope enfeebled and depressed by this cognition of the understanding; the only thing which still remains possible to him as object of hope is not the greatest possible happiness, but the least possible unhappiness. This was already seen by Aristotle (Eth. Nicom., vii. 12): *ὁ φρόνιμος τὸ ἄλυπον διώκει, οὐ τὸ ἡδύ.* Therewith, however, all *positive* significance is stripped from hope.

But even he who never, or not completely, has discovered the illusory meaning of hope, might yet, at least for his past (for instinct only misleads him as regards the future), be compelled to allow that nine-tenths of all hopes, nay, far more, are frustrated, and that in most cases the bitterness of disappointment was greater than the sweetness of hope. The correctness of this assertion is confirmed by the rule of common prudence that our expectation should always be at a minimum, as only in that case are we able fully to enjoy what good there is in things, and otherwise the immediate enjoyment of the present time might be impaired by the deceived expectation. Consequently for the instinct of hope also the result is yielded that it is both illusory, and *within* the sphere of its special illusions rather brings more pain than pleasure.

13. *Résumé of the First Stage of Illusion.*—Suppose it lay in the nature of the will to produce, as it were, in gross an equal amount of pleasure as of pain, yet the net result of pleasure and pain would in general be modified unfavourably to pleasure by the following five factors:—

(*a.*) Nervous fatigue increases the repugnance to pain, diminishes the effort to retain pleasure; thus increases the pain of pain, diminishes the pleasure in pleasure.

(*b.*) The pleasure which arises through the cessation or remission of a pain cannot by a long way balance this pain, and of this kind is the largest part of existing pleasure.

(*c.*) Pain thrusts itself on consciousness, which must feel it; not so pleasure, which must, as it were, be discovered and inferred by consciousness, and is therefore very often lost to consciousness where the motive for its discovery is wanting.

(*d.*) Satisfaction is short and quickly fades; pain endures, so far as it is not limited by hope, so long as desire exists without satisfaction (and when does not such exist ?).

(*e.*) Equal quantities of pleasure and pain united in a consciousness are not of equal value; they do not compensate one another, but pain remains in excess, or the exclusion of every sensation is preferred to the questionable union.

These five items produce by their co-operation approximately the same result as if pleasure, as Schopenhauer deems, were something negative, unreal, and pain the alone positive and real.

If one considers the several phases of life, the various desires, impulses, ambitions, passions, and states of mind, they fall, according to their importance as conducive to real happiness, into the following groups:—

(*a.*) Such as bring *only* pain, or as good as no pleasure at all (comp. No. 11).

(*b.*) Such as represent only the zero-mark of sensation, or the level of life, the privation of certain kinds of pain, as health, youth, liberty, a competence, comfort, and in largest part also communion with one's fellows, or sociality.

(*c.*) Such as have a real importance only as means to ends lying beyond them, whose value therefore can only be measured by the value of these ends, which, however, regarded as ends in themselves, are illusory, *e.g.*, striving after possessions, power, and honour, partly also sociality and friendship.

(*d.*) Such as bring indeed a certain pleasure to the actor, but to him or the sufferers a pain far outweighing this pleasure, so that their total effect, and reciprocity being supposed, also the effect for all concerned is pain, *e.g.*, wrong-doing, lust of power, choler, hate and vindictiveness (even so far as they keep within the bounds of right), sexual seduction, and the food-instinct of flesh-eaters.

(*e.*) Such as, on the average, cause those experiencing them far more pain than pleasure, *e.g.*, hunger, sexual love, love of children, compassion, vanity, ambition, lust of fame, lust of power, hope.

(*f.*) Such as rest on illusions, which must be seen through in the progress of mental development, whereupon then indeed the pain arising through them is just as much diminished as the pleasure, but the latter far more speedily, so that hardly anything remains of it, *e.g.*, love, vanity, ambition, lust of fame, religious edification, hope.

(*g.*) Such as are perceived with clear consciousness as evils, and yet are voluntarily undertaken in order to avoid other evils that are regarded as still greater (no matter whether they are so or not), *e.g.*, work (instead of want and ennui), marriage, adopted children, and also the surrendering oneself to those impulses, of which one has perceived that they bring preponderating pain, the suppression of which, however, is regarded as still more tormenting.

(*h.*) Such as bring preponderating pleasure, although a pleasure purchased by more or less pain, *e.g.*, art and science, which, however, fall to the lot of relatively few, and with still fewer meet with a genuine love for and capacity of enjoying them; which few, again, are just those individuals who feel more acutely the other sorrows and pains of life.

In all this one should bear constantly in mind the assertion of Spinoza, "*that we neither endeavour after, will, yearn for, nor desire anything because we hold it to be good, but rather that we hold it to be good because we endeavour after, will, yearn for, and desire it*" (Eth., pt. 3, prop. 9, obs.), and always and everywhere apply this truth as corrective to one's emotional judgment rebelling against the results of rational reflection.

If, then, we put together the general and special considerations, there emerges the undoubted result that at present pain not only preponderates in the world in general to a high degree, *but also in each single individual, even him who is placed in the most favourable circumstances conceivable.* It further follows that the less sensitive individuals, and those endowed with a more obtuse nervous system, are *better* off than the more sensitive natures, because with the less amount of the perceived pleasure and pain *the difference in favour of pain also* becomes less. This thoroughly agrees with empirical observation in the case of man, and has, however, universal validity on account of its deductive character, so that it may be extended also to animals and plants.

It is in accordance with experience that the individuals of the lower and poorer classes and of ruder nations are happier than those of the elevated and wealthier classes and of civilised nations, not indeed because they are poorer and have to endure more want and privations, but because they are coarser and duller. One need only remember "the shirt of the happy man," in which story there lies a deep truth. And accordingly I also maintain that the brutes are happier (*i.e.*, less miserable) than man, because the excess of pain which an animal has to bear is less than that which a man has to bear. Only think how comfortably an ox or a pig lives, almost as if it had learned from Aristotle to seek freedom from care and sorrow, instead (like man) of hunting after happiness. How much more painful is the life of the more finely-feeling horse compared with that of the obtuse pig, or with that of the proverbially happy fish in the water, its nervous system being of a grade so far inferior! As the life of a fish is more enviable than that of a horse, so is the life of an oyster than that of a fish, and the life of a plant than that of an oyster, until finally, on descending beneath the threshold of consciousness, we see individual pain entirely disappear.

On the other hand, the higher sensibility sufficiently explains why men of genius are so much more unhappy in their lives than ordinary men, to which must be added (at least among reflective geniuses) the penetration of most illusions. This is in accordance with the result of the foregoing examination, which taught us that the individual is so much the better off the more he is entangled in the illusion created by the instinctive impulse ("He that increaseth knowledge increaseth sorrow."—Ecclesiastes); for, in the first place, it has corrupted his judgment on the true proportion of past pleasure and pain, and in consequence he feels his misery less, and is not so oppressed by this feeling of misery; and, secondly, there remains to him in every direction the happiness of hope, whose partial frustration is quickly followed by new hopes, whether in the same or in another direction. He lives, therefore, always in dreamland, and in all present misery consoles himself with the illusion which promises him a golden future. (Käthchen von Heilbronn or Mr. Micawber in "David Copperfield" will readily occur to the reader.)

This felicity of the illusive reverie is especially characteristic of youth. Every youth, every girl, regards him or her self more or less as the hero or the heroine of a romance, and they console themselves for their present misfortunes or reverses, as in their novel-reading, with the prospect of the radiant conclusion; only with the difference that it never comes, and that they forget that behind the seemingly brilliant conclusion of the story lurks the common drudgery of life.

Of the rich assortment of youthful hopes, however, with advancing age and experience one after the other is seen to be illusory, and the man is relatively far poorer in illusions than the youth, ambition and the desire of property usually alone remaining.

These, too, also are perceived to be illusory by the old

man, unless ambition ossifies into childish vanity, the acquisitive instinct into avarice; and among sensible old men one finds, in fact, no more illusions having reference to the life of the individual, save, of course, the instinctive love of children and grandchildren.

The result of individual life is, then, that all is surrendered; that, as the Preacher sees, "All is vanity," i.e., illusory, worthless.

In the life of humanity this first stage of the illusion and its abandonment is represented by the ancient (Jewish-Greek-Roman) world. In the earlier Asiatic empires the tendencies of life and thought afterwards distinguished are all too intermingled. Mosaism most openly declares the faith in the attainability of individual terrestrial felicity, both in its promises and also in its general optimistic world-view without a transcendent background. In Greece the same tendency is exhibited in a nobler fashion in the enjoyment of art and science, and in a certain æsthetic conception of life. Hellenism also rejoices in an endeavour after a refined individual earthly happiness, since the πολιτεία is merely to afford maintenance and protection. Think of the utterance of the dead Achilles in the "Odyssey" (xi. 488–491)—

> "Speak not lightly to me of death, O famous Odysseus;
> Rather would I as a serf act as the serf of another,
> A man of little possessions, with scanty means of subsistence,
> Than rule as a ghostly monarch the ghosts of all the departed."

The well-known pessimistic chorus in the masterpiece of the aged Sophocles must not be taken as an expression of Hellenic feeling; it and other similar passages, as well as the significant melancholy found in masterpieces of Hellenic art in the midst of all the seeming satisfaction, prove that even at that time gifted individuals were able to peer through the illusions of life, to which the spirit of their own age surrendered itself without the faintest critical reflection.

The Roman republic certainly adds a new element:

the endeavour after happiness in and through the enhancement of the splendour and power of the strict Fatherland. After this effort at the attainment of universal empire proves illusory in respect of felicity, a degraded form of Greek speculation is adopted by Rome in the shape of the shallowest Epicureanism, and the ancient world lingers out its day in the utmost disgust of life.

SECOND STAGE OF THE ILLUSION.

Happiness is conceived attainable by the individual in a transcendent life after death.

On this extreme weariness of life of the ancient world falls the kindling ray of the Christian IDEA. The founder of Christianity completely adopts the contempt and weariness of earthly life, and draws from them their last and most repulsive consequences (comp. F. A. Müller, "Briefe über die Christliche Religion," Stuttgart, Kötzle, 1870).

Only to those who feel the misery of existence, sinners, outcasts (Samaritans and publicans), oppressed (slaves and women), poor, sick, and suffering, but not to those who feel themselves well off and comfortable in the earthly life, does he bring his gospel (Matt. xi. 5; Luke vi. 20–23; Matt. xix. 23–24; Matt. xi. 28). He rejects everything natural, not even laws of nature does he acknowledge (Matt. xvii. 20); he speaks slightingly of the ties of family (Matt. x. 35–37; Matt. xix. 29; Matt. xi. 47–50); he requires sexual continence (Matt. xix. 11–12); he condemns the world and its goods (Luke xii. 15; Matt. vi. 25–34; 1 John i. 15–16; Luke xvi. 15); declares it to be impossible simultaneously to attain earthly and heavenly bliss (Matt. vi. 19–21, and 24; John xii. 25; Matt. xix. 23–24), and demands, therefore, voluntary poverty (Matt. xix. 21–22; Luke xii. 33; Matt. vi. 25, and 31–34). Nowhere and in no respect does Christ prescribe asceticism, although voluntary restraint and the fewest possible wants, whence it is clear that he assumes pain to increase with the number of wants and desires. He regards his age as so corrupt (Matt. xxiii. 27; Matt. xvi. 2–3) that the day of judgment must be near at hand (Matt. xxiv. 33–34), and the quintessence of his teaching is, patiently to bear this life of affliction in the terrestrial vale of tears as one's cross (Matt. x. 38), and to follow him in worthy preparation and cheerful hope of the blessedness of a future eternal life (Matt. x. 38–39). "These things I have spoken unto you, that in *me* ye might have *peace*. *In the world ye shall have tribulation: but be of good cheer; I have overcome the world*" (John xvi. 33).

This is the fundamental difference between the older Judaism and Christianity; the promises of the former have reference to the life here ("that it may be well with thee, and thou mayest live long on the earth"), those of the latter to the life beyond; and this earthly vale of tears has only a meaning as preparation and trial for the life hereafter (1 Peter i. 5–7); in itself, however, of no value whatever; on the contrary, the earthly life is composed of tribulation (John xvi. 33) and daily torment and evil (Matt. vi. 34: "Sufficient unto the day is the evil thereof"). Love makes this limbo more bearable, and is also the test of worthiness (Rom. xiii. 8–10; Matt. xxii. 37–39); faith and hope of the hereafter enable us to "overcome the world" or "to be delivered from the world," *i.e.*, from evil and sin.

The redemption of the world through Christ comes to pass, therefore, through this, that all men follow him in despising the world, and in living in faith and hope of a hereafter; but not through his death with the subsequent Judaical conception of the same as a purifying sin-offering, of which Christ himself assuredly would not have heard for a moment.

This is the historical and only important content of the doctrine preached by Jesus, to which, at the most, the rejection of an outward ritual and all priestly mediation in worship is to be added. Christian virtue also follows on its negative side from contempt of the flesh, whence all sin arises, on its positive side from the supreme commandment of love.

All that relates to earthly relations themselves is so unimportant and indifferent to him, that he either fits himself to the existing order with smiling contempt (Matt. xxii. 21; Matt. xvii. 24–27), or only gently hints at what is desirable, *e.g.*, self-government and independent jurisdiction (Matt. xviii. 15–17) of the communistic society. All other ideas, which we are accustomed to regard as Christian, were already current in the ancient world, but outside India the combination of contempt of the world and intense belief in an eternal transcendent blessedness was new. It was the peculiar world-redeeming Idea which saved the dying antiquity from its despair and world-weariness, in that it condemned the flesh and enthroned the spirit, conceived the natural world as the kingdom of the devil (John xiv. 30, and xvii. 9), and only this transcendent world of the spirit as the kingdom of God (1 John iv. 4, and v. 19), which latter certainly, according to Christ himself, could *even here* have its commencement in the hearts of believers; as Paul (Rom. viii. 24) very truly says, "For we are saved by *hope*."

Contempt for the world combined with a transcendent life of the spirit had, indeed, in India already found a place in the esoteric doctrine of Buddhism; had, however, in the first place, not become known to the Western mind; in the second place, in India itself was only within the reach of a narrow circle of celibate adepts; and, thirdly, had soon been submerged in exoteric frenzy, so that the thought only attained realisation in the eccentric phenomena of hermits and penitents; fourthly, it did not originally spring up in a soil so fertile by reason of previous corruption; fifthly, it did not possess in the same degree the cosmopolitan side, the idea of the universal human brotherhood and the divine fatherhood

(Matt. xxiii. 8–9); sixthly and lastly, what is most important, it knows indeed an eternal transcendent blessedness for those finally released from terrestrial existence, but no *individual* immortality. Christianity, however, which promises a resurrection (of the flesh), and, accordingly, an *individual* everlasting life in the transcendent kingdom of God, thereby appeals more directly to human egoism, and consequently inspires the believer with a far more felicific hope. In this satisfying hope the Christian world has hitherto lived, and still for the most part continues to live.

We have already seen above, under the head of Religious Edification, that the pleasure arising from religious hope and devotion is also not without pain, partly resulting from the rebellion of the instinctive impulses against their unnatural suppression, partly consisting in the doubts concerning one's own worthiness and the procuring of the divine favour, and in the fear of the last judgment. Add to that the required repentance and contrition for one's own sins and sinfulness, even when one is, properly speaking, not conscious of wrong-doing. Whether the religious pain or pleasure predominates will essentially depend on the character; frequently, however, with the genuine believer hope will predominate. Pity only that this hope, too, like all others, rests on an illusion. I abstain here from a searching examination of the doctrine of the individual perpetual existence of the soul, and simply refer to Chaps. ii. and vii., Sect. C., according to which the individuality both of the organised body and of consciousness is only a *phenomenon*, that disappears with death, and only the substance, the One Unconscious, remains, which evoked this phenomenon partly by its own individuation as atoms, partly by its direct action on the atomic groups combined to form a body.

I may remark that the cosmic theory of Jesus was far too naïve and childish to consider possible the separation of body and soul, and the isolated continuance of the latter.

Hence also the adoption of "the resurrection of the flesh" into the third article of the Confession of Faith is quite in the sense of Christ. Passages certainly are to be found in John and Paul which throw light on the nature of the eternal life little in harmony with the promises of Christ, but their consequences were never drawn. Rev. x. 5, 6: "And the angel . . . sware by him that liveth for ever and ever . . . *that there should be time no longer.*" 1 Cor. xiii. 8: "Charity never faileth; but whether there be prophecies, they shall fail; whether there be tongues, they shall cease; *whether there be knowledge, it shall vanish away.*"

The latter passage announces the cessation of all *consciousness*, the former the ceasing of all *change* in that condition; both abolish individuality, or at least its significance. That in all the important systems of modern philosophy (apart from Kant's inconsequence and Schelling's later declension) there is no room for an individual immortality no one save the self-deluded can for a moment doubt. I shall, however, although very rapidly, summarise the opinions of certain ancient and modern thinkers.

In Plato's "Timaeus" (ed. Steph., iii. p. 69) we read: "And of the divine (existences) he himself becomes the fashioner. The generation of mortals, however, he intrusted to his own children; and they imitating, having received the immortal foundation of the soul, surrounded it with a mortal body, and gave it as vehicle the whole body, and built *in it another kind of soul—the mortal*, receptive of fearful and inevitable feelings, first pleasure, the greatest bait of evil; then pains, warding off the good, and again boldness and fear, senseless counsellors; then anger, slow to cease, and seductive hope; and having mingled these with irrational perception and love ready to attempt all things, compounded by necessity the race of mortals."

From this, together with Plato's theory of Knowledge,

it follows that he placed the immortal soul exclusively in truthful cognition, *i.e.*, the vision of the Platonic IDEAS, which in its very nature admits no individual distinctions, although this consequence may never have been clear to Plato himself.

Aristotle occupies the same point of view. De An., i. 4, 408, a, 24 ff., he denies to the **νοῦς ποιητικός**, as he calls the immortal part of the soul, not only love and hate, but also memory and discursive thinking (διανοεῖσθαι); from other passages we gather that the **νοῦς ποιητικός** (or active understanding) is the eternal, universal, unchangeable, and inaccessible to all external impressions in man; it is accordingly altogether incomprehensible how it could be individual.

Spinoza, who certainly proceeds from other presuppositions, comes to the same result. "The human mind cannot be absolutely annihilated with the body, but there remains something of it which is *eternal*" (Eth., part v. prop. 23). As is clear from the proof of this proposition, by "eternal" the "enduring" is by no means to be understood, but only the being logically contained in the IDEA of the Absolute Substance (part v. prop. 22). "Our mind can only be called enduring and its existence be defined by a certain time, so far as it includes *the actual existence of the body*" (*ibid.*) If we now ask *which* part of the mind is to be affirmed eternal, *i.e.*, contained as necessary moment in the eternal IDEA of God, we are able so far to determine it that it can only be the purely active, not the passive mind affected by the body. To the latter part belong, however, all the passions and emotions, sense-perception, ideation, and memory; they are all accordingly dependent on the existence of the body, and cannot endure after its death (part v. prop. 34, 21). Even love belongs to the transitory perturbations of the soul, and must perish with the body; only the intellectual love springing from intellectual intuition (part v. prop. 33) with which God loves himself calmly and dispassionately (prop. 17, corollary), only this purely contemplative absorption in the logical necessity of the Absolute is eternal (prop. 34, corollary). Strictly speaking, then, there is nothing eternal in mind but the third species of intellectual perception (prop. 33, proof; comp. above, vol. i. p. 22, obs.) This, however, and the consciousness of himself, of God, and of the eternal necessity of things springing from it along with the sequent mental repose, only the wise man will really possess, whilst the mind of the uncultivated is absorbed in passive sensation. As soon, therefore, as "the uncultivated ceases to feel, he also ceases to be" (prop. 42, obs.); so that, properly speaking, we can only speak of an eternal part of the mind in the cultured and wise.[1] If we ask, finally, how we are to conceive the eternal being of the active part of the spirit, the required answer is given in part ii. prop. 8, to wit, since the mind is the idea of the body, the mind, before and after the actual existence of the body, is the idea of a non-existent thing. Of such ideas, however, the proposition mentioned affirms that they must be contained in the infinite idea of God, as the formal essences of individual things or modes in God's attributes, which is elucidated in the observation by the manner in which the infinitely numerous ideas of describable rectangles are contained in the idea of a given circle, although they are not actually drawn therein. We should, however, say that only the formal possibility of these rectangles is given, and accordingly that in the eternal absolute idea the idea of a particular individual mind is only potentially contained, which implicit potentiality, however, is only explicated realiter at the moment when the individual mind

[1] As is well known, Goethe likewise inclined to this view of a reservation of immortality for the aristocracy of mind; and, in fact, if one insists on maintaining the immortality of the intellectually eminent, and at the same time does not admit the immortality of the souls of infusoria or the soul of the first fecundated human ovum, there always lies more sense in drawing the line for the immortals at the intellectual aristocracy of humanity than in arbitrarily placing it between Bushman and orang outang, or between the seventh and ninth month of the embryonic life.

attains to actual existence in an organism. With this interpretation there is just as little to be said against Spinoza's eternity of individual minds as (say) against the eternity of any particular mathematical truth.

In Leibniz this at least is deserving of notice, that he is unable to assign as the individual limitation of the monads anything but the body, and therefore ventures to assert the immortality of the soul only with a simultaneous immortality of a body peculiar to it and inalienable. At the present stage of physical science the statement of the latter hypothesis is its own criticism.

Schelling expresses himself in like manner as Spinoza (i. 6, 60–61): "The eternal element of the soul is not eternal on account of the absence of a beginning or end to its duration, but it has altogether no relation to time. It can therefore also *not be called immortal* in the sense in which this concept includes that of an *individual* perpetuity. . . . It is therefore a mistaking of the genuine spirit of philosophy, to place the immortality above the eternity of the soul and its being in the IDEA, and, as appears to us, a distinct *misunderstanding* to conceive the soul at death denuded of sensibility, and yet to possess an endless *individual* existence."—Fichte and Hegel entirely adopt this view, and Schopenhauer goes still farther, in that with him only the will, never knowledge, is eternal.

In the monistic systems, be they Naturalism, Pantheism, or Personal Pantheism, there can be no talk of individual immortality without the grossest inconsistency, and just as little in the pluralistic Materialism; it remains a matter of discussion, therefore, only in the system of a psychical Individualism or in Theism proper. As for the former, I know of no elaborated system of psychical Individualism that does not lead to the more or less open confession of impotency to stand by Pluralism as a metaphysical ultimate. Leibniz concludes with the all-comprehending central monad, which, in truth, absorbs the whole Monadology; Herbart with the double entry of the God-Creator of faith by the side of the known absolute positions of the many simple Reals. We have, then, strictly only to do with Theism, if also with a shame-faced Theism. Even in Theism, however, as we saw before (vol. ii. pp. 266–269), the individual is guaranteed continued existence only as long (we will not say) as God does not issue his annihilating fiat, but God as constantly renews his conserving action. Now one might allege the abstract possibility that God should let the individual endure to the world's end, and even appeal to the analogy of the atoms, which, although also mere manifestations of divine will, doubtless severally possess an unbroken existence from the beginning to the end of the world. In opposition to this, however, we may refer to Chaps. vi. and xi. C., in which the concept of individuality is analysed, and the great difference between the simple will-act in the atom and the very compound individual we call man is pointed out. The atomic will can be constant because it is simple; the stream of will-acts of the Unconscious, which is directed upon a particular individual organism, cannot possibly have a longer duration than the object on which it is directed. If the organism has entered into dissolution and the organic individual has lost its existence; if, in consequence, the consciousness has ceased that was bound to this organism and had stored up its ideal treasures, and possessed the determining ground of its individual character, in the molecular arrangement of the cerebral molecules of the same, then is the fasciculus of actions of the Unconscious, which afforded this individual mind its metaphysical foundation, without an object, and thereby becomes impossible as continued *action*. The *power* to will is not thereby altered, but this is no longer *individual*, but resides in the universal and unique unconscious essence. Were there even a similar organism created on which the Unconscious should direct similar actions, it would still be *another* individual, not the same as the deceased, since continuity of existence would be wanting. Unwarranted as would be the assertion that before the organic development of the ovum and the spermatozoon, whence a future man arises, the same man possessed an individual psychical antenatal life, no less unjustified would be the assumption that after the destruction of the organism the man might possess an individual psychical after-life. What is enduring is the substance that is manifested in this particular man, but this substance is not individual.

Thus, then, also, the hope of an individual duration of the soul turns out to be an *illusion*, and therewith the main nerve of the Christian promises is cut, the Christian Idea outgrown. The draft on the life hereafter, which is to compensate for the miseries of the life here, has only one fault: place and date of discharge are forged. *Egoism* finds this result *cheerless; to it* indeed immortality was a postulate of the heart; and with the observation that postulates of the heart can establish no metaphysical verities (as Jacobi and Schleiermacher fancy), *its* comfortable condition ceases. But the sterling soul that puts its trust in self-renunciation and love does *not* find this result cheerless. To the unselfish the guarantee of an endless self-affirmation appears not merely worthless, but disquieting and abhorrent, and all the attempts to demonstrate immortality as an emotional postulate on any other basis than that of the grossest self-love utterly fail (comp. my essay, "Ist der pessimistische Monismus trostlos?" in the "Ges. philosoph. Abhandlungen," No. iv.) Even the humblest form of the desire for immortality, the wish to live on in one's works, deeds, and achievements, is egoistic; for one may indeed rightly desire the continued production of good deeds and the continued influence of useful and admirable works, but the insertion of the dear self into this wish, the demand that it shall be just *my* deeds and works that shall bear fruit for the future of the world, is, if, humanly speaking, excusable, yet always an ethically unjustified *selfishness*, which becomes even *vanity* when it requires the grateful preservation of the *name* and its memory among the men who derive a benefit from the deeds and works.

Since *all* longing for immortality is egoism, it would seem to be of small importance to all who have been "saved by hope" in the immortality dogma whether, after the destruction of the hope in *individual* immortality, Christianity, with its transcendent optimism as regards the truth of an eternal blessedness in general, in contrast to the originally purely negative Buddhism, is right or wrong; for he to whom immortality is a postulate of the heart is also always so far egoist as to say, "What is the greatest future blessedness *to me*, if *I* do not feel and enjoy it?"

But how stands it in general with that everlasting blessedness according to our premisses? The only Unconscious is all-knowing and all-wise, cannot therefore become wiser; it has, as Aristotle says, no memory, therefore can learn nothing from the experience which it gets (suppose) in the world. Consequently, when the world has once ceased to be, and the fleeting moment of *contrast* between the torment of willing and the peace of non-willing is past, it is precisely in the same condition as it was before the creation of the world; as blessed as it formerly was is it now again, neither more nor less: the world-process can never help it to a greater bliss than it possessed before, unless it should find it *in* the process itself. (This latter case we do not, however, consider here, for it would be only the secular life itself, whereas we are inquiring concerning the bliss of the ultra-mundane condition.) If, then, through terrestrial life we can make no addition to the felicity of that ante-mundane state, but after the close of the world-process merely relapse into that former condition, the question arises of what nature it was. It is clear that if there had been willing, there would also have been act, therefore process, and the Unconscious would not have been acosmic; the acosmic state could only be that of non-willing. But now we have seen (Chap. i. C.)

that until the world existed thought could only be urged by volition from non-existence into existence; for in itself thought had no impulse and no motive to emerge from non-being into being, therefore *before* the occurrence of volition there was also no actual thinking; consequently, before the origin of the world neither willing *nor* thinking, *i.e.*, *nothing actual at all*, nothing but the quiescent, inactive, self-enclosed *essence* without existence. As long as volition lasts, so long will the process and its phenomenon in consciousness, the cosmos, last; if, then, one day the world shall be no more, there will be no willing, consequently also no thinking more (since the unconscious thinking always only becomes so far actual as the interest of the will requires it), *i.e.*, it will again, in the same sense of the term as above, be *nothing*. This is also the state alluded to in the words of the Apostles, that there shall be no more time nor knowledge. As long, then, as the world exists is there cosmic process, and as much happiness or unhappiness as this includes; before the genesis and after the cessation of the world and the world-process is—actually—Nothing.

Where now is the promised bliss? *In* the world it may and can not be, and the *nothingness after* the world could at the best be relatively happier or unhappier than an earlier condition, but not a positive blessedness or unblessedness (comp. Aristot., Eth. N. i. 11, 1100, a, 13). Certainly if the world is the state of the unblessedness of the creative Being of the world, *in comparison with that* nothingness will be blessedness; but unfortunately this contrast can only be drawn in the condition of existence, not in that of non-existence, since in the latter there is neither thought nor feeling—for either would be already actuality, which is excluded—the one would presuppose actual imagination, the other even actual reflection on a memory of the former intra-mundane state implying comparison with the present, and the participation of the will in this reflection, all which is simply impossible.

Thus thinks Buddhism with its "Nirvâṇa;" thus Schopenhauer; but not so Christianity. This is as little satisfied with such a reduction to the zero-point of sensation, to painlessness and absence of happiness, as the common egoistic understanding that claims the fulfilment of its instinctive striving after happiness as its natural right. Christianity does not indeed strictly allow a right to happiness, but it demands its renunciation only to enhance the value of the undeserved gift of grace of a happiness hereafter, and the individual Christian foregoes his pretended right, only because he is assured of the satisfaction of his claims by express covenant. Christianity must have a positive world-goal or renounce the principle that at bottom distinguishes it from Buddhism, *i.e.*, abdicate. As, however, no satisfactory explanation can make this practical postulate intelligible, every justification of the positive transcendent bliss that refuses to rest content with a confessedly unintelligible divine promise must issue in a more or less fantastic presentation of Nirvâṇa, which, of course, in the character of its phantasmagoria follows the direction of and changes with the culture of the time. The Christian theory of the world is simply incapable of rising to the complete resignation of happiness; even Christian asceticism is out-and-out selfish. Hence it is no wonder if we, who are still more or less entangled (I will not say, in the Christian faith, but) in the Christian philosophy, indignantly resent the complete renunciation of happiness. A prolonged historical discipline, and the discipline, moreover, of a non-Christian purely secular period, is needed to prepare mankind for this extreme demand. This period, however, we shall soon become acquainted with as the third stage of Illusion.

But now, if, on the one hand, the Christian hope of blessedness rests on an illusion, that necessarily disappears in the further course of the development of consciousness; if, on the other hand, the mission of the gospel through Jesus, and its eager reception by the nations, in spite of Greek philosophy, that had long risen above this childish standpoint, can certainly only be understood as a direct intervention of the Unconscious in the genius of the founders and the popular instinct of the rage for conversion, the question arises, *what* then was the object of this illusion? The answer is simply this, that this second stage is the necessary link between the first and the third, because through despair of the first stage of the illusion, *Egoism* is not yet so far broken as not to cling with both arms to the only egoistic hope still remaining to it. Not till this anchor too breaks, and the complete despair of attaining happiness for one's dear self has taken possession of the soul, not till then does it become receptive for the self-denying thought, to work *only* for the weal of future generations, to lose itself in the universal movement for the future good of the whole.

Rome had indeed possessed and practised this self-renunciation, but only for the sake of increasing the power of a single branch of the human family; it had, therefore, as it were, expanded individual egoism into a race-egoism, and in this spirit chased the phantoms of boundless ambition and lust of power; but now the question becomes the expansion of the egoistic into a *cosmic* consciousness and endeavour, of self-*seeking personal* feeling into self-*denying impersonal* feeling, into the consciousness that the individual and the nation are nothing but a wheel or a spring in the vast world-machine, and have no other task than to do their duty as such, to further the movement of the whole, which alone is of consequence.

For such a thought, for such a self-renunciation, the ancient world was of course not ripe, and there was an external secondary reason, as it were, for the interim existence of Christianity in the circumstance that so much technical progress had to be made before the possible opening of a world-communication, and that the future elements of telluric social life, the nationalities, had first to be created. *Apart* from all this, there is exhibited, however, a decided *advance* from the first to the second stage of the illusion, namely, in the acquired conviction that happiness is *not* to be found in the present phase of the evolution, just as in the transition from the second to the third stage the advance consists in the attained perception, that the way to redemption from the misery of the present, in the first place, is *not* to be sought outside the *world-process*, but lies *in the world-process itself;* that thus the future redemption of the world is not to be found in *abstention from life*, but in *devotion to life;* that, however, again this devotion to life, which for its own sake would be an absurdity, has only a meaning for the sake of the future of the process of the whole.

This passage from the second to the third stage is certainly with human weakness hardly otherwise to be conceived than through a partial mistaking of the latter truth, *i.e.*, than through a partial relapse into the first stage of the illusion; for how is man to attain to a sufficiently strong faith in a future happiness on earth if he regards the present state as miserable in every respect, and all attainable happiness in the life of the present as vain?

Accordingly we see with the principle of free investigation and criticism set up by the Reformation, although negatively, it is true, the commencement of the decomposition of the Christian dogma and the destruction of its promises; but at the same time we see appear, in place of the Christian "salvation in the hope of the hereafter," the regeneration of ancient art and science, the sudden growth of municipal wealth and commerce, and the progress of the practical arts, the universal expansion of the mental horizon; in a word, the *reawakening love of the world.*

The gigantic progress in all directions after so long a stagnation kindled hope into still greater expectations, and there thus arose, as ever in the epochs of much-promising progress, a period of optimism, whose chief theoretical representative is Leibniz. (At the present moment, when the formation of nationalities is nearing its end, there prevails a similar optimism in political affairs.) Only slowly and gradually can the power of an idea so great as the Christian be broken. This is especially interesting to observe in the most recent philosophy. Kant, growing dizzy at the unfathomable consequences of his principle, turns back and prescribes his soul as quickly as possible to the Christian God, solemnly reinstated by the practical categorical imperative; Hegel tries, by the juggle of a symbolic dialectic, to save, at any rate, some of the leading ideas of Christianity; Schelling, with a start, pauses at the very edge of the abyss, and meekly returns at the end of his system to the positive dogma of revelation, with a perfectly serious deduction of the three Persons of the Christian Trinity from the potentialities of being.

There is only one who completely and in all respects breaks with Christianity, and denies it all significance for the future—Schopenhauer—to be sure only to relapse into Buddhist asceticism, and without being able to rise to the thought of the possibility of a positive principle for the historical future, without the trace of an understanding and a love for the great endeavours of our time, which are abundantly represented in all other recent philosophers. Day by day secular aims palpably gain in power, extent, and interest; Antichrist is evidently advancing more and more, and soon Christianity will only be a shadow of its medieval greatness—will again be, what it exclusively was at its origin, the last consolation of the poor and wretched.

THIRD STAGE OF THE ILLUSION.

Happiness relegated to the future of the world.

Characteristic of this stage is the idea of immanent development, its application to the world as a whole, and the belief in a cosmic evolution. In ancient philosophy, with the exception of Aristotle, we can find no trace of this, but even in Aristotle the application of the conception is substantially limited to the natural evolution of the individual, and on the mental side, at any rate, exerted no epoch-making influence on contemporaries or posterity.

Rome recognised a development only as development of the power of Rome. To the inherently stationary and stagnant Judaism the idea of development is so strange and repugnant, that even a Mendelssohn could maintain and defend against a Lessing the impossibility of progress.

Catholic Christianity is likewise self-complete and perfect; it strives only after *an extension* of the kingdom of God, not after the enriching of its substance; the evolution of dogma in the first centuries takes place against its will, as it were, simply from the endeavour to attain a fixed form. The Reformers also had by no means the intention of carrying the development of Christianity farther, but only of purifying it from abuses that had crept in, and of restoring it to its original form.

Even Spinoza's rigid necessity, whose soulless and aimless character causes the ever-varying forms of existence to appear only as an indifferent, I might almost say, capricious and fortuitous sport, has no place for the notion of evolution; it is Leibniz who first discovers it, as it were, afresh, but also immediately works it out in all its significance and varied application, and in this sense may, to a certain extent, be regarded as the positive apostle of the modern world.

Lessing makes a magnificent use of the same in his "Education of the Human Race;" the works of Schiller are penetrated by it; Herder gives it expression in his "Ideas on the Philosophy of the History of Mankind," and Kant in several essays on the Philosophy of History, animated by the genuine philosophic spirit (Werke, Bd. vii., Nos. xii., xv., xix.) Most full and profound is this thought in Hegel, for whom indeed the whole world is nothing but a self-realising of the IDEA (cp. Ges. philos. Abhandl., No. ii.: "Ueber die nothwendige Umbildung der Hegel'schen Philosophie aus ihrem Grundprincip heraus").

That the whole cosmic mechanism is one great process of development emerges ever more distinctly as result of modern positive science. Astronomy no longer limits itself merely to the genesis of the planetary system; by the help of spectrum analysis it reaches farther into the cosmos, in order, by a comparison of the present states of remote suns and nebulæ, to comprehend the same as different stages of an evolution in which one part has advanced more quickly, another more slowly, but whose sum can only be conceived as a collective cosmic evolution. Photometry and spectrum analysis combined seek to ascertain the continuation of the same in the formation of the several planets; and chemistry and mineralogy unite to determine more precisely the phase of evolution of our planet before that period of refrigeration, whose gradual progress to the present time is told in the stony memorials of geology, in hieroglyphics that are being continually deciphered. Biology interprets to us from the petrified remains of past ages the history of the vegetable and animal kingdoms (cp. C. Chap. x.); and archæology, supported by comparative philology and anthropology, unveils to us the pre-historical period of development of the human race, whose magnificent tableau of advancing civilisation is displayed in history, revealing at the same time glimpses of the future (cp. Chap. x. 13). What the several sciences offer piecemeal Philosophy has to comprehend with all-embracing glance, and to recognise as the development of the world-whole providentially guided by the all-wisdom of the Unconscious according to pre-determined plan to a beneficent goal.

In the case of the individual it is not difficult to convince one's self of the fact of an evolution One sees it indeed on all hands every day. The more difficult, however, is it so to assimilate the thought of the development of a whole consisting of many individuals as to gain for it an *ultra*-egoistic *interest;* for from nothing is it more difficult to free ourselves than from the instinct of egoism.

Extremely instructive in this reference is "Der Einzige und sein Eigenthum," by Max Stirner, a book that nobody interested in practical philosophy should leave unread. This book subjects all ideals having an influence on practice to a destructive criticism, and shows them to be idols that only possess power over the Ego so far as the latter concedes such to them in its self-mistaking weakness. It cleverly and piquantly demolishes with forcible reasons the ideal aims of political, social, and humanitarian Liberalism; and shows how the Ego alone can be the smiling heir of all these ideals thus reduced to impotent nothings. If these considerations only had the purpose of confirming the theoretical position that I can as little step out of the frame of my self-hood as out of my skin, nothing need be added; but as Stirner professes to have found in the Idea of the Ego the absolute standpoint for action, he either falls into the same error that he had combated in the case of the other ideals, such as Honour, Freedom, Right, &c., and places himself at the mercy of another enthralling idea, whose absolute sovereignty he recognises, not however for this or that reason, but blindly and instinctively, or he conceives the Ego not as idea but as reality, and with no other result than the perfectly empty and meaningless tautology that I can will only my own will, think only my own thoughts, and that only my own thoughts can become motives of my willing—a fact as undeniable by his opponents as by himself. If, however, and only in that case has his conclusions any sense, he means that we ought to acknowledge the IDEA of the Ego as the only governing one, and to admit all other ideals only so far as they have a value for the former, he should first have examined the idea of the Ego. He would then before all have found that, as all the other ideals are the cues of instincts in pursuit of special ends, so the Ego is the cue of a universal instinct, egoism, that is related to the special instincts somewhat as a season to a day ticket, of which many special instincts are only derivatives in particular cases, and with which, therefore, we can get along tolerably well after all other instincts have been banished, which even, on the contrary, is never entirely to be dispensed with as long as we live.

Thus it is certainly more pardonable to accord an unconditional sovereignty to this instinct than to any other; but although in the abstract the error is the same in the two cases, the consequences are far worse in the exclusive homage paid to egoism. Other instincts, namely, if they are only sufficiently strong, can frequently be pacified, although commonly only with sacrifice of happiness on the whole, which makes them unprofitable; but egoism is, according to our former inquiries, never to be satisfied, because it always procures an excess of pain.

This perception, that from the point of view of the ego or the individual the denial of the will or forsaking of the world and renunciation of life is the *only rational course*, Stirner entirely misses. It is, however, an infallible specific for an over-balanced egoism. Whoever has once realised the preponderating pain that every individual must endure, with or without knowledge, in his life, will soon contemn and scorn the standpoint of the self-preserving and would-be enjoying—in a word, self-*affirming* ego. He who has come to hold lightly his egoism and his ego will hardly insist upon the same as the absolute pivot on which everything must turn, will rate personal sacrifice less highly than usual, will less reluctantly accept the result of an investigation which exhibits the Ego as a mere *phenomenon* of a Being that for all individuals is one and *the same*.

Contempt of the world and life is the easiest path to self-denial; *only by this path* has a morality of self-denial, like the Christian and Buddhist, been historically possible. In these fruits which it bears for facilitating the infinitely difficult self-renunciation lies the immense and hardly to be sufficiently estimated *ethical value of Pessimism*.

But lastly, had Stirner approached the direct philosophical investigation of the Idea of the Ego, he would have seen that this idea is just as unsubstantial and brain-created a phantom (cp. "Das Ding an Sich," sect. iii., "Das transcendentale Subject"), as, for instance, the Idea of honour or of right, and that the only being which answers to the idea of the inner cause of my activity is something *non-individual*, the Only Unconscious, which therefore answers just as well to Peter's idea of his ego as Paul's idea of his ego. On this deepest of all bases rests only the esoteric ethics of Buddhism, *not* the Christian ethics. If one has firmly and thoughtfully made this cognition his own, that *one and the same Being* feels my and thy pain, my and thy pleasure, only accidentally through the intervention of different brains, then is the exclusive egoism *radically broken*, that is only *shaken*, though deeply shaken, by contempt of the world and of life; then is the standpoint of Stirner finally overcome, to which one must at some time have entirely given adhesion in order to feel the greatness of the advance; then first is Egoism sublated as a moment in the consciousness of forming a link in the world-process, in which it finds its necessary and relatively, *i.e.*, to a certain degree, authorised place.

There occurs, namely at the end of each of the preceding stages of the illusion, and before the discovery of the next, the voluntary surrender of individual existence—*suicide*, as a necessary consequence. Both the life-weary heathen, and the Christian, despairing at once of the world and his faith, must in consistency do away with themselves; or if, like Schopenhauer, they believe themselves unable to attain by this means the end of the abolition of individual existence, they must at any rate divert their will from life to quietism and continence, or even asceticism. It is the height of self-deception to see in this saving of the dear Ego from the discomfort of existence anything else than the grossest selfism, than a highly refined Epicureanism, that has only taken a direction contrary to instinct through a view of life opposed to instinct.

In all Quietism, whether with brutish inertness it is content merely to eat and drink, or loses itself in idyllic love of Nature, or in reverie natural or artificially induced (by narcotics) passively revels in the images of a luxuriant fancy, or surrounded by the refinements of a luxurious life, languidly drives away ennui with the choicest morsels of the arts and sciences—in all this Quietism the Epicurean trait is unmistakable, the inordinate desire to pass life in the manner most agreeable to the individual constitution, with a minimum of effort and displeasure, unconcerned about the thereby neglected duties to fellow-men and society. But even asceticism, which is apparently the counterpart of Egoism, is also always egoistic, even when it does not, like the Christian, hope for reward in an individual immortality, but merely hopes, by the temporary assumption of a certain pain, to attain the shortening of the evil of life and individual deliverance from all continuation of life after death (new birth, &c.) In the suicide and in the ascetic the self-denial is as little deserving of admiration as in the sick person who, to escape the prospect of a perpetual toothache, reasonably prefers the painful drawing of the tooth. In both cases there is only well-calculated egoism without any ethical value; rather an egoism that in all such situations of life is *immoral*, save when the possibility of fulfilling one's duties to one's relatives and society is entirely cut off.

It is otherwise when interest for the development of the *whole* takes deep root in the heart, and the individual feels himself a member of the whole—a member filling a more or less valuable but never quite useless place in the general evolution. Then will it be requisite, for the sake of filling this place, to devote oneself with genuine joy in self-sacrifice to the life which, from the point of view of the Ego, was rejected not only as useless good, but as sure torment, because the suicide of a still capable individual not only saves the whole no pain, but even increases its torment, lengthening it out by the necessity, needing considerable time, of procuring a substitute for the amputated limb. Then there further results the obvious demand to fill up the life preserved out of self-denial for the sake of the whole in a manner subserving no longer individual comfort, but the welfare of the whole, which is not to be accomplished by passive receptivity, not by indolent repose and the timid avoidance of contact with the struggle of existence, but by active production, by untiring action, by self-denying plunging into the vortex of life, and participation in the common economic and mental work of civilisation. That alone would render Quietism a deadly sin, that its more general extension would jeopardise and convert in a short time into continually increasing retrogression all the achievements of civilisation, which mankind has conquered with such difficulty in the thousands of years. History teaches however, how boundless is the wretchedness of a people retrograding in civilisation, nay, how hardly even the mere pause of civilisation, impeded progress, presses upon a people. For as the life of the individual organism is a sum of continual acts of the *vis medicatrix*, so, too, is the life of the political and social organism only possible as a continual strain of all available force for the warding off of the disturbing and injurious influences constantly lying on the watch on all sides for points of attack.

Thus, then, the *instinct* of egoism, or instinct of individual life, is to a certain extent reinstated by *consciousness*, but no longer as absolute or sovereign power, but with the extent resulting from its *aim for the whole*, and *limited* by the recognition and respect for the striving of other individuals likewise necessary for the process.—As Egoism in general, so also those instincts are rehabilitated by consciousness which, like compassion, sentiment of equity, have a value for the whole, or, as love and honour, a value for the future; they are now voluntarily adopted with the consciousness of personal *sacrifice* for the sake of the whole and of progress. This personal sacrifice, made for life by the very devotion to it, finds then its *reward* in the *hope* of the future of the evolution, of the growing improvement of the circumstances of life, and the *felicity* beckoning the creative Being of the world, whose life is also mine.

This hope of a future positive happiness of humanity, and the *co-operation for its sake* in the process of the whole, forms the *third stage of the illusion,* whose examination is now our task. I trust and believe that most of those readers who have thus far followed the discussion with approval will not part company with me at this point. They can and must not, if they would not cease to be the children of their age, which is itself at the beginning of the third stage of the illusion, and hopefully hails and eagerly rushes to fulfil the promises of the golden future. Providence takes care that the anticipations of the silent thinker do not disarrange the course of history by prematurely gaining too many adherents. The only apparently related contemporary political and social pessimism of certain governments in the condition of youthful ferment or decay is a product of passing constellations destined to be overcome; it will and must pass over into political and social optimism, and has nothing to do with my metaphysical pessimism, which does not exclude, but includes, the political, social, or other optimism.——

When we were occupied with the criticism of the first stage of the illusion, it was not possible to avoid occasional glimpses into the future shaping of the world; nay, we may go so far as to assert that the attentive reader must have already found in that criticism of the first stage the criticism of the third.

To save repetition, I therefore beg that the *resumé* (No. 13) of the critique of the first stage may be re-read in this sense, and the reader will be convinced of the truth of my assertion that those results contain far *more* than was then concluded from them for the refutation of the first stage of the illusion. Thus, *e.g.*, the proof of the proposition that the pain of non-satisfaction is always and fully felt, but the pleasure of satisfaction only under favourable circumstances, and, with considerable deductions, holds good not merely for the present, but *quite universally*.

However great the progress of mankind, it will never get rid of, or even only diminish, the greatest of sufferings—sickness, age, dependence on the will and power of others, want, and discontent. However many the remedies found against diseases, diseases, especially the tormenting slighter chronic ills, always increase in quicker progression than medical science. Cheerful youth will always form only a fraction of mankind, and the other part be composed of morose age. The hunger due to the indefinite increase of the human race will always be the portion of a large stratum of the population, which has more hunger than it can satisfy, which, by reason of deficient nutriment, shows a long bill of mortality; in short, which continually succumbs to a considerable percentage in the bitter struggle with want (comp. ii. 23, iii. 28–30). The most contented peoples are the rude peoples living in a state of nature, and the uneducated classes of civilised peoples; with the increasing cultivation of the people grows, as experience shows, its discontent.

That stratum of the population living on the borders of hunger felt formerly, and in part now feels, its misery only as long as the stomach gnawed; but the farther the world gets the more threatening becomes the spectre of the poverty of the masses, the more fearful does the whole consciousness of their wretchedness take possession of those wretched ones. The social question of the present day rests in the last resort upon a heightened consciousness of the working classes of the wretchedness of their situation, whilst actually this situation is truly golden in comparison with that of two hundred years ago, when nothing was known of a social question.

Immorality, if one measures by the standard of the disposition, has not grown less since the establishment of a primitive human society to the present day, only the form in which the criminal character expresses itself is changed. Apart from variations of the ethical character of nations on the large scale, everywhere we see the same proportion of egoism and charity, and when the atrocities and barbarities of former times are pointed to, we should also not forget to take into account, on the one hand, the probity and honesty, the clear feeling of equity, and the reverence for consecrated custom of ancient peoples living in a state of nature, and, on the other, the growing deceit, falsehood, cunning, chicane, non-regardance of property and of the well-founded, but no longer understood, instinctive morality accompanying civilisation. (Cp. the descriptions and reflections of Wallace on the almost paradisaical purity of manners and singleness of heart of the Malays at the close of his book of travels, "The Malay Archipelago.") Theft, fraud, and forgery increase, despite the penalties annexed to them, more rapidly than the gross and serious crimes (such as robbery, murder, rape, &c.) decrease; the basest self-interest shamelessly rends asunder the most sacred bonds of the family and friendship wherever it comes into collision with them, and only the infallible execution of the punishments assigned by the state *and* society prevents the brutal cruelty of ruder times, which *immediately* breaks forth again and reveals human bestiality in all its hideousness, when the bonds of law and of order are loosened or rent, as in the Polish Revolution, the last year of the American Civil War, or the horrors of the Paris Commune in the spring of 1871. No; thus far the wickedness and the all-devouring selfishness of man has *not lessened;* it is only artificially *dammed in* by the dikes of the law and of civil society; knows, however, in place of the open overflow how to find a thousand secret paths by which it percolates the dams. The degree of the immoral *disposition* has remained the same, but it has discarded the cloven foot and walks about in conventional costume; the thing and its consequences remain the same, the form alone becomes more elegant.

The time is at hand when theft and illegal fraud will be despised as vulgar and clumsy by the more clever rogue, who knows how to keep his attacks on his neighbour's property within the letter of the law. I would, however, rather have run the occasional risk of being slain among the ancient Germans than in the modern civilised state to have to regard every man as a rogue and rascal until I have undeniable proof of his honesty. We may conclude by analogy that however refined the form in which immorality may hereafter appear, it will still remain equally immoral and equally a source of pain to those suffering the wrong. For although it may justly be objected that in the primitive and patriarchal forms of society morality rests on unconscious custom, and has declined with this foundation without, owing to the inadequateness of all religious and philosophical individual ethics, having found a substitute, but which the future will find in a social ethic elevating morality step by step through the replacement of unconscious moral tact by consciousness; if, further, one may also point to this, that the eruditio or "decrudescence" of feeling must necessarily afford, and, in part, has already afforded, in benevolent institutions, systems of poor-relief, care for the sick, the mentally imbecile, blind, deaf and dumb, criminals, societies for the protection of animals, &c., a broader field to the same extent of ethical foundation, yet such a real increase of the fund of morality, in part ameliorating the character through repeated practice, in part directly applying its lever to ethical feeling, is completely balanced by the sharpened sensibility for wrongs endured, although in the mildest and most refined form. If rude men cleave one another's skulls with the utmost nonchalance, yet the sensitive and cultured feel very acutely even the slightest want of consideration, and how much more the fine edge of subtle malice! Accordingly, as regards the question concerning the total suffering called forth by immorality, growing morality and increasing sensibility to injuries are at least balanced; nay, with increasing culture the moral standard even rises, which now brands the same action as much more immoral than formerly, and with reference to this necessary raising of the standard, one may even say that the sum of immoral action *increases*, because the augmentation of the moral fund does not keep pace with the raising of the standard for the ethical judgment, but remains behind the latter. But even supposing morality actually to increase to an *ideal* state, yet it could scarcely reach the threshold of feeling, because the exclusion of all wrong is still not happiness, and positive morality only a palliative of helpless human want (cp. p. 60, and vol. ii. 365). The latter finds expression in the saying, that the endeavours of the future must aim at rendering superfluous, and obviating by a firm organisation of the most varied forms of social solidarity, private beneficence and voluntary works of charity.——

One phase of life, which, with a certain mental constitution, may doubtless afford positive happiness, piety, is, of course, at our third stage of the illusion a surmounted standpoint, at least its principal arteries, the immortality-dogma and prayer are ligatured. Were it not so, the third stage of the illusion would not be pure, but mixed with the second, which indeed may in reality be very common, but in our rational survey, where the points of view must be kept well apart, must not be assumed. But at all events, one will not be able to deny that with progressive civilisation the average decrease of the religious illusion more and more diminishes its importance of the same for our estimation, and the time is not far off when an educated person will no longer be capable of the enjoyment of religious edification in the previous sense, but at the most will be able to fashion a sort of private religious cultus out of the consciousness of the mystical connection with the All-One.

The two other factors, to which we had accorded a positive excess of pleasure, Science and Art, will also alter their position in the future of the world. The more we look back, the more is scientific progress the work of a few eminent men of genius, whom the Unconscious creates as its organ, to accomplish what is not to be attained with the forces of the average conscious human understanding. The more we approach the present day, the more numerous become the scientific workers, the more co-operative their work. Whilst the geniuses of former times resembled magicians who cause an edifice to spring up out of nothing, the spiritual works of modern times may be compared to the construction of an industrious body of builders, in which each adds his stone to the great building, a larger or smaller, according to his strength. The method of the future will become more exclusively inductive, and the fundamental character of scientific work be not depth but breadth. Thus there will be ever less need of the men of genius, and therefore ever less wrought by the Unconscious. As society is levelled by the civilian's black coat, so also in spiritual reference we are steering more and more towards a level of respectable mediocrity. It follows from this that the pleasure in scientific production is becoming ever less, and the world is limited more and more to the receptive enjoyment of science. This, however, is only considerable where the wrestling and struggling after truth has been personally experienced, not, however, where truth is presented to one like a baked pasty. Then often the pleasure of knowing hardly balances the effort of acquiring, and the practical utility of the acquisition or ambition must yield the proper motives of learning.

A similar state of things takes place in Art, although this has a more favourable outlook than Science. In it, too, the productive men of genius will become ever rarer the more humanity leaves behind it the spontaneous life of childhood and the transcendent ideals of its enthusiastic youth, and is careful for the comfortable furnishing of its earthly home, the more in manhood the social, economical, and practical scientific interests gain the upper hand. Art is then no longer what it was to the youth, the sublime beatific goddess; it is only a distraction enjoyed with half-attention as a refreshment from the toils of the day, an opiate for ennui, or an amusement after the seriousness of business. Hence an ever-extending dilettante superficiality, and a neglect of all earnest tendencies of art to be enjoyed only with strenuous application. The artistic *production* of the manhood of humanity estranged from the ideal naturally reflects the same facile dilettante superficiality, skilfully mastering the form and living on the treasures of the past, and no longer produces men of genius, because they are no longer needs of the time, because that would be to throw pearls before swine, or even because the age has advanced beyond the stage to which men of genius belonged to one more important. To protect myself from misunderstanding, I expressly observe that I do *not* by this characteristic intend to denote the present time, but a future, on whose threshold our century stands, and of which the present offers only a weak foretaste. Art will be on the whole to humanity in its manhood somewhat what the Berlin farce is to the Berlin stock-jobber of an evening. This view is certainly only to be proved by the analogy of the development of humanity with the life-periods of the individual, and by the confirmation which this analogy finds in the previous course of development and the already tolerably distinctly perceptible aims of the next period.——

As regards the practical instincts which depend on illusion, like love and honour, there are three cases: either men never lose them *at all*,—then the pain arising from them always remains; or men *entirely* lose them,—then along with the pleasure they certainly also lose the pain, and have become relatively much happier, which means, however, nothing more than that life has become so much *poorer*, and has so much nearer approached the zero-point or level of sensation,—has, however, also become conscious of its poverty and worthlessness. One may somewhat compare both states with a miser who rejoices over the treasures in his chest, until one fine day he opens the chest and finds it empty; only in this image the torment really endured, even in the first state along with the illusion of happiness, is not expressed. The third possible, and at the same time most probable case, is that men only *partially* lose these instincts, that they indeed quite see through their illusory character, and in consequence somewhat diminish the force of the impulse by reason, but are never able completely to destroy it. This case contains the pains of both the others combined. For the miser who has seen quite well that his chests are empty now falls into the delusion of wishing to regard them, despite his clear and better rational insight, as still full, and is all the time rational enough to understand his aberration without being able to deliver himself from it. He has at the same time the rational consciousness of the poverty of his life, of the illusory nature of his pleasure and pain springing from these impulses, and of the great predominance of pain. He has therefore now also the full consciousness of the torments to which he is condemned, the rational endeavour to suppress these impulses, and the painful feeling of the impotence of his rational will over instinctive impulse. Wherefore Goethe says quite correctly, "Nature, as the sternest of tyrants, punishes that man who destroys illusion in himself and others" (vol. xl. p. 386), and yet can and will this destruction of the illusion not be spared humanity. Pitiless and cruel is this work of the destruction of illusion, like the rough pressure of the hand that wakes one sweetly dreaming to the torment of reality. But the world must onwards; the goal cannot be approached in dreams, it must be wrestled for and conquered, and only through pain lies the path to redemption. The *individual* rightly sees the reconciliation of this difference *as regards himself* in the complete surrender of egoism, and the self-renouncing thought that the love and instinct to found a household is yet to the advantage of the *future*, in that they call into existence the new generation, and thus serve the purpose of progress; but it would be a manifest contradiction if a generation should always only exist *for the succeeding one*, whilst *each by itself* is wretched. This pointing ever forward awakes the involuntary thought that progress is not for the sake of progress, but for the sake of a goal beyond the progress. The like answer may be made to the objection that the illusive instincts, as honour, the acquisitive impulse, love, help *to further evolution*. This is certainly true, but it can lend those instincts no value as regards real happiness so long as we can attribute no endæmonological value to the enhancement of the evolution. It is forgotten in these replies that the process as such is *only the sum of its moments*.

Let us now cast a glance at the belauded progress of the world. Wherein does it consist? how are we made happy? Progress in *art* one would not be warranted in rating highly; although our modern works of art are richer in ideas, yet the artistic *form* was more perfect in antiquity, and the resuscitated Greeks would with *perfect truth* declare our works of art in all departments to be thoroughly *barbarous*. (Think of our romances and stage-plays, of our statues and exhibitions of pictures, of our architecture, and the monotonous temperament in music!) The more the ideal content of our works of art threatens to burst the confining form, the further are these works removed from the *pure* notion of art, that is rooted in absolute harmony of form and matter. Space unfortunately prevents my working out these suggestions in detail.

Scientific progress contributes in a purely theoretical

reference little or nothing to the happiness of the world, but in practical reference they stand in good stead political, social, moral and technical progress. The influence of science on moral progress I may regard as insignificant, as also in political and social respects it must not be rated too highly, since in these departments theory for the most part hobbles after instinctive practice. On the other hand, it is of incalculable importance in the progress of the *practical arts*. But what do these achieve for human happiness? Manifestly nothing but afford the possibility of social and political progress and increase the conveniences of life, and *perhaps* also superfluous luxury! Partly this takes place directly, partly by the facilitation and perfection of commercial communication. Factories, steamships, railways, and telegraphs have done nothing *positive* for the happiness of mankind; they have only diminished a part of the impediments and inconveniences by which man was previously confined and oppressed. If a more rational cultivation of the soil and a facilitated importation from less populated regions has placed a greater supply of food at the command of the civilised nations, this certainly has had the result that the *number* of the population of these civilised nations have in part very considerably increased; but is the *happiness* or the *misery* of the individual and the community thereby increased? Especially when we remember that with increasing population the number of the millions living on the verge of starvation likewise increases. The augmented food-supply of the earth, the augmented comfort and the augmented luxury taken together represent the augmented national wealth or terrestrial wealth. This latter, likewise, cannot be regarded as a growth of positive happiness. In the first place, it effects nothing but an increase of the population, and therefore of misery; secondly, its high appreciation depends on the illusion created by the instinctive acquisitive impulse; thirdly, its consequence is a diminution of pain, and an approximation to the zero-point of sensation that is never attainable. The only *positive* utility of the growth of opulence is that it *sets free for mental exertion energies* that before were absorbed in the struggle with want, and that it thereby *accelerates* the *progress of the world. This* result appertains, however, only to the process as such, by no means to the individuals or nations concerned in the process, who yet imagine that they are working *for themselves* in increasing their national wealth.

The last great advances of the world which remain to be considered are the *political* and *social*. Let us assume the most perfect State to be realised and the peoples of the earth to have solved their political problem in a complete manner. What then does one get by this political framework? A snail-shell without the snail, an empty form that waits its filling up. Mankind does not live in order to be governed, but it is governed in order to be able to *live* (in the highest sense of the term). All the well-known problems of the State are of a negative nature. They are *protection* against, *security* for, *defence* from, &c. Where the State fulfils positive objects (*e.g.*, instruction) it trespasses on the sphere of Society, which, in the immaturity of the latter, may occasionally become necessity. The most perfect state does, therefore, nothing but place man in a situation where he can begin to live without fear of unwarranted attacks, *i.e.*, to unfold his forces and capabilities in all directions, which do not infringe the rights of others. Thus the ideal of the State also simply places man at the threshold of his felicity.

With the *social* ideals it is not different. They show how to lighten to a certain extent the struggle with want for the necessaries of life through the principle of the solidarity of the community and other expedients. They teach how to alleviate as far as possible the torments and cares which one draws upon oneself through the satisfaction of the instincts of founding a household by the best possible arrangement of the family relations; to fulfil the duties of the education of children at the least possible cost, &c.—The question is always only the mitigation of evils, not attainment of positive happiness. The sole apparent exception is the increase of the collective wealth resulting from co-operation, but this has been already dealt with above.

These, then, would be the main lines of the world's progress. So far as they rest on *realities*, they agree in lifting man more and more from the depths of his misery towards the level of sensation. Were the ideal goals attained, the zero or indifference point of feeling as regards these phases of life would be attained; but as ideals always remain ideals, and the progress of humanity may indeed approach, but never reach them, even in these directions the world will never attain the height of the zero-point, but always remain below it, pain being still in excess.

One may become clear with regard to the *endæmonological value* of the world's progress even without considering it in detail. One has only to reflect on the analogous case of the individual. He who comes into a better position in life will in passing from worse to better certainly feel pleasure. This pleasure, however, disappears with astonishing rapidity; the new and better circumstances are taken as matter of course, and the man does not feel himself a hair's-breadth the happier than in his former position. (The transition from better to worse worse produces a much more lasting pain.) It is just so with a nation, just so with humanity at large. Who feels himself better off now than thirty years ago because now there are railways and then there were none? And should the difference still be felt by older persons, assuredly not by those who have been born since the existence of railways. With the increased *means* nothing more has increased than *wishes* and *needs*, and in their train *discontent*. And even should mankind ever succeed in getting rid of the infectious diseases by preventive and eradicating measures—the hereditary by more rational sexual unions (contingent on a relaxation of the present unnaturally limited and almost blind struggle for existence), the rest by the progress of hygiene and medicine; should it ever succeed in preparing aliment from inorganic substances in chemical laboratories, and in limiting multiplication without restraining the instinct of propagation in accordance with the available means of subsistence,—yet all this progress would offer nothing positive, but only remove or mitigate the worst, and in part most unnatural, evils of existing physical and social circumstances. But at the same time they would cause the question to become the more burning, What then to do with this life, with what substance of inner worth it is to *be filled?* what is to *compensate* for the bearing of the burden of life rendered placid by the simplest elementary considerations?

Whereas before the discomfort of existence, so far as it was felt, was referred to external evils and defects, and the attainment of a comfortable condition hoped for from the removal of the external evils most sensibly felt at the time, the error that lies in this projection of the cause of discomfort is the more perceived the more the palpable external ills of human life are removed by the world's progress; and in proportion as this escape from the pessimistic insight into the essential nature of the personal will is cut off, in the same degree grows the perception that pain is *immanent* to will; that the wretchedness of existence is founded in existence itself, and is dependent on external circumstances more in appearance than in reality. Consequently every approach to the ideal of the best life attainable on earth must make the question as to the absolute value of this life only an *ever more burning one*, since both the continually increasing perception of the illusory nature of most positive pleasures, as the ever clearer and clearer insight into the inevitableness of the misery lurking in one's own breast, like a goblin perpetually changing its shape, co-operates to this result. As, according to Paul, the law given to the Jews was precisely the "strength" of sin (1 Cor. xv. 56), *so is the utmost world-progress the "strength" of the pessimistic consciousness of humanity.* And just because it is so, and only because it is, is the utmost possible progress *a practical postulate.* In the fact that men usually only desire progress because they hope to become *happier*, we may see the practically *wholesome fascination* of the third stage of the illusion, through which the Unconscious stimulates men to tasks which for the most part they would be incapable of imposing on themselves if they penetrated the true purposes of the Unconscious. But if it is true, that the enhancement of consciousness to the point of a general pessimistic consciousness of humanity is the purpose of the Unconscious directly preceding the final purpose (as we shall see in the next chapter), then from our standpoint the progress of the world is precisely so urgent a requirement because it leads to this goal.

In the *resumé* of the first stage of the illusion we saw that *peoples in a state of nature* are not more wretched, but *more happy*, than civilised peoples; that the *poor*, low, and *rude* classes are happier than the *rich*, aristocratic, and *cultivated*; that the *stupid* are happier than the *clever*; in general, that a being is the happier the obtuser is its nervous system, because the excess of pain over pleasure is so much less, and the entanglement in the illusion so much greater. But now with the progressive development of humanity grow not only wealth and wants, but also the sensibility of the nervous system and the capacity and education of the mind, consequently also the excess of felt pain over felt pleasure and the destruction of illusion, *i.e.*, the consciousness of the paltriness of life, of the vanity of most enjoyments and endeavours and the feeling of misery; there grows accordingly *both* misery *and also* the consciousness of misery, as experience shows, and the often-asserted enhancement of the happiness of the world by the progress of the world rests on an altogether superficial appearance. (This is especially to be laid to heart by those who perhaps are not quite in accord with me, that *at the present time* the sum of pain in the world outweighs the sum of pleasure.)

As the suffering of the world has increased with the development of organisation from the primitive cell to the origin of man, so will it further increase with the progressive development of the human spirit until one day the goal is attained. It was a childish short-sightedness when Rousseau, from the perception of increasing suffering, drew the conclusion: the world must, if possible, turn back—back to the age of childhood. As if the childhood of humanity had not been misery! No; if once backwards, then farther, ever farther, to the creation of the world! But we have no choice. We must *forwards*, even if we desire it not. It is not, however, the golden age that lies before us, but the iron; and the dreams of the golden age of the future prove still more empty than those of the past. As the burden becomes heavier to the bearer the longer the road on which he carries it, so will also the suffering of mankind and the consciousness of its misery increase and increase until it is insupportable. We may also employ the analogy with the ages of the individual. As the individual at first as child lives for the moment, then as youth revels in transcendent ideals, then as man strives after glory, and subsequently possessions and practical science, until, finally, as old man, perceiving the vanity of all endeavour, he lays to rest his weary head, longing for peace, so, too, Humanity. We see nations arise, mature, and perish; we find also in Humanity the clearest symptoms of growing older. Why should we doubt that, after the energetic activity of manhood, for it, too, one day old age will come, when, consuming the practical and theoretical fruits of the past, it enters upon a period of ripe contemplation, when with melancholy sorrow it overlooks at a single glance all the sufferings so unthinkingly of its past life-career, and comprehends the whole vanity of the previously supposed goals of its endeavour?

There is only one difference between it and the individual. Hoary humanity will have *no heir* to whom it may bequeath its heaped-up wealth, no children and grandchildren, the love of whom might disturb the clearness of its thought. Then will it, imbued with that sublime melancholy which one usually finds in men of genius, or even in highly intellectual old men, hover like a glorified spirit over its own body, as it were, and as Œdipus at Colonos, feel in the anticipated peace of non-existence the sorrows of existence as if they were *alien* to it, no longer *passion*, but only a self-*compassion*. That is the heavenly serenity, the divine repose, that breathes in Spinoza's Ethics, when the passions are swallowed up in the abyss of reason because they are clearly and distinctly grasped as ideas. But even if we assume that pure passionless state attained, if even the sorrow in self-compassion is glorified, it yet does not cease to be *grief, i.e., pain*. The illusions are dead, hope is extinct; for what is there still to hope? The dead-tired humanity drags along its frail earthly body wearily from day to day. The *highest* attainable were indeed *painlessness*, for where is positive happiness still to be sought? In the vain self-sufficiency of the knowledge that all is vanity, or that in the contest with those vain impulses reason now usually remains victor? Oh, no; such vainest of all vanities, such *arrogance of the intellect* has long been surmounted! But even painlessness is not attained by hoary humanity, for it is still not pure spirit; it is feeble and frail, and must nevertheless *work* in order to *live*, and yet does not know *for what* it lives; for it has indeed the illusions of life *behind* it, and hopes and expects *nothing* more from life. It has, as every very aged and self-knowing man, only one wish more: repose, peace, eternal dreamless sleep that may soothe its weariness. After the three stages of illusion of the hope of a positive happiness it has finally seen the *folly* of its endeavour; it finally foregoes all *positive* happiness, and longs only for *absolute painlessness*, for nothingness, Nirvana. But not, as before, this or that man, but man*kind* longs for nothingness, for annihilation. This is the only conceivable end of the third and last stage of the illusion.

We began this chapter with the question whether the being or the not-being of the present world deserves the preference, and have been obliged to answer this question, after conscientious consideration, thus, that all secular existence brings with it more *pain* than *pleasure*. As cause of this disproportion we have seen those moments collected under (1.) in the first stage of the illusion, which bring it about that all volition must necessarily be attended by more pain than pleasure, that thus all volition is foolish and irrational. Even then the only possible result was clearly to be perceived; the whole subsequent inquiry was merely the empirical inductive proof of the correctness of that consequence, which we certainly could not omit if we were to proceed surely.

If this result *appears* to the reader who has had the patience to accompany me so far a cheerless one, I must assure him that he was in error if he sought to find consolation and hope in philosophy. For such ends there are books of religion and edification. Philosophy, however, has but a single eye for truth, unconcerned whether what it finds suits the *emotional judgment entangled in the illusion of instinct* or not. Philosophy is hard, cold, and insensitive as a stone; floating in the ether of pure thought, it endeavours after the icy cognition of what is, its causes, and its essences. If the strength of man is unequal to the task of enduring the results of thought, and the heart, convulsed with woe, stiffens with horror, breaks into despair, or softly dissolves into world-pain, and for any of these reasons the practical pyschological machinery gets out of gear through such knowledge,—then philosophy registers these facts as valuable pyschological material for its investigations. It likewise registers it when the result of these considerations in the sympathising soul of the more strongly built natures is a righteous indignation, a manly wrath clenching the teeth, a fervid fury at the frenzied carnival of existence, or when this rage turns into a Mephistophelean gallows-humour, that with half-suppressed pity and half-unrestrained mockery looks down with a like sovereign irony both on those caught in the illusion of happiness and on those dissolved in tearful woe,—or when the heart wrestling with fate spies after a last way of deliverance from this hell. To philosophy itself, however, the unspeakable wretchedness of existence—as manifestation of the folly of volition—is *only a* TRANSITION-MOMENT *of the theoretical development of its system.*

XIV.

THE GOAL OF EVOLUTION AND THE SIGNIFICANCE OF CONSCIOUSNESS (TRANSITION TO PRACTICAL PHILOSOPHY).

WE saw in Chap. xii. C. (vol. ii. pp. 359–361) that the chain of final causes is not, like that of phenomenal causality, to be conceived as endless, because every end in respect of the following one in the chain is *only means;* therefore in the end-positing understanding the *whole* future series of ends must always be present, and yet a completed endlessness of ends cannot be present in it. (Cp. Ges. Phil. Abhandl., No. ii., "Ueber die nothwendige Umbildung der Hegel'schen Philosophie aus ihrem Grundprincip heraus.")

Accordingly the series of final causes must be finite, *i.e.*, they must have a *last* or *ultimate end*, which is the goal of all the intermediate ends. Further, we have seen (vol. ii. p. 365, vol. iii. pp. 60 and 106) that justice and morality by their very nature cannot be final ends, but only intermediate ends; and the last chapter has taught us that also *positive* happiness cannot be the goal of the world-process, because not only is it not attained at every stage of the process, but even *its contrary*, misery and unblessedness, is at all times attained, which besides increases in the course of evolution by destruction of the illusion and with the heightening of consciousness.

It is altogether absurd to conceive *evolution* as *end in itself*, *i.e.*, to ascribe to it an absolute value; for evolution is still only the sum of its moments; and if the several moments are not only worthless, but even objectionable, so too is their sum, the process. Many indeed call *free-*

dom the goal of the process. To me freedom is nothing positive, but something privative, the absence of constraint. I cannot understand how this is to be regarded as *goal* of the evolution, if the Unconscious is one and all, and therefore there is no one from whom it could suffer constraint. If, however, there is anything positive in the notion of freedom, it can only be the consciousness of inner *necessity*, the formal in the rational, as Hegel says. Then is an increase of freedom identical with an increase of consciousness. Here we come to a point already frequently mentioned. If the goal of evolution is anywhere to be looked for, it is certainly on the path where we, so far as we can overlook the course of the evolution, perceive a decided and continuous *progress*, a gradual advance.

This is only and solely the case in the *development of consciousness*, of conscious intelligence, but here also in unbroken ascent from the origin of the primitive cell to the standpoint of humanity of the present day, and with the highest probability farther as long as the world lasts. Thus Hegel says (xiii. p. 36): "All that happens in heaven and on earth happens eternally; the life of God and all that takes place in time has this *sole aim*, that the spirit attain self-knowledge, become its own object, find itself become independent, unite itself with itself; it is duplication, alienation, but in order to find itself to be enabled to come to itself." Likewise Schelling: "To the Transcendental philosophy Nature is nothing but the organ of self-consciousness, and everything in Nature is only *necessary* because *only through such a* Nature can self-consciousness be achieved" (Werke, i. 3, p. 273); "and consciousness is that with which the whole creation is concerned" (ii. 3, p. 369). Individuation, with its train of egoism and wrong-doing and wrong-suffering, serves the origination of consciousness; the acquisitive impulse serves the enhancement of consciousness by the liberation of the mental energies through increasing opulence, likewise vanity, ambition, and the lust of fame by spurring on the mental activity; sexual love serves it by improving mental capacity; in short, all those useful instincts that bring the individual far more pain than pleasure may often impose the greatest sacrifices. *By the way of the unfolding of consciousness* must then the goal of evolution be sought, and consciousness is beyond a doubt the *proximate* end of Nature—of the world. The question still remains open whether consciousness is really *ultimate end*, therefore also self-end, or whether it again serves only *another* end?

One's own object consciousness can assuredly not be. With pain it is born, with pain it consumes its existence, with pain it purchases its elevation; and what does it offer in compensation for all this? *A vain self-mirroring!* Were the world in other respects fair and precious, the empty self-satisfaction in the contemplation of its reflected image in consciousness might at any rate *be excused*, although it would always remain an infirmity; but an out-and-out miserable world, that can never have any joy in the sight of itself, but must condemn its own existence as soon as it understands itself, could such a world be said to have a rational, final, and proper end in the ideal apparent duplication of itself in the mirror of consciousness? Is there then not enough of real wretchedness that it should be repeated in the magic lantern of consciousness? No; Consciousness cannot possibly be the ultimate object of the world-evolution guided by the all-wisdom of the Unconscious. That would only mean *doubling* the torment, preying on one's own vitals. Still less can one suppose that the purely formal *determination of action* according to laws of conscious reason can be a rational man's aim; for why should the reason determine action, or why should action be determined by reason apart from the diminution of pain thereby to be induced? Were there not painful being and willing, no reason need trouble itself about its determination.

Consciousness and the continuous enhancement of the same in the process of the world's development can thus in no case be end in itself; it can merely be *means* to *another* end, if it is not to float *aimlessly* in the air, whereby then also regressively the whole process would cease to be *evolution*, and the whole chain of natural ends would hang aimlessly in the air; thus, properly speaking, would, *as ends*, be annulled and declared irrational. This assumption contradicts the all-wisdom of the Unconscious, therefore it only remains for us to search for *the* end which the development of consciousness subserves as means.

But where to get such an end? The observation of the process itself, and of that which mainly grows and progresses in it, leads only to the knowledge that it is Consciousness; morality, justice, and freedom have already been set aside.

However much we may ponder and reflect, we can discover nothing to which we could assign an absolute value, nothing that we could regard as end in itself, nothing that so affects the world-essence in its inmost core, *as Happiness*. After happiness strives everything that lives, according to eudæmonist principles motives influence us, and our actions are consciously or unconsciously guided. On happiness in this or that fashion all systems of practical philosophy are grounded, however much they may think to deny their first principle. The endeavour after happiness is the most deeply rooted impulse, is *the essence of the will itself seeking satisfaction*. And yet the investigations of the last chapter have shown that this endeavour is exposed to objections; that the hope of its fulfilment is an illusion; and that its consequence is the pain of disillusion, its truth the misery of existence; have taught us that the progressive evolution of consciousness has the negative result of gradually perceiving the illusory character of that hope, the folly of that endeavour. Between the will striving after absolute satisfaction and felicity and the intelligence emancipating itself more and more from the impulse through consciousness a *deeply pervading antagonism* cannot therefore be mistaken. The higher and more perfectly consciousness develops in the course of the world-process, the more is it *emancipated* from the blind vassalage with which it at first followed the irrational will; the more it *sees through* the illusions aroused in it by impulse for the cloaking of this irrationality, the more does it assume a hostile position in opposition to the will struggling for positive happiness, in which it combats it step by step in the course of history, breaks through the ramparts of illusions behind which it is entrenched one after the other, and will not have drawn its last consequences until it has completely *annihilated* it, in that after the destruction of every illusion only the knowledge remains that *every* volition leads to unblessedness, and only *renunciation* to the *best attainable* state, *painlessness*. This victorious contest of consciousness with the will as it empirically meets our eyes as result of the world-process, is now, however, anything but accidental; it is *ideally contained* in consciousness, and is *necessarily* posited along with its development. For in Chap. iii. C. we saw that the *essence* of consciousness is *emancipation* of the intellect from the will, whereas in the Unconscious the idea only appears as servitor of the will, because there is nothing but the will to which it can owe its *origin*, being incapable of self-origination (cp. C. chap. i. vol. ii. p. 59).

Further, we know that in the sphere of ideation the logical, *rational*, rules, which is intrinsically just as repugnant to the will as the will to it; whence we conclude that if the idea has only attained the necessary degree of independence, it will have to condemn everything contra-rational (anti-logical) that it finds in the irrational (alogical) will, and to annihilate it. Thirdly, we know from the foregoing chapter that there follows from volition always more pain than pleasure; that therefore the will that wills *happiness attains* the contrary, *unhappiness*; therefore *most irrationally* and for its proper torment digs its teeth into its own flesh, and yet on account of its unreason can be taught by no experience to desist from its unblessed willing. From these three premises it necessarily follows that consciousness, so far as it attains the necessary clearness, activity, and fulness, must also more and more perceive, and accordingly contest to the last, the irrationality of volition and endeavour after happiness. This contest, hitherto recognised by us only *a posteriori*, was accordingly not an accidental, but a necessary result of the creation of consciousness; it lay therein *a priori preformed*. But now, if consciousness *is* the proximate end of Nature or the world; if we necessarily *need* for consciousness a further end, and can absolutely *think* no other true end than the greatest possible happiness; if, on the other hand, an endeavour after *positive* happiness that is identical with volition is preposterous because it only attains unblessedness, and the greatest possible *attainable* state of happiness is painlessness; if, lastly, it lies *in the notion* of consciousness to have for result the emancipation of the intellect from the will, the combating and final annihilation of willing, should it be any longer doubtful that the all-knowing Unconscious thinking end and means at once has created consciousness *for that very reason, to redeem the will from the unblessedness of its willing*, from which it cannot redeem itself,—that the real end of the world-process, to which consciousness serves as final means, *is this, to realise the greatest possible attainable state of happiness, namely, that of painlessness!*

We have seen that in the existing world everything is arranged in the wisest and best manner, and that it may be looked upon as the best of all possible worlds, but that nevertheless it is thoroughly wretched, and worse than none at all. This was only to be comprehended in such wise (cp. conclusion of Chap. xii. C.), that, although the "What and How" in the world (its essence) might be determined by an all-wise Reason, yet the "That" of the world (its existence) must be posited by something absolutely irrational, and this could only be the will. This consideration is for the rest only the same applied to the world as a whole that we have long known as applied to the individual. The atom of body is attractive power, its "What and How," *i.e.*, attraction according to this or that law, is Presentation; its "That," its existence, its reality, its force, is will. Thus also the world is *what* it is and *how* it is as presentation of the Unconscious, and the unconscious idea has as servant of the will, to which it itself is indebted for actual existence, and as compared with which it has no independence, also no counsel and no voice in the "That" of the world. The will is essentially only non-rational (destitute of reason, alogical), but in that it acts, it becomes through the consequences of its volition, *irrational* (contrary to reason, anti-logical), inasmuch as it attains unblessedness, the contrary of its volition.[1] Now to bring back this irrational volition, which is guilty of the "That" of the world, this unblessed volition into non-volition and the painlessness of nothingness, this task of the logical in the Unconscious is the determinator of the "What and How" of the world. For the Reason the question therefore is to repair the mischief done by the irrational Will. The unconscious idea represents the will, if not positively as will, yet negatively as the negative of the logical, or as its own limit, *i.e.*, as the non-logical; but it has in the first place and as such no power over the will, because it has no independence in respect of it, therefore it must employ an artifice to

[1] We must not regard this alogical, which afterwards becomes an antilogical, as a something that undergoes change, but it is *per se* alogical, so far as it is out of all relation and contact with the logical, and keeps entirely aloof from this, whilst it shows itself as anti-logical by coming into relation with the logical through its activity, which latter now cannot avoid finding in this activity of the alogical a contrast to its own nature, therefore an anti-logical in contrast to the logical, and encountering it as such. Were there no logical principle, were the other principle, which is not the logical, the only one, its activity could also never be termed anti-logical, and so far it is *accidental* to the alogical that it afterwards becomes anti-logical, in the same sense as it is accidental to it that there is altogether beside and beyond it a logical principle.

utilise the blindness of the will, and to give it such a content, that by a peculiar turning back upon itself in individuation it falls into conflict with itself, whose result is consciousness, *i.e.*, the creation of an independent power opposed to the will, in which it can now begin the contest with the will. Thus the world-process appears as a *perpetual struggle of the logical with the non-logical*, ending with the conquest of the latter. If this conquest were impossible, if the process were not at the same time development to a fairly beckoning goal, if it were interminable, or even one that exhausted itself in blind necessity or contingency, so that all wit would in vain endeavour to steer the ship into harbour, then, and only then, would this world be really absolutely cheerless, a hell without an exit, and dumb resignation the only philosophy. But we who perceive in Nature and history only a single grand and marvellous process of development, we believe in a final victory of the ever more radiantly shining reason over the unreason of blind volition; we believe in a goal of the process that brings us release from the torment of existence, and to whose induction and acceleration we too may contribute our mite in the service of reason. (Cp. my demonstration of the self-annulling of the process from the notion of development, Ges. Phil. Abhandl., No. ii. pp. 50–55.)

The main difficulty consists in this, *how* the termination of this contest, the final redemption from the misery of volition and existence into the painlessness of non-willing and non-being, in short, how the entire annulling of volition by consciousness is to be conceived. There is only one attempt to solve this problem known to me, namely, that of Schopenhauer, in sects. 68–71 of the first volume of the "World as Will and Idea," which essentially agrees with the similar but more obscure designs of the mystical ascetics of all ages, and of the doctrine of Buddha, as Schopenhauer himself very plainly shows (cp. W. as W. and I., ii. chap. xlviii.)

The main point of this theory consists in the assumption that the individual, in virtue of the individual cognition of the misery of existence and the unreason of volition, is able to cause his personal willing to cease, and thereby *to be individually annihilated after death*, or, as Buddhism expresses it, to be no more born again. It is obvious that this assumption is altogether incompatible with the fundamental principles of Schopenhauer, and only his inability to grasp the notion of development renders explicable the shortsightedness which made it impossible for him to get rid of this palpable inconsistency in his system. This inconsequence must here be indicated very briefly.—The will is for him the ἕν καὶ πᾶν, the sole being of the world, and the individual only subjective appearance, in strictness never objectively actual phenomenon of this essence. But even if it were the latter, how should it be possible for the individual to negate his individual will as a whole, not merely theoretically but also practically, as his individual volition is only a ray of that Only Will? Schopenhauer himself rightly declares that in *suicide* the negation of the will is not attained, but it is said to be attained in the highest conceivable degree in *voluntary starvation* (cp. W. als W. und V., 3 Aufl. i. 474). That sounds indeed almost absurd, if one remembers his declaration "that the body is the will itself, objectively regarded as a phenomenon in space," whence it immediately follows that with the annulling of the individual will, also its appearance in space, the body must *disappear*. According to our view, with suppression of the individual will at least all the organic functions dependent on the unconscious will, as heart-throb, respiration, &c., must instantly cease, and the body collapse as *corpse*. That this too is empirically impossible will be doubted by nobody; but whoever is obliged to first *kill* his body *by refusal of food* proves by that very act he *is not able* to deny and *abolish* his unconscious *will* to live.

But supposing the impossible to be possible, what would

be the consequence? One of the many rays or individual objectifications of the One Will, that which related to this individual, would be withdrawn from its actuality, and this man be dead. That is, however, *no more and no less* than happens at *every* decease, no matter to what cause it is due, and to the Only Will the consequences would have been the same if a tile had killed that man; it continues after, as before, with unenfeebled energy, with undiminished avidity, to lay hold of life wherever it finds it and can lay hold of it; for to acquire experience and become wiser by experience is impossible to it, and *it cannot* suffer a quantitative abatement of its essence or its substance through the withdrawal of a merely one-sided direction of action. Therefore the endeavour after *individual* negation of the will is *just as foolish and useless*, nay, still more foolish, than *suicide*, because it only attains the same end more slowly and painfully: abolition of *this* appearance without altering the essence, which for every abolished individual phenomenon is ceaselessly objectified in new individuals. Accordingly all asceticism and all endeavour after individual negation of will is perceived and proved to be aberration, although an aberration only in procedure, not in *aim*. And because the goal which it endeavours to gain is a right one, it has when rare, by ever whispering in the world's ear a *memento mori*, as it were, and provoking a presentiment of the issue of all endeavour, a high value; it becomes, however, injurious and pernicious when, attacking whole nations, it threatens to bring the world-process to stagnation, and to perpetuate the misery of existence. What would it avail, *e.g.*, if all mankind should die out gradually by sexual continence? The world as such would still continue to exist, and would find itself substantially in the same position as immediately before the origin of the first man; nay, the Unconscious would even be compelled to employ the next opportunity *to fashion a new man or a similar type*, and the whole misery would begin over again.

If we look more deeply into the nature of asceticism and personal negation of will, and to the position which it occupies in the historical process in its highest flowering in pure Buddhism, it appears as the issue of the Asiatic pre-Hellenic period of development, as the union of *hopelessness* for here *and* hereafter with the still uneradicated *egoism* which thinks not of the redemption of the *whole* but only of *its own* individual redemption. As we briefly pointed out above (cp. pp. 100–101) the immorality and *perniciousness* of this standpoint for the whole of humanity and the world-process, so now the *folly* of the same is revealed for the individual who builds upon it, in that the personal hope of redemption has turned out illusory, consequently *every means made use of for this end* (thus also *Quietism*, so far as it is not to serve an individual or nationally coloured Epicureanism, but to lead to redemption through individual negation of the will) is *absurd*.

Schopenhauer, too, means at bottom something different to what he says. Before him, too, hovers in shadowy outlines, as the only goal worthy of effort, a *universal* negation of will, as, *e.g.*, the following passage proves: "After what was said in the second book on the *connection of all* phenomena of will, I think I may assume that with the *highest* phenomenon of will (humanity), the weaker reflection of the same, animality (and the still lower forms of objectification of will), would also *pass away*, as with the full light the penumbræ disappear" (W. a. W. u. V., 3 Aufl. i. 449). On the following page he points, among others, to the biblical passage (Rom. viii. 22) in which it is said, "For we know that *the whole creation* groaneth together" for the redemption; it expects, however, its redemption "from us which have the first-fruits of the spirit." Such deeper perspectives are, however, nevertheless, out of the question for Schopenhauer's expressly declared standpoint, not only because their consideration would require a surrender of the latter, but also because the following out of them is not at all possible with the unhistorical world-theory of his subjective idealism. It only becomes so when the reality of time and the positive meaning of the temporal, *i.e.*, historical, development is acknowledged, through whose cumulative progress the prospect opens up of a future attainment of such states of humanity as may enable that which now appears absurd one day to obtain realisation.

For him, who has grasped the idea of development, it cannot be doubtful that the end of the contest between consciousness and the will, between the logical and the non-logical, can only lie at the *goal* of evolution, at the issue of the world-process; for him who before all holds fast to the *universality and unity* of the Unconscious, the redemption, the turning back of willing into non-willing, is also only to be conceived *as act of each and all*, not as *individual*, but only as cosmic-*universal* negation of will, as the act that forms the end of the process, as the *last moment*, *after* which there shall be no more volition, activity, or time (Rev. x. 6). That the cosmic process cannot be thought without an end in time, cannot be of endless duration, is presupposed; for if the goal lay at an *infinite distance*, a *finite* duration of the process, however long, would bring *no nearer* the goal, that would still remain infinitely remote. The process would thus no longer be *a means* for *reaching* the goal, consequently it would be *purposeless* and *aimless*. As little as it would comport with the notion of development to ascribe an infinite duration in the *past* to the world-process, because then every conceivable development must be already traversed, which yet is not the case, just as little can we allow to the process an endless duration for the *future*; both would abolish the idea of *development towards a goal*, and would put the world-process on a level with the pouring of water into a sieve of the daughters of Danaus. The complete victory of the logical over the alogical must therefore coincide with the temporal end of the world-process, the last day.

Whether humanity will be capable of so high an enhancement of consciousness, or whether a higher race of animals will arise on earth, which, continuing the work of humanity, will attain the goal, or whether our *earth* altogether is only an abortive attempt to reach such goal, and it will only be reached, when our little planet has long been reckoned to the frozen celestial bodies, on a planet invisible to us of another fixed star under more favourable conditions, is hard to say. Thus much is certain, wherever the process may come to an end, the goal of the process and the contending elements will always be the same in this world. If really humanity is able and called to bring the world-process to a final issue, it will at all events have to do this at the height of its development under the most favourable circumstances of the earth's habitableness, and therefore we do not need for this case to trouble about the scientific perspective of a future congelation and refrigeration of the earth, since then long before the occurrence of such a terrestrial refrigeration the world-process altogether would have been arrested, and the existence of this kosmos with all its world-lenses and nebulæ have been abolished.

Schopenhauer does not hesitate to declare man equal to the task, but he is only so decided because he conceives the problem *in an individual sense*, whereas we must apprehend it *universally*, when it of course requires quite other conditions, which we shall soon examine more closely. However that be, of the world known to us we are the first-fruits of the spirit and must bravely wrestle. If victory does not follow, it is not our fault. If, however, we are capable of victory, and we should only miss obtaining it through indolence, we, *i.e.*, the creative being of the world, which is one with us, would have to bear so much the longer as immanent punishment the torment of existence. Therefore vigorously forward in the world-process as workers in the Lord's vineyard, for it is the process alone that can bring redemption![1]

Here we have reached the point where the philosophy of the Unconscious gains a principle which alone can form the basis of practical philosophy. The truth of the first stage of the illusion was despair of existence here; the truth of the second stage of the illusion was despair also of the hereafter; the truth of the third stage of the illusion was the absolute resignation of positive happiness. All these points of view are merely *negative*; practical philosophy and life, however, need a *positive* standpoint, and this is *the complete devotion of the personality to the world-process for the sake of its goal, the general world-redemption* (no longer, as in the third stage of the illusion, in the hope of a positive happiness in some later phase of the process). Otherwise expressed, the principle of practical philosophy consists in this, TO MAKE THE ENDS OF THE UNCONSCIOUS ENDS OF OUR OWN CONSCIOUSNESS, which follows immediately from the two premises, that, in the first place, consciousness has made the goal of the world-redemption from the misery of volition its own goal; and, secondly, that it has the persuasion of the all-wisdom of the Unconscious, in consequence of which it recognises all the means made use of by the Unconscious as the most suitable possible, even if in the special case it should be inclined to harbour doubts thereon. Since selfishness, the original source of all evil, which theoretically, by the acknowledgment of Monism, has already been ascertained to be naught, can practically be effectively broken by nothing else than the cognition of the illusory nature of all endeavours after positive happiness, the requisite perfect devotion of the personality to the whole is

[1] I hardly need specially call the reflective reader's attention to the point that the notion of redemption is here extended from the individual to humanity and the all-one world-essence sentient in it and the rest of Nature, *not* in respect of *sin*, but of *evil*. The former would be perfectly meaningless, the latter is an unavoidable consequence of the monistic theory.

at this standpoint *more readily* attainable than at any other (p. 98). Further, since the dread of pain, the fear of the eternal prolongation of the sensually present pain, yields always a far more energetic motive for effective action than the hope of a felicity represented as future, at this standpoint *instinct* will be *restored to its rights* far *more powerfully* than in the third stage of the illusion by the mere suppression of egoism (pp. 99–102), and THE AFFIRMATION OF THE WILL TO LIVE *proclaimed provisionally alone true*; for only in complete devotion to life and its pains, not in cowardly renunciation and withdrawal, is anything to be *achieved* for the world-process. The reflecting reader will also, without further suggestion, understand how a practical philosophy erected on these principles should be shaped, and that such an one cannot contain the *disunion*, but only the full RECONCILIATION with life.[1] It is now also obvious how only the *unity* of Optimism and Pessimism, here expounded, of which every human being carries in himself an obscure image as his norm of action, is able to give an energetic, and indeed the strongest conceivable impulse to effective action, whilst the one-sided Pessimism from nihilistic despair, the one-sided and really consistent Optimism from easy unconcern must lead to Quietism. [For those readers who regard the standpoint of our time, which I call the third stage of the illusion, the true one, and who are not inclined to deem it possible that this too will ever be recognised in the manner indicated by me as illusion by the further historical development of the consciousness of humanity, I will only remark, that the principles here expressed (to make the ends of the Unconscious ends of consciousness, &c.) remains just as valid for them, as the observations made on occasion of the third stage of the illusion with respect to egoism (suicide, Quietism, &c.) retain their validity from the point of view here reached, since it is for both indifferent

[1] Cp. Ges. Phil. Abhandlungen, No. iv.: "Ist der pessimistische Monismus trostlos?"

whether the final goal of the world-development be conceived positively or negatively.]

We have in conclusion still to deal with the question, *in what manner* the end of the world-process, the relegation of all volition to absolute non-volition, with which, as we know, all so-called existence (organisation, matter, &c.), *eo ipso* disappears and ceases, is to be conceived. Our knowledge is far too imperfect, our experience too brief, and the possible analogies too defective, for us to be able, even *approximately*, to form a picture of the end of the process; and I beg the gentle reader *not* to take the following for an apocalypse of the end of the world, but only for hints which are to prove that the matter is *not quite so unthinkable* as it might well appear to many at the first blush. But even those whom these aphorisms on the mode of conceiving that event may far more repel than the bare enouncement of the same, I beg not to be misled as to the *proved necessity* of that only possible goal of the world-process by the difficulties which attend the comprehension of the "How" at a point so remote from the end.[1] Of course, we can only contemplate the case that mankind, and not another species of living beings unknown to us, is called to solve the problem.

The *first* condition of the success of the work is this, that by far the *largest part* of the Unconscious Spirit manifesting itself in the present world is to be found in humanity; for only when the negative part of volition in humanity outweighs the sum of all the rest of the will objectifying itself in the organic and inorganic

[1] Experience has shown me that all limiting clauses in respect of the *purely problematical* nature of the following suggestions are insufficient to guard against an intentional or unintentional misunderstanding, as though positive *assertions* of any kind whatsoever were meant to be made here upon the "How" of the end. If I wrote for *success*, it would certainly have only been the commonest prudence to suppress in the first edition these four pages, literally indifferent for the book as a whole. It is always more profitable for the *author* not to expose too much the difficulties of a subject which are for the time being insoluble; for the advance of *science*, *on the contrary, the clearest exposure is most advantageous.*

world, only then can the human negation of will annihilate *the whole actual volition of the world without residuum*, and cause the whole kosmos to disappear at a stroke by withdrawal of the volition, which alone gives it existence. (That is here the only question, not as to a mere suicide of humanity *en masse*, the complete inutility of which for attaining the goal of the world-process has already been proved above.) This supposition now, that one day the major part of the actual volition or of the functioning Unconscious Spirit may be manifested in humanity, seems to possess no difficulty in principle. On the earth we see man ever suppressing other animal and vegetable life, save those animals and plants that he employs for his own use. Future still undreamt-of advances in chemistry and agriculture may permit the increase of the earth's population to a very considerable degree, although it already now amounts to upwards of 1300 millions, a relatively small part of the solid land supporting as dense a population as the means of obtaining nourishment known at our present stage of civilization allow. Of the stars only a comparatively small part have entered upon that brief period of refrigeration which permits of the existence of organisms; but not to mention that for the raising of a luxuriant organisation quite other conditions are required than merely the right temperature (*e.g.*, irradiation through rays of light, suitable atmospheric pressure, existence of water, right mixture of the chemical constituents of the atmosphere, &c.), of that insignificant number which at all support organisation, only a very small part again will be able to produce beings of a stage of organisation approximating to the human. The sidereal developments are measured by such immense intervals that it is *a priori* extremely improbable that the existence of a highly organised *species* on another star should coincide with the duration of mankind on earth.—But now how much greater is the spirit that manifests itself in a cultivated man than that in an animal or a plant; how much greater than that in an unorganised complex of atoms! One must not commit the error of estimating the strength of the active will *merely* by the *mechanical* effect, *i.e.*, by the degree of the resistance of *atomic* forces overcome; this would be extremely one-sided, since the manifestation of the will in the atomic forces is only the lowest. The will, however, has many other aims, and a contest of the most violent desires can take place without any perceptible influence on the position of the atoms. Therefore the hypothesis seems to me to be by no means far-fetched, that one day in a remote future humanity may combine in itself such a quantity of spirit and will, that the spirit and will active in the rest of the world is considerably outweighed by the former.

The *second* condition of the possibility of victory is, that the consciousness of mankind be *penetrated* by the folly of volition and the misery of all existence; that it have conceived *so deep a yearning* for the peace and the painlessness of non-being, and all the motives hitherto making for volition and existence have been so far seen through in their vanity and nothingness that that yearning after the annihilation of volition and existence attains resistless authority as a practical motive. According to the last chapter, this condition is one whose fulfilment in the hoary age of humanity we may expect with the greatest probability, when the theoretical cognition of the misery of existence is truthfully comprehended, and this cognition gradually more and more overcomes the opposing instinctive emotional judgment, and even becomes a practically efficient feeling, which, as a union of present pain, memory of former pain and fore-feeling of care and fear—becomes a collective feeling in every individual, embracing the whole life of the individual, and through sympathy the whole world, which at last attains unlimited sway. Doubt as to the general motive power of such an idea at first certainly arising and communicated in more or less abstract form, would not be authorised, for it is the invariably observed course of historically regulative ideas which have arisen in the brain of an individual, that although they can only be communicated in abstract form, they penetrate in course of time into the heart of the masses, and at last arouse their will to a passionateness not seldom bordering on fanaticism. But if ever an idea was *born as feeling*, it is the pessimistic sympathy with oneself and everything living and the longing after the peace of non-existence; and if ever an idea was called to fulfil its historical mission without turbulence and passion, silently but steadily and persistently in the interior of the soul, it is this. Since experientially the individual negation of the will *at variance* with the ends of the Unconscious furnished in such numerous cases a sufficient motive for overcoming the instinctive will to live in quietistic ascetic self-immolation (certainly without any metaphysical result), it is not obvious why at the end of the world-process the universal negation of will *fulfilling* the purpose of the Unconscious should not likewise be able to afford a sufficient motive for overcoming the instinctive will to live, especially as everything hard is the more easily executed the greater the co-operation. It should further be noted that humanity has still a life of many generations in which to gradually subdue and deaden, by habit and hereditary influence, the passions opposing the pessimistic feeling and the longing after peace, and to strengthen the pessimistic disposition by hereditary transmission. Even now we may remark that the natural force of passion and its demoniac power has to yield no inconsiderable domain to the levelling and enfeebling influences of modern life, and this enfeebling process will attain results the more considerable the more law and morals restrict personal caprice, and the more rationally life is managed according to the pattern of trivial worldly prudence from childhood upwards. It is one of the signs of humanity's *growing old* that not a growth, but a diminution of the energy of feeling and of passion opposes the growth of intellectual clearness; that thus the influence of conscious intellect in the provinces of feeling and willing, undeniably present at every stage, is, for a twofold reason, constantly on the increase, until in old age it becomes decidedly dominant. From this point of view, too, the possibility therefore appears anything but remote that the pessimistic consciousness will one day become the dominant motive of voluntary choice.——We may modify this second condition in such a way that not *all* humanity, but only a part thereof, need be penetrated by this consciousness, provided that the spirit that is manifested in it be the larger half of the active spirit of the universe.

The *third* condition is a sufficient communication between the peoples of the earth to allow of a *simultaneous common resolve*. On this point, whose fulfilment only depends on the perfection and more dexterous application of technical discoveries, imagination has free scope.

If we assume these conditions as given, there is a possibility that the majority of the spirit active in the world may form the resolve to give up willing.

There now arises the further question whether, in the nature of the will, its functional activity and the mode of its determination by motives, the *possibility* is at all given *of attaining a universal negation of the will, supposing* the preponderating part of the actual world-will to be contained in that mass of conscious mind which resolves *a tempo* to will no more, *no matter* whether this supposition be fulfilled within humanity or another species, or only under quite other conditions of existence of a future phase of development of the kosmos? We have to go back for the decision of this last question to our knowledge of the nature of volition and the laws of motivation following therefrom (comp. Chap. xi. B.), it being always assumed that these must remain identical in every possible form of objectification of the will.

It admits of no doubt that a special volition in man, a desire, affection, or passion, may, in certain circumstances, be neutralised by the influence of conscious reason in the special case. If, *e.g.*, I aim at honour by a deed or a work, and my reason tells me that those whose recognition I covet are fools and blockheads, this insight, if it is sufficiently convincing and potent, is able to allay my ambition, at least in this case. But now all psychologists are agreed that such a suppression is *not* to be conceived by *direct* influence of the reason on the desire to be suppressed, but only indirectly by the motivation or *excitement of an opposite desire*, which now on its part comes into collision with the first, the result of which is that they neutralise one another. Only in this manner is the suppression of the positive world-will to be conceived that Schopenhauer calls the will to live. Conscious cognition cannot directly diminish or suppress the will, but it can only excite an opposite, therefore negative will, which diminishes the intensity of the positive will. Quite inadmissible accordingly is Schopenhauer's doctrine of the *quietive* of the will consisting in an altogether different mode of knowledge, before which the motives are to be inefficient, and which shall be the only possible case of an incursion of the transcendent freedom of the will into the world of phenomena (cp. W. a. W. u. V., Bd. ii. p. 476–477). Such incomprehensible, utterly unjustified miracles are with our view superfluous. How beautifully, on the contrary, Schelling says (ii. 3, p. 206), "Even God cannot otherwise conquer the will than through itself."

If in the struggle of the special desires often two desires effect no reciprocal suppression in spite of the struggle, this happens either because they are only partially opposed, but partially pursue different side-ends, therefore their paths form only an angle, as it were; or it happens because the one desire is indeed in fact continually annihilated, but just as continually is instinctively *born anew* from the *persistent* ground of the Unconscious, so that there arises the *appearance* of its not being altered at all. In the opposition of the affirmation and negation of will the contrast is so mathematically strict that the former case certainly cannot occur, and for an immediate resurgence of the world-will after its total annihilation there is at any rate entirely wanting the analogy with the single desire, because in the latter the background of the actual world-will, in the former, however, nothing actually any longer remains. (For the rest, the possibility of a resurgence will receive notice in the following chapter.) As long, then, as the opposition of the will motived by consciousness has not yet attained the strength of the world-will to be suppressed, so long will the continually annihilated part continually reassert itself, supported on the remaining part, which also further secures the positive direction of the will; but as soon as the former has attained the same strength as the latter, there is no obvious reason why both should not completely paralyse one another and reduce to zero, *i.e.*, be destroyed without residuum. A negative excess is therefore inconceivable, because *the zero-point* is *the goal* of the negative will, which it *will* not transgress.

The motivation or excitement of the negative will by conscious knowledge is, according to the analogy of the excitement of a special negative desire through rational insight, *not merely conceivable, but demanded*; for here in the universal, just as in the individual, the ground on which reason sets in motion the conscious will of opposition is no other than an eudæmonological one—*regard to the attainment* of the happiest possible state, beyond which goal the positive unconscious will in its blindness darts to its misery. This endeavour after the greatest possible state of satisfaction, which the blind will only seeks from want of understanding in a perverse direction, thus belongs actually quite universally to the nature of the will itself, and wherever in the kosmos so high a consciousness may arise that it perceives the absurdity of the way to the goal, there necessarily a conscious volition is motived by this knowledge, which seeks to attain the greatest possible state of satisfaction by the opposite path, namely, by way of negation of the will.

The result of the last three chapters is, then, as follows. Volition has by its nature an excess of pain for its consequence. Volition, which posits the "That" of the world, thus condemns the world, no matter *how* it may be constituted, to torment. To obtain redemption from this unblessedness of volition, which the all-wisdom or the logical element of the unconscious Idea cannot directly effect, because it is itself in bondage to the Will, the logical in the Unconscious procures the emancipation of the Idea through consciousness in that it thus dissipates the will in individuation, so that its separate tendencies turn against one another. The logical principle guides the world-process most wisely to the goal of the greatest possible evolution of consciousness, which being attained, consciousness suffices to hurl back the total actual volition into nothingness, by which the *process* and the *world ceases*, and ceases indeed without any residuum whatever whereby the process might be continued. The logical element therefore ensures that the world is a best possible world, such a one, namely, as attains redemption, not one whose torment is perpetuated endlessly.

XV.

THE ULTIMATE PRINCIPLES.

We have in our previous inquiries ever and again met with two principles, Will and Idea, without the assumption of which no explanation would be possible, and which are really principles, *i.e.*, original elements, because every attempt to resolve them into simpler elements appears from the first hopeless, but all previous endeavours to refer one to the other are to be regarded as miscarrying. We have, however, also nowhere needed other than these two principles for our explanations, and what perhaps might be regarded as principia, feeling or sensation and consciousness, we have seen to be phenomenal consequences of our principles. *Other* elementary activities, as imagining, willing, perceiving, or feeling, have, so far as I know, never been introduced even tentatively in any spiritualistic philosophy, so that he alone could find fault with our adhering to Will and Idea who, on his part, should furnish the proof that the previously received elementary functions of the mind are not the right ones, and show what others are to be put in their place.

Now, as concerns our conceptions of these principia, we proceeded here too purely empirically, and inductively. We understood them, in the first place, as the ordinary intelligence formed in the leading-strings of the Teutonic languages apprehends them, and altered, extended, and limited them as the scientific need of explaining facts required. The starting-point of our philosophising is accordingly anthropological, so far as the linguistic popular consciousness and philosophic empiricism derive both from the *inner* experience of the mental activity of men. In fact, this starting-point appears, after a little reflection, the only possible one. Only what we are able to understand by *analogy with ourselves, only that* are we able *at all* to understand of the world; and were we not *ourselves a piece of the world*, and had not our anthropological elementary functions, like all the other phenomena of this world, grown out of the common simple fundamental principles of this world, then with the absence of resemblance and analogy between us and the rest of this world all possibility also of an understanding of the same would be cut off for us. But supported precisely on this intimate *affinity* of ourselves with other products of Nature and with the common metaphysical roots of all, we may confidently indulge in a cautious use of analogy, and risk the analogous transference of the anthropological principia to the rest of Nature, if we only proceed *critically enough* in the *separation of those peculiarities* which *distinguish* us men from the rest of Nature.

Thus we extended the anthropological principles Will and Idea by recognition of the same, first in the descending scale of animals, then in the independent lower nerve-centres of the human organism, then in the kingdom of the lower animals and protists, then in the vegetable kingdom, then, lastly, in the domain of inorganic matter. We felt, however, compelled by criticism, at the stages more removed from man, more and more *to strip off* that which in self-observing man most strikes the eye, namely, *Consciousness*, but also at the same time perceived that even in the highest forms of the mental activity of man such volition and ideation play the most significant part as is free from the form of consciousness; that man too is what he is only by this, that the same unconscious spirit dwells in him which he long admired in silence in the manifestations of the phenomena of Nature of less developed consciousness. We understood, further, that this unconscious spirit must be the common bond of the world and the support of the unity of the creative plan prevailing in it; nay, that it must altogether be the indivisible metaphysical essence, as whose objective phenomena] the only apparently substantially separated natural individuals are to be regarded. Thus before our searching glance the principles "Unconscious Will" and "Unconscious Idea" coalesced to form the one universal spiritual world-essence, which the dark impulse of mankind has always sought by the most diverse paths and denoted by the most diverse names, but yet everywhere at a certain stage of culture has apprehended as *spirit.* As said, *we can comprehend* of the nature of such a being only just so much as is revealed of this nature also in ourselves through the medium of internal experience, *as we ourselves are its phenomena* and apprehend ourselves as such, as its principles are also visibly unfolded in us; only he who denies the *essential identity and continuity of the world* and the harmony of the principles *efficient in it* with the principles *producing it*, would be able to blame our procedure as anthropopathic; and only the absolute abandonment of thought of the most thorough-going scepticism would remain if this mode of procedure were repudiated in principle. The warning against anthropopathism is only justified so far as it is limited to the sharpest critical severance from the ultimate principles of all that could anyhow belong to the special phenomenal form of the world-essence in *man* or in the *animal kingdom*, or in some narrow group of objectifications of the All-one, not exhausting Nature in its totality. In this direction, however, I believe I have in fact also conscientiously satisfied the most far-going and most scrupulous requirements, which is best proved by this, that the principles Will and Idea are apprehended in the highest degree of a universality destitute of all empirical particularity, namely, as generally as the necessity of at all retaining a positive and precise concept any way admits. Thus is every *unwarrantable* and *spurious* anthropopathism most carefully avoided, without abandoning the only path of understanding that our position in the world *renders possible* for us, but also *permits, i.e.*, justifies by results, without therefore from an ultra-scepticism distrusting and disdaining *genuine* anthropopathism, which indeed only reaches just as far as *we ourselves* are *of metaphysical essence* (or in theological language: of divine origin).

If now, according to the results of our previous inquiries, the two principles Will and Idea, conceived in metaphysical essential unity, actually suffice for the explanation of the phenomena presented to us in the known world, they form the apex of the pyramid of inductive knowledge, and it only remains to us in conclusion to take one more view of the height thus scaled, when a comparison with the ultimate principles of existing philosophical systems may not be uninteresting. This chapter forms, accordingly, the direct continuation of Chap. iv. A., Chaps. i., vii., viii. C., and in part also of Chaps. xi., xii., and xiv. C., whose contents I beg the gentle reader particularly to bear in mind.

The contents of the present chapter may perhaps possess least interest for the reader who has had but little philosophical culture, because more than all the foregoing they lose themselves in the analysis of notions which in general extend to the bounds of abstraction and of our intelligence. However, on the one hand, the relation here first more precisely indicated of my point of view to the systems of the most important philosophers, and, on the other hand, the stricter discussion of the notions whose significance and mutual relations had hitherto for the most part been presupposed, should, on account of the clearing up of many points previously left in obscurity, be a sufficient inducement to a reader who has followed what has gone before with interest not to leave this concluding chapter unread.

If the value of scientific conclusions be estimated solely according to the degree of their certainty or accuracy, undoubtedly the value of the same is less the further they are removed from the ground of the facts to be explained, because their probability becomes less, and then the value claimed by the apex of the pyramid of knowledge would be least. However, for the determination of value, yet other elements than merely the degree of probability should be taken into account, which may be summed-up in the degree of importance which these results would have in comparison with other objects of knowledge, supposing that they were all apprehended with the probability 1, *i.e.*, with absolute certainty. As for this factor, the value of the apex of the pyramid of knowledge manifestly exceeds all other possible objects of knowledge, and therefore I, for my part, shall not be weary in contributing my mite to the better establishment of the last metaphysical principles, hoping that very soon some other may come who may go still farther. On the other hand, however, I hope that my successors will find the *base* of the pyramid built so well and firmly by me as to be able to build farther thereon, and will not have cause to demolish the same in its essential parts.

1. *Retrospect of Earlier Philosophers.*—Of the great philosophers, those most in accordance with our principles are Plato and Schelling, Hegel and Schopenhauer, and indeed the two latter represent one-sided extremes (Hegel the logical element, Schopenhauer the Will), whilst Plato and Schelling so far occupy a connecting and intermediate position, that in neither does there exist a complete equilibrium of the two sides, but in Plato the Idea, in Schelling's last system the Will has chief importance.

Plato's best-known and most important principle (cp. the masterly presentation of the Platonic principles in Zeller, Philos. der Griechen, 2 Aufl., ii. 1, pp. 441–471) is the Platonic IDEA, the world of Ideas, or the nature of the many ideas included in the One (the ἕν) highest Idea or the Idea absolutely, which he more precisely defines as the Idea of the good, *i.e.*, the absolute end, and which is to him identical with the Divine Reason. Plato conceives the Idea as in the eternal repose of unchangeable independent Being, and only exceptionally, and with manifest inconsistency, does he here and there (especially, in mythical representations) ascribe to it also efficient operation, an activity.

Since the self-enclosed IDEA would never have reason for going out of itself, it needs a second, equally important principle, the ground of the Heraclitean flow of all things, the moving spring of the world-process.

This second is, accordingly, as opposed to the eternal repose of the Idea, the principle of absolute change, the ever coming and going, and never genuinely being; wherefore he also calls it the relatively non-being (μὴ ὄν); but yet it is that which receives the ideas as its content, and ushers them into the whirl of procession. Whilst the Idea is the measured, self-enclosed, that is the measureless, in itself unlimited (ἄπειρον); whilst the IDEA (even number) is in itself only qualitatively determined, that brings the element of quantity into the phenomenon. There belongs to it "all that is capable of more or less, of stronger or weaker, and of excess;" wherefore Plato calls it also the "great and little."

Whilst the Idea is the Good, and all the good in the world springs from it, the ἄπειρον is the Bad, and the cause of all the bad and evil in the world (Aristot., Metaph. i. 6, end), is that blind Necessity found pre-existent by the world-forming Intelligence, that senseless Cause, which could not be perfectly overcome by Reason, that irrational residue that we always get over when we abstract from things all that is image of the IDEA.

From the marriage of the two opposed principles arises the World, which we know through sense-perception. Both principles have this in common, that they are not affected by the change of the phenomenon, but stand above it as transcendent (χωρισταί) essences.

The agreement of the Platonic results with our own is obvious; we only need to translate the realm of the *per se* existing IDEAS into that of the unconscious Presentation (that is indeed also conceived by us as intuitive and non-temporal, *i.e.*, eternal) and the intensive principle of absolute change into the Will.

It is also remarkable that Plato asserts that this *ἄπειρον* is in no way cognisable, neither by thought nor by perception, which entirely agrees with our view, that the Will as such is a something for ever inaccessible to Consciousness. [When Plato sometimes characterises the *ἄπειρον* also as *χῶρα, τόπος,* this is certainly just as figurative as the expression *δεξαμενή* (reservoir) and *ἐκμαγεῖον* (soft substance, in which a form, here the Idea, is imprinted), and means, as the expressions *ἐκεῖνο, ἐν ᾧ γίγνεται,* and *φύσις τὰ πάντα σώματα δεχομένη,* testify, nothing more than that wherein the ideas find their stand, place, locality, or room for reception and unfolding, just as he sometimes assigns to the ideal world an intelligible supramundane place (*τόπος νοητός*). Less strict still is the expression *ὕλη* (matter), substituted, not by Plato himself, but by Aristotle and later writers for the *ἄπειρον.*]

Schopenhauer's philosophy is contained in the proposition: Will alone is Thing proper, the Being of the world. Hence it follows that the presented object is only a—manifestly accidental—product of brain, and that there is only so much reason to be found in the whole world as the fortuitously arisen brain chooses to put into it. For what can proceed from an absolutely irrational, senseless, and blind principle but an irrational and senseless world? If there is a trace of *sense* in it, it can only have crept in by *chance!* As little as a *blind* Will can propose to itself ends, so little can it choose and realise fit means to its ends; and thus the conscious intellect can with Schopenhauer in truth appear only as a *parasite* of the Will, that, far removed from being willed by this latter, has rather settled upon it in some incomprehensible fashion, God only knows whence, like the mildew on the plant. It is obvious that the absolutely irrational, taken as principle, must be very much poorer and infertile than the absolutely rational, the Idea and Thought. There is also needed a remarkable restraint to put up with the absolutely irrational and its poverty as principle. Hence the dilettante colouring, which, with all its intellectual wealth, the philosophising of Schopenhauer possesses, hence the sigh of relief when, in the third book of "The World as Will and Idea," one approaches the great inconsequence of the system, the IDEA.

On the other hand, one cannot sufficiently admire and praise the wisdom of the Unconscious, that it created so confined a genius, to show posterity what can and what cannot be achieved with that principle in its isolation. The one-sided elaboration of this principle was in the genetic course of development of philosophy just as necessary as the pointing of the opposite extreme in Hegel.

How closely the two philosophers are connected is rendered evident by the undesigned coincidence that the principal works of both philosophers appeared in the year 1818, when one at the same time recalls the utterance of Hegel (xv. p. 619), "Where several philosophers synchronously appear, they will represent different aspects of a single whole."

As certainly as Schopenhauer was incapable of comprehending Hegel, so certainly must Hegel, if he had known him, have shrugged his shoulders over Schopenhauer; both stood so far from one another, that every point of contact was wanting for mutual recognition.

If Kant's Criticism was compelled to decline every attempt at a theoretical metaphysic, and Fichte begins the positive metaphysical evolution of the most recent philosophy with the dialectic treatment of self-consciousness, Hegel sums up this development till the close of the first third of the century, in that he receives from Schelling the principle which till then had been its more or less unconscious moment: the IDEA alone is the Being of the world; logic is consequently ontology; the dialectic self-movement of the concept is the world-process. This principle is, as compared with the complete poverty of the Schopenhauerian, the absolutely rich; for all that the world is, it is indeed through the IDEA; something may be done with it, therefore, and it is not to be wondered at that it produced four systems when its antipode exhausted itself in one.

Hegel in his logic measured the Platonic realm of the *per se* existing IDEA: he tried to surprise the Idea in the process of its eternal self-deliverance from barest being, and thus far his principle was within its right. But when the realm of the *per se* existing Idea had been traversed in all directions, the principle reached its limits; for though the Idea was omnipotent in its own sphere, one thing remained unattainable by it, the *res*, *reality*; "for real is just that which cannot be created by mere thought" (Schelling, i. 3, p. 364).

The principle, however, though one-sided, was regarded as all-inclusive, and had to be worked out in this one-sidedness, in order to show here, too, distinctly how far it extends and how far not. On the other hand, however, it lay pre-indicated in the dialectic movement, that the logical IDEA, after it had exhausted itself on its own ground, must, with dialectical necessity, demand the other of itself, or the negative of itself, and this could only be —the alogical.

With this plain acknowledgment, however, the Logical would have had to renounce its absolute sovereignty, would have had to acknowledge and admit an equally authorised principle, that the truth is found in and reality depends once on the conflict and time union of these last and highest contrasts. Then, however, logic would also have had to declare that that Alogical is only accidentally, namely, looked at only from *its own* point of view, the negative, but in truth, from a higher point of view, the *positive*, which first of all realises the Logical, whereas without this positive it is, with its whole stock of ideas, *equal to nothing*.

This demand upon absolute Idealism all at once to declare its own principle negative was for man—at least for that man who had carried it to its height—too much. Certainly Hegel allows here and there the feeling to break through that the negative of the logical element deserves notice and makes possible the passage of the Idea into actuality, but he suppresses the stirrings of this feeling in their origin, only not to approach too near his dear IDEA. He tries to comply with the imperative compulsion to do justice to the alogical element, everywhere thrusting itself on the observer in the world, by preposterously drawing the alogical self-contradiction *into* the logical, in that he gives to his dialectical method (intended to be at once ideal- and real-dialectical) inner contradiction as an integral element of its process; whereas in truth the contradiction of the logical can always only be kindled by the existing logical not posited by it. But now even Hegel himself observes that, on the one hand, he does not thereby exhaust the demands of the actual as regards their alogical character, and that, on the other hand, he therewith burdens his logical IDEA with the responsibility for things which it cannot bear without losing its character of the logical. Accordingly, he takes refuge in his category of the Contingent, which must always bear the brunt when the details of a phenomenon withdraw themselves, or even only appear to withdraw, from explanation through the principle of the logical IDEA. But the contingent as little as self-contradiction has a place within the logical principle and within the "What" of the world determined by it; for the logical principle is only determined logically, *i.e.*, necessarily; and therewith the contingent is simply excluded from it (and relegated to the sphere of the alogical). But just this compulsion, *in addition* to the self-contradiction already drawn into the logical, to have recourse to the category of the *contingent* ought to have shown Hegel that, after abstracting all that is logically posited in phenomena, there is really only an *alogical residue*, and that there must therefore be an alogical *beside* the logical, not merely *in* the same. With this recognition Hegel would, however, at once have got quit of the motive which had urged him to credit the inconsistency of an alogical *in the* logical, *i.e.*, he would have been able to refine his inherently contradictory dialectical process into a consistent logical process, which the alogical only underlies as impelling moment of the process.

Thus much is universally recognised, the relation of logic to the Philosophy of Nature is in Hegel himself obscure and obliterated. From consistently carrying out his *principle*, and (with Michelet) maintaining that Nature can only be called externalised logic, or logic in its *alterity*, so far as the moments of the dialectic process united in logic have *fallen asunder*, Hegel is protected by a certain instinctive timidity which teaches him that with the consistent carrying out of his principle he sins against his own *method*, which unconditionally demands the alogical as the equally authorised negation of the logical idea; but he is again deterred from satisfying this demand by the consequences of that step, which manifestly destroy his own principle, that the IDEA is the sole substance.

This contradiction explains why the transition from the Idea to Nature, on all occasions when Hegel mentions it (*e.g.*, "Phänomenologie," p. 610; "Logik," Bd. ii. p. 399-400; "Encyclopädie," Bd. i. § 43 and § 244), is dealt with in an unusually aphoristic manner, frequently changed in new editions, and, moreover, dressed up in unsuitable and figurative expressions (sacrifice, unfolding, alienation, dismission, reflection of the Idea, &c.) The difference on this point has first clearly revealed itself in the divisions of the Hegelian school.

Let us bestow one more glance upon the question how much Hegel felt in silence the necessity of the alogical as counterpoise of the logical. At the close of the larger "Logic" he says of the absolute Idea, that, enclosed in the sphere of pure thought, it is *still* logical; whence it is to be concluded that its emergence from this into another sphere must be the passage into the no longer logical, *i.e.*, into the *alogical*.

In the "Phänomenologie," p. 610, he says, "Knowledge knows not only itself, but also the *negative of itself*, or its limit." Here, indeed, we might be inclined to suppose that the non-logical must be intended by this negative; but he again entirely weakens the effect by declaring this "*knowing* its own limit" to be *sufficient* for sacrifice or alienation. In the "Logic," vol. ii. p. 400, he further says, "Because the pure idea of knowing is so far enclosed in subjectivity, it is IMPULSE *to abolish this*." Here he feels even that the going beyond the Idea can only be an affair of the Will. Altogether impossible, however, is the thought that this "*willing* of the Idea to emerge from the Idea" can come from itself, from the eternal repose of its being-for-self, which must rather be considered equivalent to the *absolutely self-sufficient peace*, the untroubled self-enclosed *contentment*.

Not only would it be *incomprehensible* how the Idea could of its own accord come to precipitate its eternal purity into the vortex of the real process, but it would be the height of absurdity if it, that encloses all knowledge in itself, willed to sacrifice its blessed peace of non-temporal eternal calm without *external compulsion*, in order to fall a prey to the torment of the process, the unblessedness of volition, the misery of real existence. No, not absolute Reason itself can all at once become irrational, but the irrational must be a *second* or other lying outside Reason.

If it lay in the *nature* of the logical to pass out of itself into the alogical, this occurrence would be necessary and eternal, and one could never speak of a conclusion of the process, of a redemption.

It is also indeed only the *negative* relative determination (relative, namely, to the logical Idea) of that opposite of the Idea to be the alogical; its *positive* determination, however, is this, to be principle of change, origin of reality, *will;* and when Hegel in the above passage suddenly throws in this determination to be impulse, it is quite clear indeed that he has procured it purely from the empirical need of explaining the reality of Nature.

But this is also, in fact, the *only possible way* to come to the knowledge of the Will. *A priori* one could *at the most* only know *the Idea* and all that follows from the Idea; the existence of the *Will*, however, is, at all events, only to be concluded *a posteriori.* For every *a priori* purely logical or purely rational philosophy can only assert *ideal relations*, but not *real existences ;* it can at most say, "If something is, it *must* be *thus*," but it can never show *that* something is; this only experience can do, *i.e.*, the *conflict* with the extant will (existence) in the *perception* of consciousness. This answers quite to the circumstance that the Idea only determines the "*What*" of things, but the Will their "That;" thus the Idea can also only so far *comprehend* things as it *determines* them, therefore never their real existence.

This necessary step in philosophy, which Hegel had been unable to take, Schelling accomplished[1] in his last system, when, as indicated in Chap. vii. C., he perceived the purely logical character of previous philosophy, declared it to be negative, and in opposition to it raised the demand for a positive philosophy beginning with the immemorial being only to be known through experience. (Cp. Schelling's "Critique of the Hegelian Philosophy," in i. 10, pp. 126 to 164, especially pp. 146 and 151–157; further, ii. 3, fourth and fifth lectures.)

[1] Compare my memoir serving as a necessary complement and elucidation of this whole chapter, "Schelling's positive Philosophie als Einheit von Hegel und Schopenhauer," Berlin, Otto Lowenstein, 1869.

So far as Schelling's deductions are critical and preparatory they are excellent, but as soon as he begins to deliver his positive philosophy itself he becomes weak, wavers between an explanatory argumentative procedure, a dialectic method and the sudden and unmotived introduction of new leading concepts, to lose himself soon in the shoals of a mystical theogony and the details of Christian theology. This is simply due to the circumstance that, to preserve consistency with his own past, he becomes unfaithful to his better knowledge, that the principle of positive philosophy is only to be gained *a posteriori* from experience, accordingly by the *inductive* path.

[Because Schopenhauer in the main (*e.g.*, W. as W. and I., 2d Book, and "On the Will in Nature") proceeds inductively, he accomplishes so much more as regards this problem, although he is not particularly clear about his method, and why it is the only correct one.]

Nevertheless Schelling's last system (unity of positive and negative philosophy) has a high value, in that it embraces the principle of Hegel (the IDEA) and that of Schopenhauer (the Will) as co-ordinate, equally authorised and equally indispensable sides of the one principle (cp. i. 10, 242–243; i. 8, 328). Schelling very decidedly sees in that "*extralogical* nature of existence" (ii. 3, 95), in that "incomprehensible basis of reality" (i. 7, 360), the Will. *That* something is is only perceived by the resistance which it opposes; the only thing capable of resistance, however, is the Will (ii. 3, 206). It is therefore the Will that accords its *That* to the whole world and to every single thing; the Idea can only determine the *What*. In his "Treatise on the Essence of Human Freedom," that appeared in 1809 (thus long before the writings of Schopenhauer), he said (Werke, i. 7, p. 350), "There is in the highest and last resort no other being at all than volition. Volition is original being, and to this alone are adapted all its predicates—groundlessness, eternity, independence of time, self-affirmation. All philosophy only aims at finding this highest term." And in his "anthropological scheme" (i. 10, p. 289) one finds, "1. *Will* is the proper spiritual *substance* of man, the ground of everything, the *originally* matter-producing, the *only thing* in man, the *cause of being*."

In contrast to this he declares in the same place the *understanding* to be "the not *creating*, but *regulating, limiting, giving measure* to the infinite boundless Will."

With this corresponds the principles of the Pythagoreans, the ἄπειρον (unlimited), and the περαῖνον (limiting), or εἰδοποιοῦν (giving form or notion), (i. 10, 243). If the ideal principle is an Understanding in which is no Will (ii. 2, 112; ii. 1, 375, L. 14–16), the real principle is a "Will in which is no Understanding" (i. 7, 359). "All willing, however, must will *somewhat*" (ii. 1, 462), an objectless willing is only = *vague desire*, "the longing that the Eternal One feels for self-deliverance" (i. 7, 359). The *Word* of this longing is, however, the *Presentation*—that Presentation which is at the same time the Understanding (i. 7, 361), or "the ideal principle" (i. 7, 395). In the "utterance of this word" is found the union of the ideal and the real principle from which the existence to be explained arises.

In his later expositions Schelling endeavours to deduce these principles from the concept of Being as the elements of it which cannot be thought away, an undertaking which plainly reveals its infutility by this, that all real progress can only be gained by the reinstatement of the concrete determinations. Here the being-able-to-be (*potentia existendi*) answers to the Will, the purely (*i.e.*, non-potential, idealiter) being to the Idea. On the being-able-to-be he says (ii. 3, pp. 205–206), "But now the being-able-to-be of which we here speak is not conditioned; it is the unconditioned *potentia existendi*; it is that which can pass unconditionally and without further mediation *a potentia ad actum*. But now we know no other passage *a potentia ad actum* than in *volition*. Will in itself is potentiality κατ' ἐξοχήν, willing the act κάτ' ἐξοχήν. The transition *a potentia ad actum* is everywhere only transition from not-willing to willing. The immediately being-able-to-be, therefore, is that which, in order to be, needs nothing but just passing from not-willing to willing. Being consists for it simply in the *willing;* it is in its being nothing *else* than *willing.* No actual being is without an actual willing, however qualified, conceivable."—The being-able-to-be is the Will *per se*, the not yet objected, but only primitive Will, that indeed *can* will (else it would indeed not be Will), but simply does not yet Will; the Will before its manifestation (ii. 3, pp. 212–213).

If this Will is kindled into willing, if it becomes active, it therewith surrenders its freedom, its being-able-not-to-be, and lapses into blind being, like Spinoza's substance. As such, it becomes the "Sinister," "the source of all displeasure and dissatisfaction" (ii. 3, 226).

The purely being or the IDEA is neither potentiality nor act, for act is only that which proceeds from potentiality Schelling calls its state *actus purus.*—I remark here that Schelling endeavours, for the sake of the Christian Trinity, to make his principles and their substantial unity into persons, and for that end to ascribe to each of the three a will of its own, which is altogether absurd. That one may not feel the preposterousness of this too distinctly, he suppresses in his later expositions as far as possible the tenet that the concrete determination of the "purely being" is the "Idea." (See further my essay mentioned above.)——

There is a remarkable passage in Irenaeus, i. 12, 1, where the latter is giving an account of Ptolemy. As this same passage proves how early that perception attained distinct expression which declares a creation from the pure Idea to be impossible, I shall set it down here:—πρῶτον γὰρ ἐννοήθη προβαλεῖν, φησὶν, εἶτα ἐθέλησε. . . . τὸ θέλημα τοίνυν δύναμις ἐγένετο τῆς ἐννοίας. ἐνενόει μὲν γὰρ ἡ ἔννοια τὴν προβαλὴν. οὐ μέντοι προβάλλειν αὐτὴ καθ' ἑαυτὴν ἠδύνατο, ἃ ἐνενόει.

ὅτε δὲ ἡ τοῦ θελήματος δύναμις ἐπεγένετο, τότε, ὃ ἐνενόει, προέβαλε. (For first he thought to produce, then he willed.—The Will thus became the power of Thought. For Thought thought indeed the creation, but it could not itself produce from itself what it thought. But when the power of Will was added, then it produced what it thought.)

The essential agreement of our principles with those of the greatest metaphysical systems (Spinoza we still reserve) can only serve to strengthen us in the conviction that we are on the right path. Let us now consider somewhat more minutely each of the principles.——

2. *The Will.*—*Volition* represents the superiority of the real over the ideal. The ideal is the ideal object *per se*, the real is the willed idea of the Idea as content of Will.

Equally diffused with the belief in Matter is the conception of the vulgar Theism, that the *real* is not the *apparition of the will-action itself of the creative Being of the world*, but a dead, arrested product, a *caput mortuum* of a former long-extinct activity of Will, the act of creation, and that the proper representative of this *caput mortuum* is *matter*. From this prepossession we have already, in Chap. vii. C., delivered ourselves, where we saw that there is only the Unconscious and its activity, but no third. As long as this notion of a dead matter was not overcome, there certainly only remained the two ways of apprehending it: either as uncreated eternal substance, with Materialism, or as *caput mortuum* of a former act of creation, however difficult it might be to form a clear idea of such a dead product; but after material substance had been perceived by us to be a chimera, pure matter a system of atomic forces, and the material world an ever-changing *state of equilibrium* of very many *intersecting will-activities* (cp. vol. ii. pp. 241–243), there remained no longer any reason for assuming dead remnants of former productivity, and we now perceived the Real at every moment of the process to be *present* will-activity, therefore the existence of the world a *continuous act of creation* (cp. vol. ii. pp. 268–269). This is doubtless also the meaning of the "second corollary" at the beginning of Schelling's "Philosophy of Nature" (Werke, i. 3, p. 16): "Nature nowhere exists as product; all the several products in Nature are only apparent products, not the absolute product, in which the absolute activity exhausts itself, and that always *becomes* and ever *is*."

This conception by no means, as might appear at first sight, contradicts the physical axiom that the effect of a once-acting cause persists; for the state newly induced, in which consists the physical effect (*e.g.*, a movement of this or that direction and velocity), certainly persists, *supposing* the object to persist whose state it is, *i.e.*, supposing that this object is continually posited anew.

It is coherent with this view of the persistence of the world as a continuous act of creation that we can no longer regard volition as separated from the act: *volition is itself the act.*

This truth appears clearer in the case of the atomic will, as discussed in Chaps. v. and xi. C. If it appears otherwise in psychology, this is to be explained thus:—

(1.) When act is employed in the wider sense, it must be understood as external activity of the will; if, on the other hand, act is taken in the narrower sense, namely, only as the *intended* mode of efficiency, undoubtedly only that willing is identical with the act *which accomplishes its will*, but not that which indeed does and works, but is impeded in the execution of the deed *in the intended manner* by external unconquerable impediments.

(2.) Only the volition directed to the *present* is identical with the act, a volition directed to the future, however, is also no proper categorical *volition*, but only a hypothetical volition, a *resolution* or an *intention*.

(3.) By act one understands in psychology only a doing of the whole person, but not those movements of the brain-molecules caused by the Will, which in themselves are not powerful enough to call forth an *external* action of the body, or are hindered by other cerebral vibrations acting in the contrary sense.

Therefore in psychology certainly only the *whole* present volition of the individual, *i.e.*, the resultant of all the simultaneous single wills or desires, is identical with the act, whilst the simultaneous components exhaust their *mutual* action in the brain so far as they do not become act in the resultant. Strictly taken, however, the movement of the cerebral molecules is also a coming of the will into external operation, *i.e.*, an act, and in this sense is also every single desire in the individual an act, only that it is perhaps prevented by other cerebral vibrations from realising itself in its whole possible range; *e.g.*, hunger produces cerebral vibrations in the beggar, that would compel him to stretch out his hand to the bread in the baker's shop; the dread of the theft produces other cerebral vibrations, which prevent this particular movement; but both, the positive as the negative desire, are in act expressed as cerebral vibrations.

"The Will *per se* is potentiality κατ' ἐξοχήν, volition actuality κατ' ἐξοχήν." This declaration of Schelling must certainly be assented to. Thus much is at least universally recognised, that volition is to be regarded as an act dependent on a power, and this potency, this being-able-to-will, of which we know nothing more than this, that it can will, we call Will. Whatever be a being-able-to-will, the possibility must be open to it to be, under certain circumstances, a non-willing,[1] *i.e.*, the notion of the being-able-to-will includes that of the

[1] "To a certain extent it is *a priori* obvious, in common language *self-understood*, that that which now *produces* the phenomenon of the world must also be *capable of not doing* this, consequently of *remaining at rest*, or, in other words, that there must also be a ἀναστολή to the present διαστολή. If, now, the former is the phenomenon of the *willing* of life, the other will be the phenomenon of the *non-willing* of the same. In reply to certain silly objections I remark, that the negation of the will to live *by no means* imports *the annihilation of a sub*

being able not-to-will, or the being-able-to-will is only a correctly chosen name if that which is denoted by it is at the same time also a being-able not-to-will on occasion. If, namely, the being-able-to-will were deprived of this possibility of not-willing on occasion, it would be a not-being-able not-to-will or being-obliged-to-will, and, indeed, not a being-obliged-to-will conditionally under certain circumstances or for a certain time, but an eternally unalterable being-obliged-to-will. This would, however, upset the notion of the being-able-to-will or of potentiality, and only leave the notion of the absolute groundless willing that wills to all eternity. Superfluous as would be the notion of force in presence of an eternal motion, so *superfluous* would be the notion Will (as potentiality of volition) in presence of an eternal willing; willing would then be non-potential *actus purus.* On this assumption all possibility not only of an individual, but also of a universal redemption, would be cut away; all hope of a cessation of the process (whether intended and striven for, or accomplished according to blind law and fortuitously) would be destroyed. The cheerlessness of such an assumption can of course be for us no argument against its admissibility or probability; we shall, therefore, in another direction, have to test its validity.

The *eternity* of *willing* conditions the *endlessness* of the

stance, but the mere act of not-willing" (*i.e.*, the negation of the act of volition); "*the same* that has hitherto *willed* wills *no longer.* Since we know *Substantial Being,* the *Will* as Thing *per se*, merely in and through the act of willing, we are incompetent to say or conceive what it can further be or do" (this addition "or do" is very inapt). "after it has renounced this acting: therefore negation is *for us,* who are the phenomenon of willing, a passage into *nothing*" (Schopenhauer, "Parerga," §162). The inactive *Substantial Being* "remaining in repose" is undoubtedly for us, who are at the point of view of actual reality, equal to nothing; yet we may well try and conceive what it intrinsically is, namely, the *being able* to will and not will. This Schopenhauer overlooked, although properly in the above word "*capable*" (of producing or not producing the world) he has himself enounced it. The quoted passage shows that those adherents of Schopenhauer who conceive the Will as Essential Being obliged to will, and not capable of abstaining from willing, cannot here appeal to their master, but have only modified for the worse his deeper views.

process, and indeed both forwards *and* backwards. In the endlessness of the process forwards there lies no difficulty, because the same is at every moment, at every now, merely ideal, postulated, not real, given. It remains for ever pure problem, posited progression with negation of an end, and therefore never lies under the contradiction of the completed endlessness. On the other hand, the part of the process realised at every moment always succumbs to this. *Thought* can just as easily from the given Now follow the path backwards indefinitely as the path forwards, but that proves nothing at all as regards the *real* process, which pursues its course in an *inverse* direction to this ascent of thought into the past. The infinity that remains an unsatisfiable ideal postulate to regressive thinking is to be complete accomplished result to the forward process; and here occurs the contradiction that an *infinity* (if also only one-sided) is given as finished realisation. Schopenhauer, too, is perfectly clear concerning the impossibility of this (W. a. W. u. V., 3 Aufl. i. p. 592, l. 23–27, and p. 539, l. 9 to the foot), only for our problem this is of no account, because he denies the reality of time, and therewith of the process, and deals with the question of the world's beginning or non-commencement only in the subjectively idealistic sense, where thought just as little finds a limit *in itself* backwards as forwards (ibid., p. 594). The *reality* of the process, however, includes the finiteness of the same backwards, *i.e.*, its beginning before a finite time reckoned from the present moment. The point of commencement of the process (with and through which time begins) is therefore the boundary-point between time and *timeless* eternity; only in the former was the Will willing, in the latter it was accordingly not-willing. It is herewith proved that the willing can under certain circumstances be also a not-willing, whereby at once the necessity is posited of supposing behind the actual willing a being-able-to-will (and not-to-will), a potentiality of willing, a will. Since, on the other side of the commencement of the process, this potentiality was without actuality, the possibility remains that fresh circumstances may occur where it again becomes a potentiality without actuality, *i.e.*, it is now *possible* that the real process is also finite forwards. (The *necessity* of the future end of the process is not to be proved from the notion of the process or of time, but only from that of *development*, on the assumption that the world-process is development,—as I have shown at the close of the frequently mentioned essay, "Ueber die Umbildung der Hegel'schen Philosophie," in the Ges. Philos. Abhandl., No. ii.)

It follows, then, from the impossibility of a regressive or progressive infinite world-process that volition as such cannot be eternal; that it is not an ultimate capable of and needing no further explanation, but that before its rise there must have been something that was not indeed itself volition but yet contained the power of willing. But this we call the pure will. When we come to this conception from the recognition of the fact that one and the same now wills, now does not will, we have in this conception established the elements of being-able-to-will and being-able-not-to-will. This is, however, to be taken as a contradictory, not as a contrary opposition. A contrary opposition is the counter-struggling of volition split into a positive and a negative part, as we have assumed at the end of the world-process. Here two opposed species of the genus "willing" are given, but the not-willing, of which there is question before the beginning of the process, is the purely privative negation of the genus willing in general; for only when a positive willing is already given can an antagonistic negation arise as actively-negative willing. The being-able-not-to-will is consequently also not, like the being-able-to-will, to be understood as active power, but as merely passive possibility of the intermission of the use of the active power.

The now justified relation of potentiality and act, will

and volition, appears indeed eminently clear and obvious; it becomes, however, again more involved as soon as we direct our glance to the real passage of the pure potentiality (still without actuality) into the act of volition. We know, namely, from Chap. iv. A., that volition can only truly exist when it is definite volition, *i.e.*, when it wills something determinate, and that the determination of that which is willed is an ideal determination, *i.e.*, that volition must have a presentation for its content.

On the other hand, we know, from Chap. i. C., that the Idea cannot of itself become existential,—not pass from non-being into being,—for otherwise it would be potentiality or will, or contain this in itself,—that thus only the Will can give it existence. But here we are caught in a circle. Volition is first to become existential through the presentation and the presentation first through volition. Through the Will *per se*, *i.e.*, so far as it is mere potentiality and *not* actual, certainly no effect (action) can be produced on the Presentation, but the Will can manifestly only act so far as it is not mere potentiality. If now, on the one hand, the Will as pure potentiality cannot act at all, thus also not on the Idea; if, on the other hand, Volition as act *proper* only becomes existential *through* the Idea, and yet the Idea *cannot of itself* become existential, there only remains the hypothesis that the Will acts on the Idea in a condition intermediate as it were between pure potentiality and true act, in which it indeed has already emerged from the latent repose of pure potentiality, thus seems to be actual as compared with the latter, but still has not yet attained to real existence, to complete actuality. This may be considered to be relatively potential. Not as if this intermediate state were intercalated as time-interval between the ante-mundane repose and the real world-process—this is, as we shall see hereafter, impossible—but it represents only the moment of the *initiative*. Any one accustomed to think under the notion Will or faculty of initiation might say that there is no will at all in his sense within the world-process, since Volition is here continuous state become fatal, in which merely the ideal content is changed, and that only that moment of the initiative determining the elevation of the will for the whole duration of the world-process is the true will-act. Thus much is certain, that of the two, Will and Idea, the initiative can only be ascribed to the former, and that the state of the will at the moment of the initiative is other than it was before the same, and other than it will be when the original impulse has done its duty, and has become full-action by participation of the Idea. As we must consider still more closely this condition of the Will in the initiative (in the "impulse" of Fichte transferred to the absolute), we require a fixed designation for the same and choose the expression "*empty* (*i.e.*, still devoid of content) willing."

Schelling, too, is acquainted with this empty willing. He says (ii. 1, p. 462), "But now a distinction important for all that follows presses on us of itself—of the willing, that is properly objectless, that wills *only itself* (= Sucht), and of the willing, that is filled and remains as product of that first willing."

Empty volition *is* not yet, for it lies still before that actuality and reality which we are accustomed alone to comprehend under the predicate Being; it *is substantive*, however, not merely like the Will *per se*, as pure potentiality, for it is indeed *a consequence* of this, and accordingly is related to it as act. If we desire to apply the right predicate, we can only say: Empty volition *becomes;* becoming is employed in that eminent sense in which it signifies not transition from one form into another, but *into being from absolute not-being* (*pure essence*). Empty willing is the *struggling for being*, which can only attain being if a certain external condition is satisfied. If the will in itself is the will able to will (consequently also able not to will, or *velle et nolle potens*), the empty volition is the will that has decided itself to will (thus can no longer not-will) the will willing to will indeed, but not yet able to accomplish the willing by itself alone (*velle volens, sed velle non potens*), till the presentation is added, *which* it can will.

Empty volition is thus actual so far as it *struggles* after its realisation, but it is not actual so far as it cannot *attain* this realisation of itself without the accession of an external circumstance. As mere form it can only become actually existential when it has attained its *fulfilment;* this fulfilment it can, however, not find in *itself,* because it is *only form* and nothing more. Whilst, therefore, the endeavour of definite volition has the realisation of its content (its assertion against opposite endeavours) for goal, the effort of the empty willing has no other goal than this, to realise itself, itself *as* form, to obtain possession of itself, to be, or, what is the same thing, to will, *i.e.*, *to come to itself.*

Another tendency than this, to emerge from the vacuity of the pure not yet existent form, cannot be at all imagined in the absolutely idealless and blind Will. One might say its content or goal is the negation of its want of content, if this were not self-contradictory and at the same time materially false, so far as by that a notional, *i.e.*, ideal, content was indicated, so that the empty volition would then again have an ideal content, and would be capable of existence through this alone. The relation is rather a positive one; the potentiality contains in itself the formal element of the act as abstract being, not yet posited, and the initiative strives also to *posit* it as that which it intrinsically is, *i.e.*, as pure form of the act, which, however, never could succeed as long as the other equally indispensable, namely, material moment of the act is wanting. Thus it remains, so far as the latter is not added to the empty volition, in an unceasing *preparedness to spring,* without ever coming to the point: it remains at the stage of a becoming, from which nothing becomes, in which nothing emerges. The willing-to-will *pines* for fulfilment, and yet the form of the will cannot be realised till it has grasped a content; as soon and as far as it has done this, volition is again no longer *empty* volition, no longer willing *to will*, but *definite* willing, willing *something*. The state of pure volition is therefore an eternal pining for fulfilment, which can only be given to it through the idea, *i.e.*, it is absolute *unblessedness*, pain without pleasure, even without pause. So far as empty volition is only *momentary* impulse, that immediately, at the same moment at which it emerges, grasps the idea as content (identical with it, therefore not able to withdraw from it), so far it does not attain realiter to the separate existence of such an ante-mundane unblessedness, although the latter is the condition of the origin of the world, thus *natura prius*. But undoubtedly it also attains realiter an *extra*-mundane unblessedness of empty willing *beside* the satisfied world-will. For the Will is potentially *infinite*, and in the same sense its initiative, empty volition, is infinite. The Idea, however, is *finite* in its notion (although *in itself* capable of infinite perfection), so that also only a finite part of empty volition can be satisfied by it (and only a finite world can arise). There remains, therefore, an infinite excess of the hungry vacant willing besides and beyond the satisfied world-will, which in fact, until the return of the total will to pure potentiality, falls irretrievably into unblessedness. The reader may remember that, according to Chap. iii. C., every non-satisfaction of a will *eo ipso* begets consciousness. The *sole* content of this single extra-mundane consciousness is, as we saw above (vol. ii. pp. 257–258), not exactly an idea, but absolute pain and unblessedness, whilst in the world (in the fulfilled volition) there exists only a relative pain, *i.e.*, an excess of pain over pleasure.

Will and Presentation, both of which were before the commencement of the real process, something pre-existent, or, as Schelling says, "super-existent," are therefore united in the (partial) fulfilment of empty volition through the (whole) idea into fulfilled volition or the willed idea, wherewith the act is attained as real existence. We may call this combination of willing and picturing to form existing filled volition, which, regarded from the side of the will, is an *educing* and *seizing* of the idea, by the same right from the side of the presentation a *surrendering* to the will; for devotion also is an altogether *passive* fact which demands no positive activity, but only *excludes* all negative activity, *all resistance*. It appears here very clearly that Will and Idea are related to one another as *male* and *female*, for the truly feminine never goes beyond an unresisting passive devotion. If we would carry the image further, the Idea is before being (as purely being) in the state of blessed innocence; but the Will, that has put itself into the state of unblessedness through elevation from pure potentiality into empty volition, drags the Presentation or Idea with it into the whirlpool of being and the torment of the process, and the Idea gives itself up to it, sacrifices its maiden innocence, as it were, for the sake of its final redemption, that it cannot find in itself. In that the Idea is not at all capable of an active resistance to the Will, and that the blind roving Will cannot at all avoid seizing this, because it is the only thing seizable, and lies before its nose, as it were; in a word, in that the essential identity of the Will and the Idea makes a non-concurrence of both, after the impulse has once been given, impossible, nothing is changed in that relation of the two to one another. What was before an unintelligible fact is now elevated into the sphere of necessity, and thereby at the same time the proof of the above assertion is given that an interval of empty volition between the moment of the initiative and the real world-process is impossible, because the Idea necessarily sees itself in the first moment of the initiative of the will dragged into the vortex of the process, so that the beginning of the *vague* time posited by empty volitive is likewise the commencement of the time *determined* by the Idea. From this *embrace* of the two super-existent principles, of the being-able-to-be that decides to be and of the purely being is therefore *being engendered;* as we already know, it has from the father its "That," from the mother its "What and How."

We saw that the Will is *insatiable;* however much it has it always wants more, for it is *potentially infinite;* and yet its satisfaction can never be infinite, because a satisfied or completed infinity would be a realised contradiction. Strictly it is therefore quite indifferent whether that piece of the empty volition which has found a fulfilment in the Idea is great or small, *i.e.*, whether the world is great or small (in the intensive sense), for the satisfied volition will always be related to empty volition, as something finite to an infinite, which is possible because it is related to it as actuality to potentiality. Since accordingly empty volition is and remains infinite, it is also altogether indifferent for the infinite absolute unblessedness of this empty volition whether, besides its infinite unblessedness mitigated by no pleasure, however slight, a world of pain and pleasure exists or not.

We certainly detect none of that extra-mundane unblessedness of the void willingly, for we belong *to the world*, to the *fulfilled* willing. Lastly, we can by no means adopt the opinion that the will furnished with an ideal content, *e.g.*, the atomic forces, is not obliged to endure considerable non-satisfactions and *painful* sensations, although we can say with certainty that *before* the origin of the organic consciousness it can feel no satisfaction as *pleasure*. According to all this the infinite unblessedness would be perpetuated if the possibility of a radical redemption were not given.

This possibility exists, however, as we know, in the emancipation of the Idea from the Will through consciousness. The latter certainly demands in the course of the process still greater sacrifices; for although it indeed enables pleasure to be felt, it also renders pain the more oppressive through reflection, so that the intra-mundane pain, as we have seen, does not fall, but rises with the enhancement of consciousness on the whole; but through the final redemption this enhancement of pain becomes purposive. This ultimate redemption is perfectly compatible with our principles, for although at the end of the world only the *satisfied* will is directly brought to turn round, yet this is the only actual and existential will, and is consequently related *as regards its real power* to the mere empty willing struggling for existence as an *actual* to a *non-actual*, as a something to a nothing, although of perfectly homogeneous nature. If, then, the existential volition suddenly becomes nothing through an existential willing-not-to-will, the willing in this manner itself determines itself to the willing-no-more, in that the whole volition parting into two equal and opposite directions swallows up itself, thus as a matter of course also the empty willing-to-will (not-being-able-to-will) ceases, and the return to the *pure* independent potentiality is accomplished, the Will is again what it was *before* all volition, will able to will and not to will;—for the *being able* to will is certainly not in any way to be taken from it.

To wit, there is in the Unconscious neither an experience nor a memory; the Unconscious can therefore also *not* be *altered* through the accomplished world-process; it can neither have acquired anything that it did not possess before, nor have lost anything formerly possessed; it can neither have filled its former ante-mundane emptiness with the memory of the wealth of the process passed through nor receive any instruction through the experience had in the same, to guard itself henceforward from the repetition of its former *faux pas* (for for all this reminiscence and memory, nay, even reflection would be required); in a word, it is in no other situation than before the first commencement of that process. Is this so, however, and in the impossibility of maintaining a memory in the Unconscious must the flattering illusion of the hope of final peace rejoicing perhaps in its finality after the close of the world-process be set aside as a pious delusion (cp. pp. 89–90), the possibility undoubtedly remains open that the potentiality of the Will decides once again to will, whence then the possibility immediately follows that the world-process may often have played the same tune before. Let us pause for a moment in order to determine the degree of the probability.

The Will able to will and not-will, or the potentiality which can determine itself to being or not, is the absolutely free. The Idea is by its logical nature condemned to a logical necessity; volition is the potentiality that has lost itself, which has forfeited its liberty to be able *not-to-will;* only potentiality before the act is free, is the determined and determinable by *no reason*, that abyss that is itself the abyss of all. As little as its freedom is limited outwardly so little is it inwardly; it only becomes *limited* inwardly at the moment when it is also *annihilated*,—when the potentiality itself *externalises* itself. We see at once that this absolute freedom is the stupidest thing that one can imagine; which is quite in accordance with the circumstance that it is only conceivable in the Alogical.

If, now, there is nothing at all that determines volition or non-volition, it is mathematically speaking *accidental* whether at this moment the potentiality wills or does not will, *i.e.*, the probability = $\frac{1}{2}$. Only when the probability of each of the possible cases is = $\frac{1}{2}$, only where absolute chance comes into play, only then is absolute freedom conceivable. Freedom and chance are, as absolute notions, notions, *i.e.*, deprived of all relations, identical. In the same manner Schelling conceives the relation when he says (ii. 1, p. 464), "Volition, that is for us the commencement of another world posited outside the idea . . . is the primitively accidental,—the primitive chance itself."

Now, were the potentiality *in time*, the probability would, as time is infinite, be = 1, *i.e.*, certainty, that the potentiality resolves *in time* once again to become actual; but, as the potentiality is *outside* time, which indeed the actual first creates, and this extra-temporal eternity is not at all distinguished in temporal reference from the moment (as great and small are not distinguished as regards colour), so is also the probability that the potentiality determines itself to volition in its extra-temporal eternity equal to this, that it determines itself thereto instantaneously, *i.e.*, $= \frac{1}{2}$. It follows from this that the redemption from volition can be regarded as no final one, but that it only reduces the pain of volition and being from the probability 1 (which it has during the world-process) to the probability $\frac{1}{2}$, thus always affords a gain not to be despised in practice.

Of course, the probability of future events cannot be influenced by the past, consequently the co-efficient of probability of $\frac{1}{2}$ for the repeated emergence of the willing from potentiality cannot thereby be diminished, that the latter had already once before resolved to will, but when one *a priori* considers the probability that the emergence of volition from potentiality repeat itself with the whole world-process n times, it is manifestly $= \frac{1}{2^n}$ just as the *a priori* probability of throwing heads n times in succession with a coin.

Since with the end of one world-process time ceases till the beginning of the next there is *no time-pause*; but the state of affairs is precisely the same as if the potentiality had at the *moment of the annihilation* of its former act externalised itself anew into act. It is, however, clear that n increasing, the probability $\frac{1}{2^n}$ becomes so small that it is practically sufficient for consolation.

3. *The Presentation or Idea.*—Let us now pass to the other super-existent, *Presentation*, and once more take particular notice of its relation to the Platonic idea.

Aristotle calls the Platonic ideas *οὐσίαι*, a term that Plato himself to our knowledge never employed, which at any rate with Aristotle means something altogether different from what we now understand by "substance," and which would be best translated by "entities." For Plato himself one can hardly assert more than that he conceived the Ideas as objective existences, and denied that they are only in the mind, that they are mere knowledge of some person; further, indeed, he did not go in the discussion of their nature, but he is contented with opposing them to the perishable flux of the sensible world as the truly being (*ὄντως ὄν*), as the independent being (*ὂν αὐτὸ καθ' αὐτό*), and the unchangeable (*οὐδέποτε οὐδαμῇ οὐδαμῶς ἀλλοίωσιν οὐδεμίαν ἐνδεχόμενον*). If Aristotle strives after more precise definition by calling the Ideas *οὐσίαι*, the later Platonists and the Neo-Platonic school on the other hand conceived the Ideas as *eternal thoughts of the Deity.*

Both interpretations it is probable were in the mind of Plato himself; for although the eternal thoughts of the Deity cannot be substances in the modern sense of the phrase, yet it is no contradiction at all to call them *οὐσίαι* in the Aristotelian sense, just because they are *eternal* thoughts of the Deity, therefore have an essential being for ever self-identical.

Certainly Plato would never have allowed that they are a *knowledge*, that they are *conscious* thoughts of Deity, for thereby they would be altogether deprived of their objectivity, which was the chief point to him. When Plato identifies the Idea with the Divine Reason, this can only mean that, by a very explicable license of speech, he identified the essential being with its sole eternal activity.

It is clear, therefore, that we have to understand by the Platonic ideas *eternal unconscious thoughts* (of an impersonal Being), where the "eternal" does not mean an endless duration, but that which is out of time, elevated beyond all time. For us too the unconscious presentation is an extra-temporal, unconscious, intuitive Thought, which represents to consciousness an altogether objective essentiality. The main difference between the Platonic and our view lies in the meaning which he assigns to the word "being," namely, whilst after the precedent of Parmenides, he regards *unchangeableness* as the criterion of true being, unchangeableness appears now to us *indifferent* for being, but on the contrary we demand unconditionally that true being should have *reality*.

Thus Plato comes to declare the Idea to have being in the most proper sense, whereas we are obliged to regard it as somewhat non-being, of which more hereafter.

With Plato there takes place such an interpenetration in the abstract realm of ideas, that all are contained in One Idea. I, too, have repeatedly pointed to the mutual interpenetration of the presentations in the Unconscious, and their coinherence (*e.g.*, of end and means), a state that simply follows from the non-temporal character of the unconscious presentation, where the moments of thought separated in time in discursive thought must necessarily be found *in* one another. But whereas Plato denotes the coinherence of the whole world of ideas in the peculiar Pythagorean abstract fashion as the One, and then determines this One materially as the Good, we shall not be able to rest content with any of these determinations. Since the notion of the Good in the ethical sense, as already often remarked, must not be referred to the All-One existence, which Plato too seems to feel, we shall be obliged to interpret the good itself in the Platonic sense as the higher logical end, as the final end determining all the intermediate ends and means, that the all-wise World-Reason assigns to itself. Thus understood, we too may appropriate the Platonic unity of the Idea. The Idea actualised in every moment of the world-process is one embracing in itself all the separate ideas to be simultaneously realised as integral elements, and the uniting point of this collective Idea is the self-identical world-end unchanged from the beginning to the end of the process, or true end of the world-process, which indeed is only *implicitly* thought in each single moment, but which teleologically determines the whole content of the intuition of each instant as means to it. The end is posited by the Idea itself, and the determination of the special matter of intuition of the All-One is again logically determined by the end; accordingly the total content of the intuition of the All-One is from the beginning to the end of the process pure self-determination of the Idea.

We can, however, not stop here, but must further ask, why does the Idea determine itself in this way and not otherwise? If this self-determination is a necessary one, following from its own nature, as we must assume, the question is properly only how to perceive the peculiar nature of the Idea, in consequence of which it sees itself compelled to determine itself thus and not otherwise. When we have perceived this inmost nature of the Idea, we possess that from which the whole content of the Idea necessarily follows in virtue of its pre-formed self-determination; we have gained the most precise expression for the principle that we hitherto have called Idea, but which in strictness is only Idea when and so far as it has entered into being, *i.e.*, become content of a will. The required determination for the inmost nature of the Idea now can no longer be a material one, for it must indeed also hold good beyond all ideal content (before the beginning of the world-process); the matrix of the unfolding of the whole material wealth of the world of ideas, the ground of the self-determination of the Idea to this and no other content, can only be a formal, no longer a material principle; it must be the same immanent formal principle of the Idea that is manifested in its self-determination of the ideal means to the ideal end, *i.e.*, the *logical* formal principle.

By logic was formerly, and in part still is, understood theory of thinking in the widest extent; but in order to understand what is here meant by the logical, we must first of all abstract from that too general conception all that is specifically psychological and anthropological, *e.g.*, the special *doctrine of method*, which provides a guide to research in the various departments of human inquiry, and the *theory of knowledge*, which investigates the problem whether and how consciousness may transgress its immanent sphere and attain to being *per se*. We must further remove from it the framework of Ontology, which the human consciousness has contrived with the help of the categories for the better understanding of existence, but which itself is only an implicit part of the material *content* of the Idea, and only *seems* to be formal because it is abstract. Finally, we must deduct all that appertains only to the discursive form of the manifestation of the logical in consciousness, and not to the logical as such, thus the diremption of the logically connected moments, which may be likened to the exhibition of an illuminated point as a shining line in a quickly rotating mirror. It is the logical formal principle that causes the moments successively related in the discursive-logical thought-process of consciousness (*e.g.*, the terms of a conclusion) to stand to one another in actual *logical* relation; but that the related moments are discursively sundered is due only to the nature of conscious thought, not to the logical principle, which is ever inherently unconscious, and even in the discursively logical process of consciousness is interposed between every pair of terms as a timeless unconscious factor, so that it is not to be wondered at, that it is also manifested as such in the implicit intuitive thinking of the unconscious Idea and its self-determination (cp. Chap. vii. B., vol. i. pp. 314–316). The logical principle is in theological language the divine reason; in metaphysical, the very simplest primitive reason, from which everything rational is derived. As primitive reason it is the formal regulator of the material self-determination of the Idea; it is generally the formal aspect of the unconscious intuition of the All-One, whose material aspect is the Idea in the narrower sense. Lastly, it is the *matrix* from which the not yet existing Idea is unfolded at the beginning of the world-process.

If we would now more precisely specify what the Logical or the primitive Reason is, not for the Idea, but in itself, we shall be obliged to keep to the old enouncement of the logical formal principle under the form of the laws of identity and contradiction, *i.e.*, not to the discursive expression of these laws, but to the logical element contained in them. The two are one, and only the positive and negative expression of the same thing, but at the same time also the positive and negative mode of manifestation of the same principle. The logical formal principle in the shape of the law of identity is absolutely unproductive (the A = A leads to nothing); it has been the error of all logistic philosophers that they regarded the logical principle as positively creative, and even imagined it possible to attain, by its means, to a positive content of the world, to a positive final aim of the same. All positive teleology is therefore a still-born child, because the positive end must be a creation of the logical principle in the positive sense, but the latter is in the positive form altogether uncreative, nay, of itself could never attain to a process, but must persist in pure identity with itself.

Not so the negative aspect, although here certainly the logical formal principle can only be manifested if a non-logical is present, which the logical can oppose with its negation. The inner conflict of the void Will that wills willing and yet cannot will, that aims at satisfaction and reaches dissatisfaction, is such a non-logical; the volition itself is the negation of the Law of Identity, in that it annuls persistence in identity, and demands that A (pure potentiality) do not remain A, but change into B (the act); it is therefore the negation of the positively logical, and therewith challenges the logical formal principle to manifestation in a negative sense.[1] The logical negates the negation of itself: it says, "The contradiction (namely, to me, the logical) is not to be;" and in saying that it proposes to itself an end, namely, the abolition of the alogical, of volition. Certainly this end, that follows from the negative mode of manifestation of the logical principle, is itself only negative, directed against the genuinely positive in volition, that only from the standpoint of the logical appears relatively negative. In the same sense will also, from the point of view of the logical, the end — the suppression of volition—appear as negation of the negation of itself, *i.e.*, as double negation, *i.e.*, as something relatively positive, but from the point of view of the alogical the end remains a purely negative one, as is confirmed by the result, reduction to nought. Accordingly we too must hold by the expression of a negative final end, in contrast to the impossible positive final end (in the sense of an emanation from the logical principle in its positive form), and shall have to lay stress on the fact that here teleology altogether, in the last resort, has only been saved by the absurdity of all search after a positive end and the untenability of all *positive* teleology being apprehended through the principle of the logical itself,

[1] It can hardly be necessary to call to mind that the determination of the "Alogical" and "Logical," here deduced from the nature of the two principles "Will" and "unconscious intuitive Idea," had already been proved by the inductive path. The chapter on the Misery of Existence, namely, had inductively proved that the existence of this world is worse than would be its non-existence; that therefore the "That" of the world, or its existence, must owe its origin to an irrational or alogical principle, but at the same time also that this irrational principle, which proceeds to make the world into a wretched one, is *volition*. On the other hand, it has been shown by all the preceding investigations that the "What" of the world is contrived most judiciously and wisely, and thereby points to the action of a wise and logical principle, which we have perceived in its manifestation to be unconscious intuitive *presentation*. It seemed to me expedient to show here once more that the contrary course also leads to the understanding of the Whole, *i.e.*, that from the very nature of the psychical elementary functions "willing and perceiving," expanded into attributes of the All-One, follows at once the alogical and logical character of the same, because in this manner the organic connection of all the terms in the traversed circle of thought becomes far more conspicuous.

and by the adoption of a negative teleology, *i.e.*, a teleology with absolutely negative end, but which from the point of view of logical speculation is, on account of the double negation contained in it, just as positive as a directly positive teleology could ever be.

We see, then, that we may and must go beyond Plato's determination of the One Idea as the Good or the end, to the higher determination of the ideal principle as the formal-logical. The eternity of the Ideas is not to be understood, as if they one and all, just as they are afterwards realised, lay from the very first and for ever boxed up in the ideal, and only waited for the Will to realise them; for then the infinite empty volition must realise the whole mass of Ideas at a stroke, which would only yield an eternal chaos, but no development. Rather must the Ideas always unfold themselves by self-determination from their formal principle only in the extent in which they are to be realised by the Will in the course of development; and this extent is determined by the constant final purpose on the one hand, and by the stage of development of the world at any time attained on the other. The eternity of the Ideas is therefore not to be understood as eternal, even if only ideal, *existence*, but only as eternal pre-formation or possibility. The logical is in itself to be regarded as a purely formal principle, which is stimulated to the ideal productivity of its content only by the other of itself, the alogical. We may say there is no *pure* logic, *i.e.*, no manifestation of the logical purely in and by itself; there is only *applied* logic, *i.e.*, manifestation of the logical in and by its other, the alogical. Only through *applied* logic is the ideal principle that is *primo loco* pure formal principle filled with an ideal content (first the end, and then the succession of means to attain this end).

Thus understood, our ideal principle also essentially agrees with that of Hegel (for the Absolute Idea of Hegel is nothing more than that to which the empty husk of thought, the notion of pure being identical with nothing, has determined itself in virtue of its immanent logical formal principle in the progress of the evolution itself), except that one has in the word "Absolute Idea" an empty sign, which is only filled when the whole development has been gone through; whilst the more familiar "logical" denotes the formal moment of the self-determination in the extra-temporal ideal evolution.

The process in the Idea *per se* is, as Hegel himself says, an *eternal, i.e., extra-temporal* one, consequently it is also strictly again no process but an eternal result, a being-in-one of all the moments mutually determined to all eternity; and this being-in-one of the moments determining one another *appears* to us only as process when we artificially sunder them in discursive thought. For this reason I cannot allow that the logical determination of that which at every moment emerges into actuality takes place through dialectic in the Hegelian sense, because in the sphere of the ultra-temporal eternity, where we might at any rate speak of a peaceful juxtaposition and intermingling of contradictory representations, no process is possible than that which necessarily presupposes time, and on the other hand, again, in the piece of the Absolute Idea emerging at a particular moment into reality the main requirement of the Hegelian dialectic, the existence of contradiction, is wanting,—quite apart from this, that a dialectic process in the Hegelian sense can only take place between concepts, these crutches of discursive thinking, whereas all unconscious thinking occurs in concrete intuitions.

When Plato, who, properly speaking, had no idea of laws of Nature, assumed also transcendent ideas of everything of which he could abstract common notions, this was a childish point of view, which, as Aristotle reports at a later period, excited suspicion even in his own mind.

We know now that all inorganic Nature is a consequence of the atomic forces acting according to their *immanent laws* (which are comprised in their Idea), and only with the origin of organisms is there an accession of genuinely new Ideas. We know also that as all the Ideas receive their determination from the Logical, and in strictness are altogether nothing but applications of the logical to given cases, the idea of the world-process is the *application of the logical to empty volition.* With Hegel the latter is represented by that which forms the commencing and starting-point of logic, pure being, identical with nothing; for this is the only form under which the *impulse* to self-alienation foreign to the logical can exhibit itself to the logical principle.

We have seen that the Idea first becomes existent when the Will grasps it as content, and consequently realises it; but what then is it previously? At all events, *not yet existent*, a super-existent like the Will or empty volition. As the Will in volition passes out of *itself* (as potentiality), so is the Idea put outside *itself* (as super-existent) by the Will. This is the radical difference between the two: the Will *itself* ejects itself; the Idea *is* translated into being by the Will (as one in the condition of not-being).

Could the Idea pass of itself into being, it would indeed be *potentiality of being*,—would therefore be itself Will. But, on the other hand, the Idea not yet translated into being can also not *absolutely not be* (οὐκ εἶναι), else the Will could also make nothing of *it*; it can only be a not-yet-being in a special sense (μὴ ὄν). Now, if it is to be neither active being nor potentiality of being, nor also absolutely nothing, what then remains? *Language wants* an appropriate word for the designation of this concept. One might be inclined to call this state *latent being*, which, even when it is made manifest by the Will, yet never becomes free being, but always only being as ideal content of a being *in actu*. From the *actus* the latent being of the Idea before its seizure by the Will is distinguished by this, that by the word *actus*, on the one hand, one involuntarily always thinks of a preceding potentiality that is here wanting, and, on the other hand, of *an actual* being, an efficient activity, whose strict contrary is that still, calm, latent being, altogether self-enclosed, never spontaneously going out of itself. The word *actus* therefore is at most suitable so far as this state like the *actus forms a contrast* to potentiality, but a contrast that is of quite a *different* kind from that of *actus*. Schelling seeks to make this relation of the concepts evident by terming this state *actus purus*, *i.e.*, an *actus* that is pure or free from potentiality, or translates this μὴ ὄν, "the purely (*i.e.*, non-potential) being." It is, however, clear that these expressions are by no means happy, since, in spite of the most satisfactory elucidations, they must always leave the impression of a "wooden iron." This defect of expression, which arises through a vain struggling with the limitations of language, however, by no means prejudices the result, that the Idea before being sucked into the vortex of being by the Will elevated to being must be thought in a relatively non-existent state, which, elevated above the real Being arising from the co-operation of Will and Idea (*i.e.*, super-existent), must be thought in this super-existent sense as a non-potential (*i.e.*, also unsubstantial), hidden, still, pure being. Inevitably as Schelling was led to this definition so was Hegel also obliged to give to the Idea as first and most original determination that of pure being, which, in comparison with a later filled being, is as good as nothing, except that in Hegel's panlogism by this determination the alogical is at the same time smuggled in as moment of the initiative of the process.—As we called the Will before its elevation pure potentiality or pure *faculty*, we may describe the Idea before its transportation into being the realm of pure *possibility*. Both expressions agree in determining their object by a reference to something future; the difference, however, is that this relation is in "faculty" an *active*, in "*possibility*" a *passive* one. The

Will as *per se* simply and purely formal admits of no distinction; in the Idea, however, we have to distinguish first the ideal *principle* as formal moment of self-determination, and, secondly, the Idea as the infinite wealth of the possible forms of development which it hides in its bosom. So far as the latter collectively are predestined by the "purely being" formal element of the logical for the possible case of their birth, they stand implicitly as mere ideal possibilities precisely in the same eternal logical relation which is revealed on their entrance into being. But so far as they form in a special sense the realm of pure possibility, in an altogether different sense to the formal-logical principle underlying them, from which they are unfolded when once their hour is come, so far can the principle of latent (or, according to Schelling, pure) being appertaining to their *matrix* never be attributed to them, but must be reserved for the Idea as formal-logical principle of the ideal self-unfolding.

We have seen that it is in truth the Will, more precisely empty volition, which entrudes the Idea out of its purely independent being into a being with external relations, in that it seizes it once for all as its content, but that the Idea *as* fulfilment of the Will determines and develops itself in virtue of its logical formal moment.

This proposition holds good from the first moment when the Idea is externalised by the Will to the moment when Being is extinguished with the turning back of the Will; at every moment the sum of presentations which forms the content of the Will is a definite one, and indeed that definite, phase of the evolutionary process of the One World-Idea whose inner multiplicity it composes, and it is, since this evolutionary process of the World-Idea is a purely logical one, altogether and exclusively *logically* determined, or, what comes to the same thing, *posited* as regards its "What" with *logical necessity*. But since, as we know, the "What" of the world is at any moment only the realised content of the Will, the "What" of the world is at every moment of the world-process determined by logical necessity. Because it is logically necessary (for the main aim) that there be development (in order to the genesis and enhancement of consciousness), because the necessity of evolution includes the necessity of time, thus time and the change of content in time belongs to the logically necessary content of the Idea itself, therefore the realisation also of this content is presented as a definite process in time (cp. what was said regarding Space, vol. ii. p. 181).

The above proposition holds for every single event just as much as for the whole, for each individual forms indeed an integral part of the whole, and is as such an integral part *determined* by the whole, since each several existence and event is, as regards its "What," only and wholly Idea, therefore a link in the inner organic manifold of the one and whole World-Idea at any time. If now the *total content* of the world-idea at every moment is *logically* determined throughout (namely, on the one hand, by the stable final end, on the other hand by the phase of development of the process attained at the last moment), and if each single *part* is determined by the *whole, each single* existence and happening is also at every moment *logically* determined and conditioned. If, *e.g.*, this liberated stone falls, the falling takes place with this or that velocity for no other reason than because it is *logically* necessary under these circumstances, because it would be illogical if at this moment something else happened to the stone. Certainly *that* the stone altogether can still fall at this moment, that it is still there to fall, that the earth is still there to draw it to itself, this depends on the persistence of the Will; for did the Will cease at the moment to will, therefore the world to be, it would *no longer be logical* that the stone should fall.

We see here the two elements which go to make up causality. *That* the stone which I now let go falls, depends on the continuance of the willing beyond this moment; but that it *falls*, and falls indeed with such and such velocity, depends on this, that it is *logical* that it is thus, and would be illogical if it were otherwise. That in general anything comes to pass, that the effect *follows*, depends on the Will; that the effect, *if* it follows, follows *with necessity as this* and no other, depends on the Logical. That indirectly the cause is determinative of the effect is quite clear, for *only under those circumstances* which collectively are termed "cause" is it logical that this effect follows.

According to this, causality is another name for logical necessity, that attains actuality through the Will.

Having thus perceived purpose to be the positive side of the logical, we shall now be able unconditionally to subscribe the proposition of Leibniz, "*causæ efficientes pendent a causis finalibus*;" but we also know that it only expresses a part of the truth, that the *whole* world-process is in its content only a logical process, but in its existence a continual act of Will. Only by this, that phenomenal equally with final causality is comprehended as logical necessity; only by this, that the logical necessity of the process is admitted in all its phases, and physical causation and final causality (we may add as a third "motivation") are perceived to be only different *projections*, in which universal determination, regarded under different points of view, presents itself; only, by this, I say, has at bottom a universal teleological apprehension of the world-process become possible. For if every moment of the process is to be altogether and without residue a link in the chain of physical causation, and each at the same time altogether and without residue a link in the chain of final causality, this is only possible under one of the following three conditions: either causation and final causality have their identity in a *higher unity*, of which they form merely different aspects of the apprehension through the discursive thinking of man, or both chains stand in a *pre-established harmony*, or the present link in the chain of causation only *accidentally* agrees with the present link in the chain of final causes (as one and the same event). Chance would once and a way be possible, but not in constant repetition; the pre-established harmony is miracle or the renunciation of comprehension; thus only the first case remains, if, with Spinoza, one will not entirely abandon final causality.

The notion of logical necessity is the superordinate of causation, final causality, and motivation; all necessity, causal, final, and deterministic (by motive), is *only* necessity therefore because it is *logical* necessity. It is *false* to maintain, with Kant and so many moderns, that there is no other than a *subjectivistic* notion of necessity, but it is *true* that all happening and existence as such would be *mere factness* devoid of all necessity if the *formal-logical moment did not import* the compulsion of necessity into objective reality, *precisely* as we are conscious of it in our subjective thinking. But whoever concedes the objective reality of the world (*i.e.*, independent of the consciousness of the subject) *can* no longer deny the necessity of the operation of the laws of Nature, unless he commits the absurdity of assuming that quality of matter-of-factness, which the abstraction of empirically exceptionless *rules* affords and imposes upon us, to be fortuitous. Since the probability of such a continually recurring accidental order which compels us to formulate abstract laws, is infinitely small, the probability that an objective necessity answers to and underlies the subjectively abstracted rule borders on certainty. Certain as is the existence of an objective necessity in the world, so certain is it that everything happening in the world is logically determined and conditioned, simply because the notion of necessity is only tenable as *logical* necessity. Thus and only thus are the difficulties resolved which the concept of causality has caused from Hume to Kirchmann.

4. *The Identical Substance of both Attributes.*—We now approach the question whether the Idea is attribute or substance, whether it is the thought of a Being before, behind, or above it, or whether it in its turn is itself *an*

ultimate? We have seen that Plato did not definitely decide in favour of any of these views. Hegel asserts that the Concept is sole substance, that the Idea is God, whilst Schelling denies the self-movement of the Concept postulated by Hegel (Werke, i. 10, p. 132): "There lies therefore in the asserted necessary movement a double illusion: (1.) In that for thought the *Notion* is substituted, and *this* is represented as something moving itself, and yet the Notion would of itself lie perfectly immovable if it were not the notion of a thinking subject, *i.e.*, if it were not thought; (2.) In that one imagines thought is only impelled by an inherent necessity, whilst it yet manifestly has a *goal* towards which it strives."

In the first place I would remark, that the difference of the two views, although important enough theoretically, yet is hardly so important as it might appear at the first glance, because we find ourselves here already in a region of the super-existent, where our conceptions finally leave us in the lurch; and even when they appear to us sufficient, are indeed hardly able to cover that transcendent objectivity in the way in which metaphysics only too easily imagines.

Nevertheless thus much stands firm, that of whatever kind this or the final metaphysical principles of a system may be, our thinking always finds itself under the inevitable compulsion to conceive the same either as functioning substances, or, however, to assume a substance behind them as whose attributes they appear, and which is functional as active subject when the principles become operative. Thus we cannot think the IDEA of Hegel or the unconscious intuitive Perception otherwise than as either itself raised to substance, or, however, as supported by another substance as attribute. We have likewise in the Will of Schopenhauer only the choice of substantialising the Will itself or of regarding it as attribute of a substance lying behind it. Our thinking is absolutely unable to think a function without active subject, which at the same time must, as ultimate principle resting upon itself, be metaphysical substance. We cannot think perception without a perceiving, volition without a willing subject; and the only question is, whether we will think and can think as perceiving subject the Idea itself, as willing subject the Will itself, or whether we find ourselves caused to assume a support of the attributes of willing and perceiving lying behind them. This necessity of thought goes even behind the functions as such, and tracks the principles into the condition of their super-existent calm and concealment. Even there we must distinguish in the "being-able-to-be" and "purely being" between *that which* can be or purely is, and the *states* of the being-able-to-be, or purely being. The necessity of this separation in our thinking is not to be disputed. The only question is whether one is to ignore it as merely subjective, or whether one must allow it to be transcendent and objective, a question which is hardly to be decided *a priori*.

Hegel would have had to do the former if he had dealt with this alternative; the latter is the point of view of Schelling. In the former case one speaks of the *whole* Idea or the *whole* Will irrespective of this distinction as Substance: in the latter, the subject that is functional or that supports the state is posited as substance, the function or the state as Attribute. In the former case, the *Idea* or the Will is the *whole*, therefore *substance* and attribute *at once*; in the latter, they are in the narrower sense only the function, or that which is state, thus only *attribute*, and presuppose a substance behind themselves as their functioning substance or their substrate.

The difference only becomes important when we have to do with a duality of principles and with their mutual relation. Hegel and Schopenhauer, each of whom only allows one of the two principles, have logically no reason, to make that separation, since it would be *needless* for them; but as the *need of the unity* of the two principles, Idea and Will, makes itself felt, is the carrying out of that division called for. Although, namely, the functions or states of ideation and volition are different, still this does not prevent our positing the substantial element of the two principles, or the subject of both functions, *that which* knows and *that which* wills, as *one and the same*. So far as the substantial identity and only functional difference of the two principles is recognised, we have *reached Spinoza's one substance with two attributes*.

The indispensable requirement of the essential or substantial identity of Will and Idea is thus at the same time decisive also for the question as to the substantial or attributive character of the Idea by itself and of the Will by itself. That requirement is altogether inevitable. If Will and Presentation were separate substances, the possibility of their influence on one another would be as little obvious as the possibility of a real action on one another of distinct individuals is conceivable according to the principles of a consistent pluralism (cp. above, vol. ii. p. 230 ff.) It would not be apparent how the one is to enter into relation with the other, how the Will can grasp the logical as its content, how the logical can find itself compelled to react against a foreign alogical not appertaining to it at all and its anti-rational doings. If, on the contrary, it is *one and the same* essence which is these two, *i.e.*, of which and in which they are attributes, the intimate connection of both is so much *matter of course* that its contrary even becomes impossible. The same that is the one is also the other; the willer is the perceiver, and the perceiver is the willer,—only the willing and the perceiving is different, not the willer and the perceiver. Volition is non-rational, but the reason of the willer is just the idea; perception is without energy, but the power of the perceiver is simply volition. It is no contrary opposition of opposed tendencies of one and the same activity, for such would annul each other, or at best allow the excess of the *one* quantitatively superior tendency to subsist; it is also no negatively contradictory opposition between two terms, of which only the one is positive, the other, however, negative or privative as regards the first, but it is a positively contradictory opposition, in which each term is positive in a quite different sphere, thus certainly, in relation to the other, is not what the other is. Such a contrast involves also no inconsistency; the Will and the Logical, or power and wisdom in the Absolute, contradict one another as little as, say, the redness and the perfume in a rose or goodness and truthfulness in a man. There are not two drawers in the Unconscious, in one of which lies the irrational Will, in the other the powerless Idea, but they are two poles of a magnet with opposite qualities, on whose opposition the world rests in its unity; as in a magnet we do not succeed in isolating the north magnetic function from the south magnetic, but with continued division of the magnet the double activity or polarity itself appears bound to the smallest pieces, so also are the two attributes of the Unconscious inseparably united, in each single function of the All-One however insignificant, as matter and form, as ideal and realising moment. It is not a blind man who carries a lame man showing the way, but it is a single whole and sound one, that certainly, however, cannot see with the legs and walk with the eyes.

If Will and Presentation were separate substances, an insurmountable dualism would pervade the world, and leave its mark in the soul of the individual — but of such a dualism there is nowhere any trace. Monism, towards which, as we have seen, all tends, would therewith be absolutely annulled, and a pure dualism put in its place. Now at length is the secret dread of this division, which was a disturbing element, especially in Chap. vii. C., removed by our recognising the same as a dualism only of *attributes*, which does *not* prejudice the unity of the substance, but which cannot possibly be done away with when in general an existence is to be explained. A pure and absolute *one* is equally a self-contradictory conception with a pure and absolute *many*, as Plato long ago showed in his "Parmenides." To be possible, whether as concept or as existent, the unity of the One must be unity of an inner manifoldness or plurality, which plurality is most simply duality. The inner duality is accordingly an indispensable condition of the All-One on the side of its existence, or, in other words: untenable as is every absolute dualism, so indispensable a supposition is a relative immanent dualism for the truth of absolute Monism.

This becomes still clearer if we consider the necessity of the explanation of the *process*. Could even a non-plural *One* exist, it yet could only exist as absolutely rigid, identically self-persistent, and we should never reach the possibility of a process. To explain a process we necessarily need a peace-disturber in the rigid repose of the All-One, that seizes the initiative in order to interrupt the same. But even such moment of the initiative alone would yield no actual process, but would at the most reach the mere velleity of the process (empty volition). That an actual process may come to pass there must be, beside the *commencing* factor, at least *one* more that encounters the former, and indeed in the double sense of the term of succouring and opposing; for only from the co-operation and counteraction of at least two moments can a process result. The second only helps the first to attain that which it wills to attain with its initiative, the process, as we saw more fully above; on the other hand, however, only two factors are required, because from the standpoint of the second the first is *a something that should not be*, against which the second feels itself compelled by its nature to turn, in order to make that which ought not to be again the not-being. In this sense Schelling also says (i. 10, 247), "There would altogether be no process if there were not something which *should not be*, or which at least was *in a way in which* it should not be" (namely, the being-able-to-will *as* blindly willing, or, as Schelling usually says, the being-able-to-be *as* blindly being).

That something ought not to be as it is can always only be said from a certain point of view, and indeed only from a point of view opposed to that of the being in question;

thus, *e.g.*, it can only be said from the point of view of the Logical that the Alogical as such should not *be*, so that in the last resort the turning-against-willing of the Logical, and therewith the possibility of the process, rests on this, that a logical opposition exists between the two attributes, *i.e.*, that the one is not what the other is (the Will not logical, and the Idea not endowed with Will). Only from the logical opposition of the two in the One can a process arise. Not, indeed, that this logical opposition forthwith and immediately becomes a real antinomy, in the sense in which we apprehend the contradiction between the divided will-acts of the All-One as a real conflict, for to this end there is wanting, as we know, to the logical Idea self-dependence and independence of the Will, as well as all energy of action; rather this opposition remains eminently a logical one, and only indirectly leads to a real opposition, in that a part of the Will is in the course of the process brought by means of the emancipation of the conscious Idea to turn as negative volition against the positive volition, until with continued enhancement of consciousness the negative part of volition is so far augmented as to be able to paralyse the positive, and thus to hurl back that which ought not to be into non-being. That which forms the real opposition is accordingly always volition with opposite content, and Will and Presentation as such never come into real opposition, but remain in the logical opposition appertaining to them by nature. But undoubtedly the halves of volition turned against one another bear the stamp of this opposition, because in positive volition the (still unconscious) presentation, while bound to surrender itself to the will-to-live, serves to bring the latter to the point where the conscious presentation in pessimistic self-knowledge comprehends the folly of the Will, and now motives the willing of the willing-no-longer.

The exclusion of such a misunderstanding seemed desirable in order not to render difficult, or to prevent, by this *erroneous* assumption of a *real* conflict between the attributes, the understanding of the inseparable *unity* of both attributes, as we have just expounded it.

Precisely in the same manner does Schelling apprehend the Dualism in Monism (Werke, ii. 3, p. 218): "The identity must rather be taken in the strictest sense as *substantial* identity. The meaning is not that potential being and pure being are *severally* conceived as *independent* being, *i.e.*, as Substance (for Substance is what exists in independence of aught else). They are *not themselves Substance*, but only *determinations of the One super-actual*. The meaning, therefore, is not that there is potential being *and* pure being, but the meaning is, that the very Same, *i.e.*, *the same Substance*, is in its unity, and without thereby becoming twain, potential being and pure being."

One might call this Substance identical in Will and Presentation, this individual Single Being, which only supports those abstract generalities, "the absolute subject," as that "which can be related to nothing else, and to which all else is related as Attribute" (Schelling, ii. 1, 318); but unfortunately the word Subject is so ambiguous that one may easily call forth misunderstandings by its employment (*e.g.*, if we should take it here as correlated to an object). On the other hand, if one is entitled to call anything original the *Absolute Spirit*, assuredly every reader not prepossessed by Hegel's arbitrary limitation of the word Spirit to its manifestation in the restricted form of consciousness will allow that it must be this unity of Will and Perception, of Power and Wisdom, this One Substance, that everywhere both wills and perceives,—as we have hitherto called it, the Unconscious. The One "super-existent, which is all that is," we may therefore now define as pure, unconscious (impersonal, but indivisible, therefore individual) *Spirit*, according to which our Monism may be more precisely characterised as spiritualistic Monism. Herewith have we reached the apex of the pyramid, and have advanced the elucidation of the concept "the Unconscious," provisionally outlined in I. 3 to cognition of the first order.

To come to an understanding with Spinoza we have, lastly, still to emphasise the following points of difference. It would be a great error if we tried to conceive the relation of our substance to our attributes in the way in which this has been done by many interpreters of Spinoza, namely, as if the former were the *potentiality* of the Attributes, and these were its *actus* or activities. With regard to the notion of Potentiality we are quite out of danger, for the potentiality of Being or Willing is itself *the One* of the Attributes, and the other we have expressly defined as the pure Being, which has issued from *no* Potentiality. To neither of these, therefore, can Substance stand in the relation of Potentiality, and neither is *Actus*, which proceeded from a Potentiality. This is a cardinal difference from Spinoza, with whom manifestly Substance appears as the potentiality of the Attributes. But we may agree with Spinoza in this, that *Existence* is only to be found in the ejected (*ἐξιστάμενον* or *ἐξεσταμένον*) Mode; to Substance as such, with all its attributes, however, only *subsistence* appertains (which underlies the eject, *subsistit*).

The second difference lies in the definition of that one of the two Attributes which Spinoza, after the precedent of Des Cartes, calls *Extension*. But now Thought and Extension are no contrasts, for Extension is indeed *also in Thought*. Only Thought and *real* Extension, which is intended by Spinoza, form a contrast. However, between the concepts Thought and real Extension, the opposite again is not between "Thought" and "Extension," but between "Thought" and "Real" or "Ideal and Real;" it is not Extension that makes Reality, but it itself must first be made real, in order to form a contrast with Thought. The second attribute of Spinoza must therefore be that which *makes real*, not merely Extension, but also all the rest of the Ideal: but this is no other than Will. Then first, when for Extension we put Will, does Spinoza's Metaphysic become what it should be, but then also the apex of our pyramid coincides with the One Substance mystically postulated by Spinoza.

Beyond that which is the Substrate of everything Existing no Philosophy can go. Here we stand at the inherently insoluble *problem of problems*. The earth rests on the elephant, the elephant stands on the tortoise, and the tortoise ?? The ability to become rigid before the problem of groundless subsistence, as before a Gorgon's head, is the true touchstone of metaphysical talent. The *contentment* with the regress to God-Creator, or a surrogate of the same, is the proper mark of speculative indolence. An attempted dialectic self-generation of the first beginning would be the acme of a reason-killing sophistic. For Conception, Nothing and Something are at least equally warranted, but only for conception, which always presupposes the subsistence of Thought. But whence this subsistence preceding the Concept? If nothing at all were, no World, no Process, and no Substance, as also no one to philosophically marvel, there would be nothing wonderful in that—it would be eminently natural, and there would be no problem to solve; but that there is a self-subsistent, an ultimate, on which everything depends (were this only the Hegelian Concept itself), that is so unfathomably wonderful, so absolutely alogical and senseless, that poor little man, after he has once realised this last of all problems, and has beaten a long time with the arms of his reason impotently at the bars of this prison of the not-non-being, completely ceases to wonder at the details of the world-contrivance, pretty much as an illuminated modern scientist, meeting on an aerial journey beyond the clouds, undertaken for scientific purposes, with a fairy castle of the spirits of the air, might, in measureless astonishment at the mere existence of this castle, hardly find breath enough to wonder at the interior arrangements. It is for this metaphysical problem also absolutely indifferent what we regard as ultimate, whether a self-conscious God or Spinoza's Substance, the Notion or the Will, the Subjective Dream or Matter—it is all the same; there remains a self-subsisting Somewhat with its peculiar constitution as an ultimate. This Somewhat, with its constitution, however, how comes it to subsist, and to subsist with such characters, since from Nothing nothing can come? A self-conscious God must, in despair at the insolubility of this riddle of his eternal subsistence, go mad, or, if it were possible, turn suicide! The nature of the human mind certainly stands in its obtuseness far too low not soon to grow accustomed even to the highest of the marvels surrounding it, and at last to regard the exact *formulating* of the problem, not its *solution*, as its office; and yet it is well as it is that the philosophical pathos only flames up in moments of exaltation, *in order*, viz., *that* the subordinate problems may receive their due of wonder.

5. *The Possibility of Metaphysical Knowledge.*—Here our course ends; we will, however, in conclusion, pay some attention to the question *whether and how, from the standpoint of the Philosophy of the Unconscious, metaphysical cognition is possible.*

This question is not unimportant, for often the most considerable metaphysical systems, that explain the whole world in a coherent and even acceptable fashion, stand puzzled before the problem how, according to their own presuppositions, the cognition of metaphysical connection maintained by them is possible. At this place, of course, a Theory of Knowledge cannot be expected, but only a sketch of the point of view at which we find ourselves as regards that question.

The Græco-Roman philosophy issued in Scepticism because it did not succeed in finding a criterion of Truth, and consequently despaired of a settlement of the question whether Knowledge is possible. The dogmatism of modern philosophy was in like manner broken by Hume, whose pitiless criticism Kant carried still further and deeper.

But at the same time Kant was on the other side the genius who initiated the phase of evolution of the most recent philosophy. Whilst Greek philosophy had uselessly tormented itself with the impossible demand to find in knowledge itself a mark that should impress on it the stamp of truth, Kant went hypothetically to work, and asked "Apart from the question, whether there is a true cognition, of what sort must the metaphysical conditions be if such is to be possible?"

All the most recent philosophy, with the exception of Schelling's last system, stands with more or less consciousness at this point of view: *the conditions of the possibility of knowing form their metaphysic.* As first and fundamental condition of the possibility of all knowledge, the homogeneity of thought and its transcendent-objective object may be asserted, since with a *heterogeneity* of thought and thing absolutely no *harmony* of the two, *i.e.*, truth, and still less a consciousness of this agreement, *i.e.*, cognition, is possible. Without this assumption only two standpoints are possible: that of naïve Realism and that of Subjective Idealism. The former fails to see that everything that I can express in words and reach with my thoughts can always only be my own thoughts, but never a reality lying beyond the same; that thought can never denude itself of the character of thought, and erroneously confuses thought itself or the thinkable (intelligible) with that which lies beyond thought (trans-intelligible), which as a truly imaginary quantity is *believed* by thinking when it *thinks its* thoughts. The second standpoint corrects this error (as regards the things *per se* still remaining for Kant), but it commits the other fault of *denying* that which is placed beyond the limit of thinking, because it is *unattainable* to thinking, and therewith annihilates the possibility of all knowledge, in that thinking is lowered to a dream without object and therewith without truth. This is opposed by the Philosophy of Identity, in that it supposes the transcendent element in cognition to be consubstantial with thinking, and urges with justice "*that on no other possible supposition is a knowledge conceivable*" (Schelling. i. 6, 138), because on no other supposition is a harmony of thought with its presumed (transcendent) object possible. This identity of Thought and Being thus quite indirectly established (of which the ancients had hardly an inkling) is henceforth the unshakable fundamental proposition of all philosophy, is however variously apprehended. In Schelling's "System of Identity" it is, as with Leibniz, a species of pre-established harmony, in virtue of which the individual consciousness unfolds its subjective world from its limited point of view according to the same forms, categories, and complete determinations as the world beyond is developed, although this harmony more easily finds a foundation in the Monism of the one absolute intelligence or reason of Schelling than in the Monadology of Leibniz. Hegel overcomes the difficulty by resolving everything into the one dialectical process of Idea, in which no one thing opposes another as alien or distinct (as with Schelling and Leibniz the "windowless" monads do), but each posits itself with regard to each in all possible kinds of relations (among which are also Causality and Reciprocity). If Hegel thus, on the one hand, makes a great advance beyond Schelling, on the other hand he takes a step backward when, in the great confusion of the general dialectic, he completely obliterates the distinction between thought and its object, the distinction between subjective thought and that which is beyond it, by systematically confounding the point of view of the individual and the absolute thinking, of conscious and unconscious thinking. To render these distinctions perfectly clear, to separate these points of view anew and strictly, I took for my task. To me the Beyond of conscious thinking is unconscious thinking; it is an unattainable Beyond, for consciousness cannot think unconsciously; if it thinks "unconscious thinking," *it thinks its own* conscious thought and yet *supposes* something else, precisely as when it thinks "the thing that has being." (Cp. "Das Ding an sich und seine Beschaffenheit," pp. 74–76.) But yet the hither as the further side is *thinking*, and so far as this consubstantiality reaches, reacts the possibility of an agreement, truth, cognition. It is to be observed here, first, that the Beyond of conscious thinking lies just as much *within* as *without* one's own individuality; secondly, that the concrete agreement of the thing with the conscious thought of the same is effected by a double causality—between the thing and the unconscious part of the individual (to which also the body belongs), and between this and one's consciousness; and thirdly, that the causal constraint felt by consciousness and referred to a transcendent reality and the distinction made between the same and the logical necessity of purely ideal relations is only intelligible on the supposition, that from both sides a *Will* enters into the ideal conflict and makes this a *real* one. This Will is, no matter whether one contemplates an alien will or one's own, no longer merely beyond *consciousness* (like unconscious thinking), but it is beyond the *ideal altogether*, both conscious and unconscious thinking. That it nevertheless gives rise to far fewer difficulties than unconscious thinking is due to this, that it *does not at all affect* the ideal content, but only impresses on it the meaning of reality, otherwise however leaves the perceived object unchanged.

According to these considerations it can no longer be doubtful how the Philosophy of the Unconscious is related to those contrasts: Thought and Thing, *mens* and *ens*, *ratio* and *res*, Spirit and Nature, Ideal and Real, Subjective and Objective. We know that Being is a product of the non-logical and logical, of Will and Representation; that its "That" is posited by volition, its "What," however, is the ideational content of that volition, thus not merely *homogeneous* with the Idea, but, because itself Idea, *identical* in the strictest sense of the term, but that the Real is distinguished from the Ideal by that which lends reality to the Ideal, by the Will. Thus also Spirit and

Nature are no longer different, for the *original* unconscious spirit is that in its independent being which in the actual combination of its moments is Nature, and as *result* of the natural process conscious spirit, or spirit in the narrower (Hegelian) sense of the term. But as concerns the Subjective or Objective, these are altogether relative conceptions, which *first* appear *with the origin of consciousness*, for in the unconscious Volition and the unconscious Presentation these have no place; the Unconscious is exalted above those contrasts, since its thinking is by no means subjective, but *for us* objective, in truth, however, transcendent-absolute. We can therefore also in strictness not say that the Unconscious *is* the Absolute Subject, but only that it is what alone can *become* Subject, just as it is what alone can become Object, simply because there is nothing beside the Unconscious: and *thus understood*, we may certainly *call* it the absolute Subject and the absolute Object, notwithstanding that as Unconscious it is exalted above the opposition of the Subjective and Objective.

We have seen that consciousness only occurs on a collision of different directions of the Will, of these then each is the objective for the other, and each the subjective in opposition to the other objective to it, presupposing that both directions of the Will occupy relations, which do not prevent the possibility of the arising of consciousness by their lying beneath the threshold of consciousness.

If, *e.g.*, one supposes the atoms above the threshold of consciousness, the atomic force A would become objective to the atomic force B, and conversely; the atomic force A, on the other hand, itself become, in contrast to the objectivity of B, subjective and conversely. Thus would the Unconscious become in two ways conscious in A and B, both objectively and subjectively.——

After having thus seen that the union of all the above-named contrasts results from our principles, we come back to the question as to the possibility of knowledge. It was then proved by the most recent philosophy that a system resting on the sublation of those contrasts is the only true one, *in case* there be at all a genuine cognition; but *whether* there be such, of this all proof was wanting after as before. It was in assuming the same as *dogmatic*, as the pre-Kantian dogmatism, nay, the possibility did not even occur to it, that any one with justice may deny and must deny the possibility of an absolute knowing (Reason) till proof thereof has been obtained (cp. Schelling, ii. 3, p. 74).

Its whole philosophising rested, therefore, on a condition that perfectly hovered in the air, the whole was a hypothetical philosophising from an unproved supposition.

Accordingly our latest philosophy likewise could consistently only dissolve in Scepticism. That this Scepticism is in the younger philosophically educated world (so far as it has surmounted an immature Dogmatism) the prevailing one, can hardly be disputed; that the same has received no scientifically consistent elaboration (Aenesidemus only attacks *Kant*) lies only in this, that the palpable results of the exact sciences and the practical interests now absorbing all attention are altogether unfavourable to Philosophy, in that they too much distract theoretical thinking and discourage the pursuit of it to its last consequences. To proceed further, there are manifestly only two ways: either we must, in order to establish the hypothetical result of the Philosophy of Identity, *directly* prove that a genuine cognition exists,—yet with such an endeavour one would only relapse into the inherently vain efforts of the Greeks (cp. Kant's Werke v. Roskr, ii. p. 62–63), or we must really avail ourselves of the most recent progress, and approach the problem at the *opposite* end to the Greeks, *i.e.*, we must by a path altogether different from that hitherto attempted, accessible and evident to all, *directly* prove the material identity of Thought and Being. This path can only be that traversed by us, the successive inductive ascent from experience.

Now certainly the proof led by this path must itself be a knowledge, if it is to prove anything; we might therefore think that we have merely only in appearance got a step further, but in reality, just as before, stand with our feet in the air. This is, however, not so; rather the state of the case is as follows:—

Formerly it was said: "*If* there is a knowledge, it is material identity of Thought and Being;" go beyond this simple conditional proposition we cannot.

Now we say: "(1) If there is a knowledge, it must rest on material identity of Thought and Being, therefore also be to be found in immediate experience (affection of thought by being) and the logically correct inferences from the same; (2) the inferences from experience establish the material identity of Thought and Being; (3) from this identity follows the possibility of knowledge."

Herewith we have entered into a closed circle, where each term conditions the others, no matter with which we begin, whilst before we had only a conditional proposition without back- and breast-work as it were. There accordingly undoubtedly remains still the *possibility* that this whole circle of psychological and metaphysical conditions is a *merely subjective appearance*, which consciousness is compelled to form for itself by an inexplicable necessity; that there is therefore in fact still *no* knowledge and no identity of Thought and Being, and the circle of mutually supporting relations built thereon a mere chimera. For certainly the transcendent and not merely subjective existence of that circle cannot in all strictness prove to be absolute truth, just because consciousness is condemned to this circle, and can never assume a standpoint outside the same, from which the nature of that circle could be judged, for the single reason that the possibility of cognition cannot be known without knowledge.

Although then the absolute impossibility of the contrary

cannot be proved, yet by that circle the probability that there is both knowledge as well as identity of Thought and Being has become very much greater than it was before in that simple conditional proposition, devoid of all support both in front and behind; it has become so great that the possibility of the contrary is no longer practically of account. Scepticism is, therefore, not annihilated, but acknowledged to be theoretically warranted, as it is also in fact the *preservative* against all relapse into the *dogmatic narrowness* of belief in absolute knowledge, *i.e.*, in the attainableness of an *absolute truth* as the only worthy office of the science of sciences, philosophy. But whilst we must thus acknowledge absolute scepticism to have for all time and notwithstanding any possible advance of science to a justifiable existence, we have at the same time reduced its *range* to such a degree that its importance disappears, for the practice not only of life, but also of science.

If we contemplate this result concerning the possibility of knowledge in general, it agrees remarkably with that which must by degrees be on all sides granted for the knowledge of every special truth (so far as it is not of a *formal* logical kind), that there is for us no truth, *i.e.*, probability of the value 1, but only more or less considerable probability, which never reaches 1, and that we must be perfectly content when in our cognition we reach a degree of probability which robs the possibility of the contrary of practical importance (cp. also Introductory, I. b.)

APPENDIX.

THE PHYSIOLOGY OF THE NERVE-CENTRES.

I.

Introduction.—The deep obscurity in which the functions of the central organs of the nervous system were wrapt until a few generations ago, has in the course of the present century been cleared up at many points, and in the last decennium these points, illuminated by the light of knowledge, have so increased that a certain comprehension of the facts as a connected whole is now within our reach. However conscious the possessors of this knowledge may still be of its incompleteness and superficiality, it must yet be welcomed as a first foundation of the physiology of the central organs, and is already in a position to furnish hints in different directions, which are of value partly for the psychological, partly for the natural-philosophical elaboration of experience.

Unfortunately, until a short time ago there existed no work which collected into a clear whole, and thereby made accessible to wider circles the communications with respect to this particular branch of physiology that are scattered in scientific books and journals. Perhaps *Maudsley* in the first physiological part of his "Physiology and Pathology of Mind" had come nearest to the mark; however, the second edition of this work bears the remote date 1868, and cannot therefore contain the results of the most recent progress of science.[1] On the other hand, the "Grundzüge der physiologischen Psychologie" of Professor *Wilhelm Wundt*

[1] [Since the original was stereotyped another edition has appeared: *The Physiology of Mind*, being the first part of a third edition, revised, enlarged, and in great part rewritten, of *The Physiology and Pathology of Mind*, 1876. *The Pathology of Mind*, being the third edition of the second part of *The Physiology and Pathology of Mind*, recast, enlarged, and rewritten, 1879.—Tr.]

(Leipzig: Engelmann, 1873 and 1874) fulfil the function of a compendium in an eminent degree, and along with a physiology of the sense-preceptions (in the 2d and 3d secs.) offer substantially a physiology of the nervous system, and specially of its central organs (in the 1st, 4th, and 5th secs.) To be sure this compendium, just on account of the wealth and the concentration of its contents, is more a book for study and for reference than for the general reader, and the sobriety of the elaboration of the mass of material amounts almost to dryness, by the author avoiding with almost painful anxiety every flight of thought beyond the empirical data. Of unfavourable influence in this direction was evidently the influence of the dry and unfruitful Herbartian philosophy, by which Wundt is unmistakably affected, notwithstanding his frequent criticism of the fundamental views of Herbart. The doctrine of the emotions and impulses (in chap. xx.) loses almost all value by this dependence on Herbart and by the retention of his error, "That it is not the emotions which govern the ideas, but that the emotions rather spring from the ideas themselves" (p. 818), or that "all manifestations of will arise from ideas" (and those conscious ones) (p. 622). This perverse conception of course prevents him from at all comprehending the unconscious life of the feelings and impulses, its connection with the inmost core of individuality, the character, and the thoroughgoing dependence of the intellectual life both in the healthy and in the morbid condition on the sphere of the will. But just that which is wanting in Wundt is with Maudsley a regulating fundamental idea of his conception of the healthy and morbid life of the mind, and he attains by means of it the most surprising results.

Thus Wundt and Maudsley are complementary to one another. To the richer and more precise material of the former the latter brings the fine psychological observation of a tried mental physician, and by his often ingenious side-remarks offers an abundance of valuable stimulus to thought. The fundamental importance for the conscious of the unconscious psychical life, the thorough dependence of the former on the latter, as well as the primacy of the will, is with Maudsley a firm conviction. As predecessors in respect of the knowledge of unconscious mental life, he cites, in his unacquaintance with German philosophy, hardly any one but Hamilton, Carlyle, and Jean Paul Friedrich Richter.

For Wundt, who, in his earlier studies on the genesis of sense-perception, had independently reached the theory of unconscious inferences, the hypothesis of Herbart that the will results from the dynamic of ideas was fraught with serious consequences, in that he was induced thereby to limit the scope of his own earlier doctrine. And undoubtedly the theory of unconscious inference cannot but appear a very venturesome and doubtful hypothesis when completely isolated and arbitrarily limited by the denial of unconscious mental life in all other directions. Nevertheless Wundt's restriction of the doctrine of unconscious inference (which, according to his own statement on p. 708, is *thoroughly accepted* by the more recent "Psychology," so far as it does not take a Nativistic direction) merely amounts to this, that the unconscious connection of those moments which we reproduce in discursive logical form is *not* to be regarded *as a discursive one* (which I myself have always and everywhere emphatically asserted); and only because Wundt does not observe that the form of Logic in and of itself is *anything but discursive*, but first becomes so through reception into the form of consciousness, only for that reason does the acknowledgment of a *logical* connection in the unconscious genesis of perception appear to him hazardous (cp. pp. 424, 460–461, 637, 708–711). The error of Wundt, in refusing to acknowledge the essence of the *logical* save in the discursive form of reflection, seems to stand in close connection with his other erroneous opinion, that *consciousness* also only consists in the form of discursive reflection, *i.e.*, in the connection between ideas separated in time, brought about by memory and reflection (cp. pp. 825–827, 829, 837). It is, however, not evident why a conscious centre should not be conceived which once in a lifetime, and then never again, has a perception, and yet retains this in full clearness of consciousness. Whether this perception leaves behind a memorial trace, whether this trace suffices to lead to reproduction on renewed excitement, and whether the intelligence of the organ suffices to recognise this reproduction as such (*i.e.*, as memory), all that is for the consciousness of the first perception entirely indifferent and without influence. Wundt thus mistakes in two directions the derived and secondary character of conscious reflection. In the first place, he fails to see that all discursiveness of conscious ideation is composed of single acts of consciousness, each of which possesses the intuitive evidence of sense; and, secondly, that all that is logical in the discursive sequence rests on the implicit logical connection of the moments of unconscious intuition. By taking as the type of consciousness in general his cerebral consciousness in the form most familiar to him of discursive reflection, without going back to its genetic elements, Wundt lapses into false conclusions on two sides; he denies the character of the logical as of consciousness when he misses the characteristics of discursive reflection.

These preliminary remarks may suffice to prove that even the two best books which we possess for acquiring an insight into the physiology of the central organs of the nervous system, taken singly, do not meet the wants of the layman, whilst to treat them as complementary requires a tolerable amount of labour and independent criticism. I think therefore that the following attempt to discuss the most important points of our present knowledge, in all brevity, and leaving on one side all anatomical and physiological detail, will not be unwelcome to wider circles of the scientifically educated public.

2. *Nerve-Fibre and Ganglion-Cell.*—All the nervous elements of the organism are divisible into two clearly distinguishable kinds—conducting fibres and ganglionic cells. When the organism is intact, the conducting fibres are not determined to isolated, independent action, but merely serve to propagate or transfer a stimulus: (1.) From the peripheral sense-organs to ganglionic cells; (2.) from ganglionic cells to bundles of muscular fibres or secreting membranes; (3.) from one ganglionic cell to another. They thus serve to connect periphery and centre, or to unite several centres. The ganglionic cells, on the other hand, exercise the central functions; they receive the impulses propagated from the periphery, independently modify the same, and either neutralise them by their internal resistance, or are determined to a partial liberation of their reserved force, which then leads to peripheral actions by shorter or longer circuits and by centrifugal paths. The ganglionic cells, moreover, influence the nutrition of the nerve-fibres which proceed from them; nerves severed from their centres of innervation become atrophied (Wundt, p. 107).

But now it would not be correct so to conceive the differentiation as if the conducting elements were *only* passive translators, the ganglionic cells *only* active organs; the conducting fibres also possess their own activity, and also the grey nerve-substance made up of ganglionic cells may serve to propagate stimuli. Only because the path of resistance in the nerve-fibre is relatively much smaller than in the ganglionic cell is it more suited for conduction than the latter; and only because in the ganglion-cell the stored-up force is much greater than in the nerve-fibre is it more fitted than the latter for active operations. Until the transferred excitement is extinguished through the resistance on conduction every stimulus is also propagated in the grey matter, unless the energy therein contained can be discharged in another direction, where the path of resistance is less. Thus, *e.g.*, the grey matter of the spinal cord after section of the white strands consisting of conducting fibres is unmistakably capable of the propagation of not too feeble stimuli; and the circumstance that with often-repeated conduction in a particular direction the nerve-substance adapts itself to this function, thus the resistance is diminished by habit, makes possible the phenomenon so important for the existence of the organism of the spontaneous compensation of disturbances by the vicarious function, not only of other plexi of fibres, but also even of the grey matter (Wundt, p. 271).

The molecular accommodation of nervous matter to the work most frequently thrust upon it also makes it explicable why the nerve-fibres that are in connection with the organs of sense are most exercised in centripetal, the fibres ending in muscles, on the other hand, most in centrifugal conduction, and meet with less resistance in the corresponding direction. That they do not under normal circumstances conduct in the reverse direction is in any case not provable, since we have no means of making the effect perceptible, if such a conduction takes place. In *motor* nerves the already-mentioned dependence of the nutritive condition on the corresponding ganglion cells, in *sensory* nerves the centrifugal current of innervation of attention and the central mode of origin of illusions of the senses, tells, however, *for* the existence of such opposite nerve currents. However, these reversed nervous currents are in any case of another constitution and form in their vibrations than the normal ones, and since the adaptation and customary diminution of the path of resistance has always reference only to one particular kind of stimulus, the same nerve may very well be employed in the centrifugal conduction of *this* and the centripetal propagation of *that* vibration, whilst it opposes considerable resistance to the particular conduction in the opposite sense. That for the rest this resistance also is not insurmountable has been shown by the experiments of Philipeaux and Vulpian, in which they succeeded in forming a union between the cut ends of neighbouring motor and sensory nerves, and in thereby obtaining a considerable inversion of the direction of function (Wundt, p. 227). The experiment proves beyond a doubt that the most important thing for the nervous process is the form of vibration, which is determined by the peripheral and central end-organs and handed over to the fibre, and that there can henceforth be no more talk of "specific energies" of nerves in the sense of an absolute immutability. When, on the other hand, Wundt grants (p. 361 ff.) that exercise in processes of a particular form of vibration and direction of propagation is able to impregnate nervous matter with such a molecular disposition "that every disturbance of the molecular equilibrium that occurs calls forth this particular mode of motion;" when further he is obliged to admit that this adaptation is only partly individually acquired, but rests in the main on an innate, inherited predisposition, it is not obvious why the older expression "specific energy" should not be also further retained in the revised modern sense; at the most, one might convert it into the other: "specific disposition."

This "specific disposition" becomes an actual "energy" by representing *not merely* a diminution of the resistance of the path to a particular form of vibration, but, at the same time, a certain tension or potential energy, which with given stimuli is liberated as living force or energy of motion. Thus the work which, *e.g.*, the galvanised motor nerve-fibre performs in preparing a muscular contraction is by no means a mere propagation of the received energy in unchanged form, but it is an effect from its own store of force, for whose liberation the stimulus only gives the external impulse. But now without an internal regulation any stimulus which oversteps the threshold would suffice to discharge the *whole* force stored up in the nerve-fibre; the reaction would be violent, and the nerve would for a long time be incapable of the repetition of a similar performance. In the mechanism of the nerve, therefore, along with the exciting potencies inhibitory ones must also be inserted, which help to fix the threshold-value of the stimulus, and to limit the discharge of nerve-fibre according to intensity and duration. If the curve of contraction of a stimulated frog's thigh be graphically represented on a vibrating pendulum, which renders perceptible to the senses the course of the reaction, there first occurs a well-marked rise, which illustrates the growing predominance of the exciting potencies, but then a quick descent, which terminates in a depression below the level of zero. After this transitory predominance of the inhibitory influences, the excitement dies away in weaker waves (Wundt, pp. 247–253). The more capable of performance the nerve is, the greater are not only its exciting, but also its inhibitory powers; the exhaustion is shown in still higher degree in the diminution of the inhibitory influences (whereby especially the duration of the reaction is prolonged) than in diminished strength of the reaction. The difference of the reaction on weak and strong stimuli is less in the exhausted than in the fresh nerve.—An increase of irritability results with quickly succeeding repetition of the same stimulus, when the impressions are in a certain measure added together.

Quite analogously, only in changed relations of intensity are the processes set up in the ganglion-cell. One is able to make a comparison between them by causing the same scale of stimuli to act at one time directly on the motor nerve, at another time on the sensory nerves of the same half of the body issuing at the same height of the spinal cord. Ganglion-cell and nerve-fibre are related to one another pretty much as a boiler with a valve not easily to be moved to one furnished with a valve moving with facility. From the latter the steam more easily escapes because with less tension, whilst with the former the valve is only opened by vapours of greater tension, thus also streaming out with greater force (Wundt, p. 268). Because the ganglion-cell offers a far greater resistance than the nerve, it absorbs stimuli which call forth considerable reactions on direct application to the nerves; the threshold of stimulation is thus raised. In the same way, also, above the threshold of stimulation the period of latent stimulation is longer, because greater resistances, stronger inhibitory potencies must be overcome. If, on the other hand, the reaction has once occurred, the greater store of energy of the ganglion-cell discharges also a greater energy, *i.e.*, the reaction is stronger with similar stimuli, and is, moreover, even with such a choice of the stimuli that the heights of contraction become equal, of longer duration (Wundt, p. 261 ff.) The summation of rapidly succeeding similar stimuli is still more perceptible and of still greater importance in the ganglion-cell than in the nerve. The aggregate activity of rhythmically recurrent stimuli, which taken singly lie below the threshold of stimulation, is the key to the understanding of the genesis of most sensations of moderate strength, which are almost all of them due to the combination of stimuli, each one of which would by itself (as, *e.g.*, an isolated wave of sound in a tone) be ineffectual. The condition of exhaustion, too, is manifested altogether in the same way as in the nerve; a special form of exhaustion is, however, that due to nerve-poisons (*e.g.*, for the ganglion-cells of the spinal cord by strychnine). Although the duration of latent stimulation is increased in poisoning by strychnine, yet the irritability is considerably enhanced (even beyond the irritability of the motor nerve), and every stimulus acts in the same manner as with the healthy ganglion-cell a whole series of similar stimuli; all reactions become stronger and more persistent, vehement even to convulsion; small and great stimuli soon call forth reactions of like strength, and finally, the spinal cord reacts on every stimulus with convulsions (Wundt, pp. 263-264).

Pathologically this condition is designated as "irritable weakness;" an understanding of it is, as Maudsley shows, the foundation of the correct understanding of all the morbid states of the central organs of the nervous system. The loss of the normal proportion of stimulus and reaction is the sign of a morbid disorder; it is the simplest form of the "aberration" of the ganglion-cell. The "errant" ganglion-cell has no more force at its disposal than the healthy one, but it wastes the same in reacting on every feeble stimulus; it squanders it in tetanus.

The madness of little children and of the brutes (with the exception of those nearest to man) consists essentially in an aberration of the ganglion-cells of the medulla oblongata and spinal cord, in a disturbed grouping of the nerve elements in any cell, and in consequence thereof also in a disturbed co-ordination of the single central cell-groups. These are here no longer functional as a purposive physiological whole, but every group reacts tetanically on the small organic stimuli affecting it, which remain unnoticed in the healthy life, and thereby becomes incapable of retaining feeling with its neighbouring groups. The result is incoherent convulsions, as in St. Vitus's dance. The convulsions may, however, also proceed from higher central points, which mediate the reflexes to sense-perception; then they stand in relation to actual or imaginary sense-perceptions, and manifest themselves as combative, destructive, or murderous impulse. Of this kind is the raging of a mad elephant, or the delirium of a maniac, who perceives the smell of sulphur in his nose, sees his supposed persecutors as devilish shapes surrounded with fiery flames, and believes he has to contend with them or an imaginary lion for his life.—Lastly, aberration in the sphere of conscious volition and ideation is an aberration of the ganglion-cells of the cerebral hemispheres; frenzy consists of spasmodic ideas and feelings, as St. Vitus's dance consists of motor reflex convulsions.

It would be altogether wrong if one tried to see in the molecular disorder of the ganglion-cell, which squanders its store of energy in a manner disproportional to the stimuli, a condition of *heightened* power and capacity of execution; the morbidly degenerate irritability, in spite of its externally destructive effects, can only be interpreted as a symptom of *weakness.* Even the explosion of a steam-engine proves nothing with respect to the efficiency and solidity of the machine, but rather that it had a weak place. The elevated self-satisfaction and the extravagant merriment of an incipient maniac, or the delirium of a raving madman are just as little a proof of the strength and efficiency of the grey matter of their brains as the motor reflex convulsions of that of a spinal cord poisoned by strychnine; in both cases only the morbidly enhanced *consumption* of energy is revealed, and therefore the irritable weakness must in all cases draw after it *torpid* weakness. All mania ends in derangement of intellect or weakness of mind, all cramps in complete exhaustion of the organs concerned, or of the whole organism. The irritable weakness of the ganglion-cells spontaneously appearing in the organism is only the first stage of a process of degeneration, which is accelerated by irritability the more the *increased consumption of energy* coincides with an already *diminished* potential energy.—If we comprehensively consider wherein consists the difference between the nervous matter in the ganglion-cell and in the (alone active) axis cylinder of the nerve-fibre, it may be thus succinctly stated, that in the latter the chemical decomposition, in the former recomposition during functional repose preponderates (Wundt, p. 266). The former is evinced by this, that the nerve-fibre, abandoned to itself, *i.e.*, separated from its province, has no power to maintain itself, but degenerates; the latter follows from this, that the ganglionic substance during functional repose not only repairs its own waste which it has suffered in the exercise of function, but also provides the nerve-fibres that spring from it with energy for defraying their expenditure. Thus, under normal circumstances, in the fibre the consumption of force, in the cell the production of force preponderates. If, now, the condition of irritable weakness occurs in the cell, not only is far more force consumed in all functional exercise, but also in consequence of the more frequent exercise of function the total duration of functional rest is diminished, when not (as in the maniacal, often deprived for weeks of sleep) reduced approximately to zero, and this, moreover, in a condition in which probably the capacity for chemical recomposition is diminished. In that case the occurrence of total exhaustion of the organism, and with a longer duration or more frequent recurrence of the attacks, the morphological and chemical degeneration of the nerve-centres is the necessary issue.

The stated fundamental distinction between the nervous matter in the ganglion-cell and that in the axis cylinder of the nerve-fibre is consequently, as is also shown by the occurrence of pathological degeneration in the grey nerve matter, *not one of kind*, but only *of degree*. Expenditure of energy takes place in the cell by decomposition, as well as storing up of energy in the fibre by recomposition, and only in the *normal* physiological condition of the organism is the opposite tendency *predominant* in either. Accordingly, in this gradual difference no reason can be found for a heterogeneity of substance in cell and fibre. The actions are, on the whole, similar in both, and the difference extends no further than the differentiation of a physiological organ into several subdivisions for the better fulfilment of modified purposes by more perfect division of labour. This result is important for the understanding of the truth that the psychical life does not cease with the ganglion-cell, but extends even to the nerve-fibre and beyond.

3. *The Spinal Cord.*—If we neglect the ganglion-cells united in the sympathetic plexus of nerves and dispersed in various organs, all the rest are massed in the grey matter of the spinal cord and brain. In the former the

grey matter forms four united columns, of which those situated right and left correspond to the lateral halves of the body, whilst the two anterior ones are distinguished from the two posterior by the motor nerves issuing from the former, the sensory nerves from the latter. These four columns now are surrounded by an envelope of white nerve-matter, in which are collected the ascending sensory and the descending motor fibres.

From this it first of all results that there is *no direct* path to the higher nerve-centres for the nerves of the body issuing from the spinal cord, but that the same spot of the grey matter of the spinal cord from which the particular nerve springs must always be passed in centrifugal and centripetal conduction. In other words, the conducting fibres in the spinal cord are *not directly*, but only by the intervention of ganglionic cells, *united* with the nerves of the body; and in every conduction from the brain to the muscles or conversely, ganglionic cells of the spinal cord co-operate as active links, which reflectorially propagate the stimulus, so far as it lies for them above the threshold.

It further results from the above-named arrangement that sensory and motor fibres never spring simultaneously from one and the same ganglion-cell of the spinal cord; that thus a reflex from a sensory to a motor fibre is compounded of several separate reflexes of at least two ganglionic cells (one in the posterior and one in the anterior cornu). The simple reflexion in a single ganglion-cell of the spinal cord can always include only *one* kind of trunk-nerve, and the other term must consist of fibres connecting other ganglion-cells—be they neighbouring and co-ordinate, higher and superordinate or lower and subordinate cells—be it a plexus of primitive fibres connecting neighbouring cells, or an ascending or descending nerve-fibre. It is important to make clear this co-operation of several ganglionic cells of different functional importance in the occurrence of the simplest reflex of the spinal cord, in order thereby to open the way for a better comprehension of the entangled co-operation and subordination between the different central organs.

If the conducting fibres that run in the white substance of the spinal cord always remained on the same side on which they arise, the two halves of the body would have no communication with one another at all for *weak* stimuli of sensation and movement, which are extinguished by the resistance of the grey matter; on that account there takes place a partial transference of nerve-fibres from the one lateral half of the spinal cord to the other. Since a co-operation of the two halves of the body only appears to be requisite with *stronger* motor stimuli, which besides are conducted through the grey matter, this decussation of the *motor* fibres extends only to a small fraction, as follows from this, that with unilateral section of the spinal cord only weak disturbances of movement become visible on the uninjured half of the body; with stimuli producing sensation, on the other hand, an exact connection of the two halves of the body is requisite for weak stimuli, and therefore the decussation of the sensory conducting fibres is a far more considerable one (Wundt, pp. 114–115). In the higher central organs, too, this order everywhere recurs, that the connection between the two halves of the body is established partly by bridges of grey matter or by special commissures (*i.e.*, conducting communicating strands), partly by decussation of the paths.

Of special interest is this relation in the chiasma of the optic nerve, which was formerly regarded as the point where the two optic nerves crossed. But that is only true of animals with outwardly-turned eyes, which have no common field of vision for the two eyes; whereas, on the contrary, with man and animals with a binocular field of vision, only the half of the fibres of any nerve, and that too the one turned inward, passes over to the other side, whereas the outer halves remain uncrossed. The consequence of this is, that the left halves of both retinas are combined in the left, the right halves of both retinas in the right corpus quadrigeminum. In animals with outwardly turned eyes injury of a corpus quadrigeminum causes blindness of the opposite eye, but in man disease of one corpus quadrigeminum, *hemiopia, i.e.*, blindness or destruction of vision in the left or right half of the two retinas (Wundt, p. 146). It is obvious that only by this blending of the similarly situated halves of the two peripheral organs in one-half of the central organ is the blending of corresponding impressions on the two retinas explained, *i.e.*, the riddle is solved of *single vision with two eyes*, and I have specially discussed this example because we have according to its analogy to imagine the whole arrangement of our nervous system, which, in spite of the *two-sidedness*, both of the central and also of the peripheral organs of sensation, yet leads to an *indivisible* sensation of our body even for the weakest stimuli. Only the *union* by central bridges or commissures with partial peripheral decussations of the paths makes this result possible, and helps us out of a condition in which we should feel the two halves of our body as if they were two separate bodies; and it only remains to the thinking consciousness to grasp these separate sensations into a unity, just as the owner of an estate can manage two properties entirely separated from each other with the help of a single ledger. It is true the necessity of the *union* by commissures with *partial* decussation of the paths holds good only for the spinal cord and the hinder and middle parts of the brain, but not for the fore-brain or cerebrum, and that for the twofold reason that in the first place the union of the cerebral hemispheres by commissures and arcuate fibres into a single indivisibly functioning organ is a far more intimate one than in the afore-named centres; and, secondly, because the motor-impulses of the cerebrum must always first pass through media (at any rate through the motor ganglia of the peduncle of the cerebrum), in which the blending in question is already performed by partial crossing of the paths, so that a repetition of these means would be superfluous. The cerebral hemispheres are therefore in man the only organ in which the decussation of the afferent unilateral paths is not a partial but a total one.

That the spinal cord in its grey matter is a central organ of lower order with a certain relative independence may now be considered as pretty generally acknowledged. Maudsley says: "There can be no difficulty in admitting that the spinal cord is an independent centre of so-called aim-working acts that are not attended with consciousness" (*i.e.*, brain-consciousness). "It is the centre, however, not only of co-ordinate action the capability of which has been implanted in its original constitution, but also of co-ordinate action the power of which has been gradually acquired and matured through individual experience. Like the brain, the spinal cord has, so to speak, its memory, and must be educated" (p. 149). "In fact, if any one attends to his ordinary actions during the day, it will be surprising how small a proportion of them are consciously willed, how large a proportion of them are the results of the acquired automatic action of the organism" (p. 152). "Of these unconscious or involuntary actions a great part is plainly due to the independent power of reaction which the ganglionic cells of the spinal cord have" (p. 136). "The anencephalic infant, in which absence of brain involves an absence of consciousness, not only exhibits movements of its limbs, but is capable also of the associated reflex acts of sucking and crying" (p. 137). "Pflüger[1] touched with acetic acid the thigh of a decapitated frog over its internal condyle; it wiped it off with the dorsal surface of the foot of the same side; he thereupon cut off the foot, and applied the acid to the same spot; the animal attempted to wipe it off again with the foot of that side, but, having lost its foot, of course could not. After some fruitless efforts, there-

[1] Pflüger, "Die sensorischen Functionen des Rückenmarks" (Berlin, 1853).

fore, it ceased to try in that way, seemed unquiet, 'as though it were searching for some new means,' and at last it made use of the foot of the other leg, and succeeded in wiping off the acid. . . . Notably we have in this striking experiment not merely contraction of muscles, but combined movements in due sequence for a special purpose; we have actions that have all the appearance of being instigated by will and guided by intelligence in an animal the recognised organ of whose intelligence and will has been removed. So much was Pflüger impressed by this wonderful adaptation of means to an end in a headless animal, that he actually inferred that the spinal cord, like the brain, was possessed of sensorial functions. Others, who would scarce admit Pflüger's supposition to be true of man, have thought that it might be so of some of the lower animals. Instead of grounding their judgment of the complex phenomena in man on their experience of the simpler instances exhibited by the lower animals, they have applied to the lower animals what I believe to be their subjective misinterpretation of the complex phenomena in man" (p. 138).

Maudsley here announces an important methodological principle for comparative physiology and psychology, which I have also followed above in Sect. A. Chap. i., and for the observance of which I have often been reproached by scientific specialists. Nevertheless, this principle ought to be self-evident to every naturalist, and it is only the psychological prejudice: that no consciousness can inhabit my organism of which *my* consciousness, *i.e.*, the consciousness of my cerebral hemispheres, is not aware,—which has closed even to a Wundt the comprehension of the *fundamental fact* of physiological psychology, namely, the capacity *of every* ganglionic cell to be conscious.

4. *The Inner Psychical Aspect of the Reflex Process.*—The conception of reflexion may be taken in a narrower and a wider sense. In the former case it signifies the im-

mediate passing over of a stimulus of sensation to the motor nerve issuing in the same centre; in the latter case it signifies any reaction of a centre on a stimulus conducted from any quarter whatever. We have already seen that even the apparently simple reflexion of a centre of the spinal cord is a complicated phenomenon, which is compounded of single actions of several ganglion-cells of the posterior and anterior cornua, each of which is only to be subsumed under the notion reflexion in the wider sense. In the same way also, however, the apparently immediate reflexion passes gradually into ever more complicated forms, as I have already shown above in Sect. A. Chap. v., so that the collective mental functions of man fall under the notion of reflexion in the wider sense. For the latter says nothing more than that no ganglionic cell performs its office without a stimulus, but it says nothing about the kind of stimulus or the kind of function. As the stimulus acting on a sensory nerve may arise from a mechanical, chemical, thermal, or electrical source, so can the stimulus of a sensory nerve-fibre soliciting a ganglionic cell to be functional arise from a neighbouring ganglion-cell, from a fibre communicating between a co-ordinate, superordinate, or subordinate centre, or perhaps from a motor nerve-fibre;[1] and the reaction need by no means be immediately an innervation of a motor nerve, but may consist of a propagation of the actively modified stimulus to neighbouring cells or to conducting fibres which lead to co-ordinate, superordinate, or subordinate centres. Every function of a brain-cell which appears subjectively as abstract idea would then be a reflex due to a stimulus received from another cell or from a sensory nerve, which would be subjectively presented as excitement of the conception through association of ideas or through sense-perception.

[1] On the assumption namely that the direct sensations of the muscular contractions (which are not effected by tactile sensations of adjacent tissues) are conveyed by the motor nerves themselves to the central organs, which however is a hypothesis not to be accepted without consideration.

If, on the other hand, one characterises as "reflex" only the *whole group* of individual reactions which lie between the irritation of sensory nerves as first term and the function of motor nerves as final term, one does not thereby avoid the fact that the highest functions of the mind come under the notion of Reflexion. For if the stimulus at all lies above the threshold of reflexion, *i.e.*, if it is not absorbed and extinguished on its way in the central organs through the resistance in conduction, it must also, under all circumstances, finally lead to motor reaction, however long it may in the mean time wander about within the central organs from one ganglion-cell to another, or, to speak psychologically, however many reflections and conflicts of desire may be intercalated between perception and voluntary resolution. In this way of looking at the matter likewise the question then is only concerning a difference *of degree* in the number of connecting links between stimulus of sensation and movement of reaction; and this number *gradually* rises from the simplest reflex contractions to the most complicated processes needed for the control and management of the external world.

"For moderate irritation of a limited part of the skin with a certain mean degree of excitability draws after it a reflex contraction only in that group of muscles which is provided with motor roots, issuing at the *same elevation* and on *the same side* as the irritated sensory fibres. If the stimulus or irritability *increases*, the excitement also first passes over to the motor root-fibres of the *other* half of the body which issue at the *same* height; lastly, with still greater increase it spreads with increasing intensity *first up* and *then down*" (the former on the sensory, the latter on the motor paths of the spinal cord), "so that finally the muscles of all parts of the body, which receive their nerves from the spinal cord and medulla oblongata, are sympathetically affected. Accordingly, every sensory fibre by means of a branch path of the *first* order stands in connection with the motor fibres arising on the same side and at the same level, by one of the *second* order with those emerging on the opposite side at the same level, by branches of the *third* order with those emerging higher up, and finally by that of a *fourth* order also with those arising far lower down" (Wundt, pp. 116–117). While with increasing intensity of stimulation greater resistances are overcome (or with increasing irritability all resistances reduced), the branch paths of the higher orders must *pari passu* be brought into requisition; and in the same proportion also increases the number of the central intermediate links concerned in the total motor reaction. This increase now takes place very rapidly as we pass from the spinal cord to the co-operation of the higher centres; the reflexions then increase in complication in quick progression, without thereby losing their reflex character.

However, then, one may look at the matter, the conclusion is not to be resisted that all the functions of the central nervous system, and therewith all our manifestations of life and mental activity, fall under the conception of reflex action. We must make this thought entirely our own, when it loses the character of a paradox. It imports, in fine, nothing more than the axiom of sufficient reason in metaphysics. If the latter be translated into the language of nervous physiology it runs, "No ganglionic cell is functional without a sufficient reason, which is called a stimulus;" and translated into the language of psychology it runs, "No volition without motive." Both are familiar self-evident truths, but which perhaps open up a fruitful prospect if we bring them into connection by help of the notion "reflexion" under the point of view of physiological psychology. We have, namely, before us the problem to make internal experience more intelligible by means of the external, and conversely.

The *physiologist* causes his beheaded and poisoned frog to make a movement of contraction, and thereby obtains indubitable evidence that the relatively simple reflex action observed rests on a *mechanism*. The *psychologist* sees in motivation a reflex act, and gains the equally indubitable conviction that reflexion is a *psychical process* in which a *volition* uniformly follows on a *sensation* in accordance with the true nature of the *character*. The *physiological psychologist*, as soon as he perceives that the essence of reflexion must in both events be *homogeneous*, has to advance to the conclusion, "Consequently reflex contraction is a volition excited by sensation in the particular centre, and the genesis of volition is a mechanism conformable to law." The materialistic physiologists do not need much pressing to accept the last half of this conclusion; but *per contra* the first, although they cannot fail to see that logically they must allow either *both* or *neither*. For the rest, psychology long ago dreamt of a "physiological psychology," talked of a statics and dynamics of desires and ideas; and after all nothing is excluded by the admission of the mechanics of reflexion but the indeterminism of the will, long ago perceived to be untenable. If one once admits that the subjectively psychical acts correspond to objectively material functions, of course all objective mechanics of molecular motions in the nervous system must correspond to the subjective mechanics of desires and ideas, and conversely. All the more astonishing must it, however, appear when the physiologists, who confirm this afresh, will not see the psychological reverse of their apparently materialistic medal, namely, that every, even the smallest, reflex action is a *volition* which is motived by a *sensation*. Sensation *is* only so far as it becomes conscious (certainly, however, only becomes conscious for the particular ganglionic cell or the centre in question); volition stands *in and of itself beyond* all consciousness; and whether in the particular case it appears in consciousness formally as intensive feeling of innervation, or materially as qualitative perceived motion, is dependent on circumstances, and in any case highly improbable for simpler reflexes in subordinate centres.

Wundt has precluded himself from this insight both by his above-mentioned prejudice in regard to consciousness, as also by his distorted conception of the will. His remark is correct: "If one tries to determine where the mechanism ceases and where the will begins, the *question* is altogether *falsely proposed*. For one here opposes conceptions to one another which are *not opposites at all*" (p. 822). But he does not draw from this the unavoidable inference that in that case either sensation and will, in defiance of internal experience, must be denied even in the highest mental functions, or they must also be admitted in the lowest reflex processes, because both sides are related to each other as inner and outer. Were these notions "a mere fiction" (*ibid.*) in the *latter case*, they must be so also in the *former;* were that inner, psychical side of the process and the metaphysical substance of an "unconscious soul" which supports it after the admission of the external mechanism in the simple reflexion "a superfluous and meaningless addition" (*ibid.*), it would be so also in the achievements of the genius and the hero.

Maudsley comes very near the truth, but he is too much of an Englishman to grasp what is apparently so paradoxical with a firm hand. He says: "Wherever an afferent nerve issues from the cell or group of cells in the cortical layers of the hemispheres, and an efferent nerve issues from the cell or group of cells, there is the possible or actual centre of a particular volition; . . . volition or will simply expresses the due co-ordinate activity of the supreme centres, not otherwise than as the co-ordinate activity of the spinal cord or medulla oblongata might be said to represent its will" (p. 444).

This not merely "might," but "must" undeniably be said, if one desires to be a physiological psychologist in the true sense of the word, and would not by such timidity in drawing conclusions forfeit the right of inference in a reverse direction, namely, from the physiological to the psychological aspect of phenomena, from material to psychical mechanics. Maudsley had the less reason to evade the acknowledgment of a *will* in the lower centres, as he even admits the necessity of the *perception* of the stimulus in the same, which indeed requires the genesis of a consciousness, which the will does not. On the other side, the unwonted step is made more difficult for him, in the first place, by the English not having, as the German, two different designations for *Wille* and *Willkür;* and, in the second place, because, like a true English empiricist, he entertains an almost superstitious dread of treating the abstract conception of the will as an ideal entity, *i.e.*, of straying into the province of metaphysics.[1]

In this question also it holds good that for comprehending the complicated events in human consciousness a sure foundation for judgment must be gained from the simple relations in lower animals. On this point Maudsley himself writes as follows: "The simplest mode of nervous action in man, comparable to that of the lowest animals that possess nerve, is exhibited by the scattered ganglionic cells belonging to the sympathetic system which are concerned in certain organic processes. The heart's action, for example, is due to the ganglionic cells diffused through its substance. Meissner has shown that nerve-cells disseminated through the tissues of the intestines govern their motions; and Lister thinks it probable that cells scattered in the tissues preside over the contractions of the arteries, and over the remarkable diffusion of the pigment granules which takes place in the stellate cells of the frog's skin. The separate elements of the

[1] I should much like to know what such an empiricist understands by "explanation" and "principles of explanation," and whether he imagines it possible without ascending to "general principles" to give any explanation, were it only of the simplest physical phenomenon. Concrete reality is of course only possessed by the attraction of the atom A and the atom B; but if Newton had had the same ghost-fear of the "abstract idea" of attraction which Maudsley has of that of Will, he would never have been able to set up gravitation as a universal principle of matter.

tissues are co-ordinated by the ganglionic nerve-cells of the sympathetic system; and these co-ordinating centres, again, are found to be under the control of the cerebro-spinal centres. In the spinal cord the ganglionic nerve-cells are collected together, and so united that groups of them and connected groups of them become independent centres of combined movements, simultaneous and successive, in answer to stimuli; this arrangement representing the entire nervous system of those animals in which no organs of special sense have yet appeared" (p. 108).

Only those who "have applied to the lower animals their subjective misinterpretation of the complex phenomena in man" (p. 139), will be prepared to dispute that these lower animals have sensation and will; for the common objection, that in these organisms all vital manifestations are only reflexes, no longer avails, since we have perceived the like in the highest mental functions. On the contrary, it is precisely the lowest animals that are suited to demonstrate visibly, as it were, that every reflex action even of the simplest ganglionic cell has just as much a subjective and psychical as an objective and physical side, and that the former again falls into a conscious and an unconscious psychical part. The stimulus or the motive must be conscious in the ganglionic cell as sensation if it is above the threshold; the reaction of the will or the result of the reflex process, looked at from within, only becomes conscious at higher stages of intelligence by comparative reflexion; the passage from stimulation to reaction, from motive to volition, the properly *punctum saliens* in reflexion, remains for ever concealed from the light of consciousness; and yet there lies therein just the enigmatic problem, Why then does *this* particular sensation act as a *motive* to *this* volition?

The materialistic conception finds the answer very easy by simply seeking the reason in the objective physical mechanism of the movements. But that means allowing the two-sidedness of a psychical and physical character only to the first and last term of the process, and refusing it to the middle term, the spark which passes from one to the other; in other words, it means degrading the psychical factor in the reflex to the dead passivity of a mere mirroring of certain members of the then alone actual external process, or the depressing of the psychical to a sort of accidental appendix of the external event, which in certain phases of the latter emerges in an inexplicable fashion.

In opposition to such an external conception it must be remembered that the objective material event, just as the inner events of consciousness, are only two parallel and polar-opposed phenomenal forms of one existence revealing itself in both, which is always more transparent to the view from the subjective than the objective side, because the former view is at any rate a *direct one*, but the latter only *mediated* by the subjective appearance of the objective phenomenon. Whether there is an objectively real physical process, apart from a consciousness apprehending it, is at the very least a *disputed question*, which is even *answered in the negative* by the idealistic theory of cognition; but even if the Realism which affirms it is in the right, it is so *only on the ground of inner* subjective phenomenal experience, which is equally indisputable for idealists as realists. To the latter consequently appertains once for all the *higher* certainty; *on it* alone can the realistic belief in an external reality *be supported*, and every inference of the latter, which leads it to a negation of the certainty of immediate inner experience *withdraws from under itself the ground* on which it stands. Therefore *psychological* experience must always *remain the immutable standard* by which the supposed external experience and the inferences therefrom have to be verified.

The being underlying the appearance begins for the inner psychological series of events just where consciousness ceases, and the unconscious-psychical foundation of the consciousness of the sensation is itself that which, turned towards others like itself, constitutes the objective phenomenon. This unconscious-psychical foundation of the reflex process in the ganglion-cell is, however, definable most accurately as a will, which is subject to a law such that a certain motive determines it to a certain volition. (It remains here perfectly obscure whether this will is a result of the combination merely of the molecular wills of the cell, or whether other volitional factors enter into it in addition.) In no case is it justifiable to ignore this unconsciously-psychical foundation, and to affix the subjective inwardness as *accidental appendix of certain* moments of the *external* physical process, *which is itself only objective phenomenon.* Volition is a psychical act not merely in its conscious or unconscious existence (as result of material mechanics, as Materialism supposes), but also in the whole history of its origination as due to the psychical motive and the law of its psychical reaction.

5. *The Teleological Character of the Reflex Function.*—The most certain proof of the inner psychical side of the reflex process is the *teleological* character of this reaction, which is expressed in the thoroughgoing purposiveness of the physiological (not pathological) reflexes.—As a matter of course, this purposiveness cannot take place with a scale of stimulation unlimited above and below. As our ear in the deepest tones does not hear a tone, but a droning noise, in the highest is aware no longer of a tone, but of an acute pain, as our eye does not distinguish objects with a very feeble illumination, and is dazzled and destroyed by a brightness all too bright, without the adaptation of these organs being thereby defective, the purposive reflexes can also be looked for only within certain finite limits of the scale of stimulation, but these limits will *themselves again be teleologically determined.* Should the centres react on all too feeble stimuli, they would, as a morbid centre actually does, squander their store of force by reason of the weak

stimuli ceaselessly playing around them, instead of sparing it for the uses where its expenditure is of value for the life of the organism. On the other hand, should the centres be constituted so solidly and firmly that even the most violent attacks could not disorganise them, they would possess a constitution, which would make them less suited to their more delicate offices, without ever satisfying the intrinsically absurd demand of an absolute indestructibility. The fact that abnormally strong stimuli produce convulsions in the centres and act in a disorganising fashion is therefore just as little as the other fact, that the suitable reaction only begins with a certain intensity of stimulation, calculated to render doubtful this teleological character of the reflexes, but rather only serves to set it in the true light.

Further, it is to be noticed, as we said above, that with increasing strength of the stimulus ever *more* and *higher* centres are drawn into action; hence it results that the character of the reaction must change with the intensity of the stimulus. But even this does not tell *against*, but *for* the purposiveness of the reflexes; for it is precisely for *the good of* the organism that it does not respond to weak stimuli merely with *weaker*, but also with *other* motor reactions, than to strong stimuli, which act at the same point. These purposive differences, now, are reached by the threshold of stimulation being different for the reflex actions of the different centres. With the weakest stimulus only the centre in which the particular sensory nerve immediately terminates solicits to reflexion, and the consequence is a simple contraction, which, *e.g.*, suffices to drive away a fly from the hide of an ox, or to push aside the oppressive fold of a man's dress, or to change the uncomfortable position of a leg during sleep.

Purposeless, therefore, the reflexes cannot be called even with the weakest stimuli above the threshold (as by Wundt, p. 823); only the motor sphere of innervation for the centre, which alone reacts on the weakest stimuli, is a confined one, and therefore also the change of the external circumstances to be effected by it very narrowly limited. As *more* and *higher* centres are reached by the propagated stimulus, this motor sphere of innervation of all the centres sharing in the reflexion extends, and therewith the possibility of combined muscular movements to change the external situation announced by the stimulus. To the sphere of motor innervation governed by a central spot must the impulses of innervation proceeding from it of course correspond, if they are not inadequate from the very first, and therefore to be called unsuitable, and therefore, in fact, for a single ganglionic cell that reflex action which is teleologically demanded is *a quite other one* than for a larger group of ganglionic cells acting in concert, and for a cell in the lower part of the spinal cord quite other than for one in the upper, and for this again another than for one in the medulla oblongata. The reaction can only be called purposive at any point when it has regard to the maximum of what is attainable from this point. This is not sufficiently estimated by Wundt, whilst he cannot of course avoid the acknowledgment of the too evident purposiveness in the case of mean intensities of stimulation.

"A decapitated frog moves its leg against the pincers with which it is irritated, or it wipes away with its foot the drop of acid applied to its skin. It sometimes tries to withdraw from a mechanical or electrical irritation by a leap. When brought into an unusual position, *e.g.*, placed on its back, it perhaps returns to its previous posture. Here, then, the stimulus does *not* introduce *merely* a movement in general, which spreads from the irritated part with increasing intensity of the stimulus and growing irritability, but the movement is *adapted to the external impression*. In the one case it is a movement *of defence*; in a second it aims at *getting rid of the stimulus*; in a third at *removal of the body* from the sphere of the irritation; in a fourth, finally, at restoration of the previous posture. Still more clearly does this purposive adaptation to the stimulus stand out in the experiments conducted by Pflüger and Auerbach, in which the ordinary conditions of movement are somewhat changed. A frog, for example, whose leg has been cut off on the side on which it is irritated by acid, first makes some fruitless attempts with the amputated stump, then, however, pretty regularly chooses the other leg, which is wont to remain at rest when the animal is unmutilated.[1] If the decapitated frog be fastened by its back, and the inner side of one of its thighs be sprinkled with acid, it tries to get rid of the latter by rubbing the two thighs against one another; but if now the moved thigh be separated far from the other, after a few vain attempts it suddenly stretches this one out and pretty accurately reaches the point which was irritated.[2] Lastly, if one breaks the upper thighs of decapitated frogs, and cauterises, whilst they are stretched on their bellies, the region of the anus, in spite of the disturbing nature of the treatment, they correctly touch the cauterised spot with the feet of the broken limbs. These observations, *which may be varied in diverse ways*, show that the animal entirely deprived of its brain can adapt its movements to the changed condition in a way which, if consciousness and will were concerned, would manifestly presuppose a perfect knowledge of the position of the whole body and of its several parts" (p. 824).

That Wundt, with the latter inference, so far as it relates to a *conscious* knowledge of one's own body, overshoots the mark he himself allows in the observation that even man, *with his very clear consciousness*, and though perfectly *master of his will, does not possess the same*; whence he should conversely have concluded that in those actions of the spinal cord also *consciousness and will may be present without* the need of a *conscious* knowledge of the relative position of the parts of the body. Had he not omitted this

[1] *Pflüger*, "Die sensorischen Functionen des Rückenmarks," p. 125.
[2] *Auerbach* in *Günsburg's* "Zeitschrift f. klin. Med.," iv. p. 487.

conclusion he would also have found no reason in the *mechanical* conception of the reflex processes for doubting the existence of consciousness and will in the same, since indeed the same mechanical conception in the case of the functions of the cerebral hemispheres does not seem to give rise in him to any doubt.

He says: "It is certainly admitted that the self-regulations, which must be presupposed in order to explain the manifold modifications of animal movements without consciousness, are partly *of an extraordinarily complicated* nature; but if one once admits the principle of mechanism, where is the limit to the animal machine?" (p. 822). However, Wundt would have to apply the same remark also to the mechanics of the cerebral hemispheres, thus by his argumentation would arrive at the denial of consciousness and will altogether. If the argument fails in this latter case, *it has no weight at all*—an inevitable consequence of its dependence on the *opposition* of mechanism and will, already declared by him himself to be *faulty*.—The Cartesian doctrine that animals are walking automata, which merely ape us with the semblance of a psychical life, is looked upon to-day by every feeling man as an almost revolting error. How long will it still last before our modern physiologists finally free themselves from the not smaller error in principle, that the organic manifestations of life of the lower central organs of the nervous system are mere mechanical contrivances without any spark of inner life?

It is precisely physiological psychology which must feel itself compelled to conclude in a contrary sense and to say: "If the whole life of the central organs when objectively regarded consists in molecular mechanics, and yet in our consciousness a purposive thinking and willing corresponds to this mechanics, this purposiveness which makes its appearance in the cerebrum also in the form of consciousness must already inhere from the first in all the functioning of ganglion-cells, although it be not everywhere conscious as such, for in the last resort nothing can emerge but that for which a foundation has already been laid in the lower phases of development." It is just the materialistically inclined physiologist, who looks upon conscious thought and volition as a merely passive reflex of the external order, as a transitory accidental appendix in certain phases of the molecular mechanics of nerve, who is entirely precluded from ascribing independent activity to consciousness, and consequently has no choice at all but to explain the undeniable purposiveness which appears in conscious thought and volition as a purposiveness of molecular nerve-mechanics, *i.e.*, it is precisely Materialism which cannot avoid recognising purposiveness in the function of the ganglion-cell, if it will not cut itself off from every explanation of purposiveness in consciousness, in its own reflections and resolutions.

Actual purposiveness Materialism can of course only acknowledge with the help of Darwinism, which represents the purposive molecular dispositions as arising in the ganglion-cells by natural selection. If this attempted explanation proves generally insufficient[1] without the foundation of metaphysical teleological principles, it particularly does so in this special case; for it is not exactly clear how, beside so many other far more important individual variations, an altogether trifling more or less of reflex dispositions in the grey matter of the spinal cord can be *decisive* for the competitive capacity of an animal. *Lamarck's* principle of gradual perfection by exercise avails here just as little; for even if we conceive the purposive modifications of function which are to be established by exercise as proceeding from the spinal cord or higher centres,[2] yet *passive consciousness* cannot explain the *pur-*

[1] Comp. my memoir: "Truth and Error in Darwinism: A Critical Exposition of the Theory of Organic Development." Berlin, C. Duncker, 1875.

[2] The functions of the spinal cord in the higher animals may be likened to the performances of a man who is prevented by his servitude to a strict master from working out his many-sided tendencies, and is obliged to constantly devote himself to a well-defined and limited sphere of labour. The spinal cord of

posiveness of these modifications, because the purposiveness of its own psychical associations *is*, according to the materialistic view, *only to* be *itself* explained by the purposiveness of molecular *mechanics*. Wherefore Wundt is also entirely in the right when he warns us to hold fast to this, that the assumption of a spinal *consciousness* and will *does not in any way contribute* to the clearing up of the problem of *purposive* actions (p. 829); only he ought in consistency to go further, and admit that a higher degree of consciousness can just as little contribute thereto as a lower one; that a *brain-consciousness* is for the explanation of design in bodily movements *just as much* a fifth wheel in the waggon as a spinal consciousness; that the brain consciousness can least of all serve to explain the purposiveness of the spinal reflexes, and that therefore the principle of Lamarck also, so long as merely conscious consideration is regarded as cause of the purposive modification of function, moves in a *circle*.[1]

One only escapes this fallacious *revolution in a circle* by assuming that those purposive modifications of function, which come about with frequent repetition by the fixing of molecular tendencies and diminished resistance, proceed from an *unconscious teleological principle*, whose efficacy in

the higher animals is, as it were, simplified by its constant necessitation to hodman's services for the behoof of the brain; but the inference is illogical that it has lost consciousness and will (which it manifestly possesses in the lower animals), since indeed in the sphere of activity reserved to it it displays distinct intelligence, and in abnormal pathological cases is wont to take part also in the vicarious execution of more independent tasks.

[1] *Maudsley*, who, from his *materialistic* point of view, keenly feels the insolubility of the unavoidable teleological problem, gets rid of the difficulty in genuine English fashion by appealing to the *unsearchable divine counsels*. The *locus* is too characteristic of English science for the writer to resist the temptation of transcribing it:—"If it be said that the gradual building up by education of this embodied design into the constitution of the nervous centres is itself evidence of design, then we can only answer that such a proposition is merely a statement in other words of the fact that things are as they are" (*i.e.*, are here constituted and operate teleologically), "and add the expression of a conviction that science cannot enter into the councils of creation" (p. 156). One wonders how an English scientist has courage to go on investigating. Even a Maudsley is still green wood!

this perfecting of the nerve-centres is only a special case of its *general* teleological efficiency as *organising* principle. As the external mechanics of the material processes and the inner mechanics of conscious ideas and desires are co-ordinate phenomena of one and the same metaphysical substance, so is also the *regularity* of this outer and inner mechanic (not the parallelism of a pre-established harmony, but) a coherent efflux from the indivisible essence of this metaphysical substance. Even at this point of view there remains the passivity of consciousness, but the latter now no longer appears as an attribute of matter, but of an immaterial substance, whose other attribute is the manifestation of material energy; thus the psychical is not here confined to the sphere of consciousness, but reaches *deeper* than this, namely, into the metaphysical Ens itself. Then also conscious design in thinking and resolving is no longer regarded as a passive reflection from the sphere of purposive molecular mechanics, but it is like this, an immediate manifestation of the teleological nature of the metaphysical substance itself (the unconscious spirit); what is there dead externality, whose spiritual stamp is first discovered by a thinking mind, is here immediate perception of the inmost nature of the spirit itself in itself.

Without comprehending the parallelism of the two problems, both remain insoluble, *i.e.*, both the teleological character of the external mechanisms and their origin, and also the conscious purposive activity of the human mind must in their *isolation* from one another appear as *transcendent* questions, to penetrate into which is a hopeless undertaking. On the other hand, from the moment when inner and outer are perceived to be two-sided phenomena of One Being, and the *sameness* of the teleological problem in *both* forms of the phenomenon is comprehended, the single reason for the teleological character both of the external material mechanics and of the conscious mental function must be sought in *one and the same* constitution of the metaphysical substance, of which *both* sides of the phenomena are only accidents, and it is now the purposive character *immediately* known to us of our own mind which affords the *key* to the understanding of that nature of the metaphysical substance which is in question, to wit, causes us to perceive it as the *unconsciously Logical*, which must be *teleologically* active as content of a will or a force. Therefore is it also so important to see clearly that the inner psychical aspect of the process intervening between stimulus and reaction and conscious perception appertain to *all*, even the lowest nerve-centres,—not as if the attribution of consciousness to the same could contribute anything directly to the explanation of the purposiveness of the functions (which I have never asserted), but because it is important to remain always aware of the two-sidedness of the phenomenon, and never to let the key which most directly opens the teleological nature of the metaphysical substance drop from our hands.

How the higher unity of causality and teleology which is here maintained is to be conceived cannot be more fully entered upon in this place.[1] I will here only remark this much, that the time is approaching with giant strides when our natural science will cease to speak of "dead matter." Already the most distinguished natural philosophers recognise the interior, psychical side of atoms;[2] and already there is the glimmering of an apprehension that the key to the nature of the simplest laws of the mechanics of the atom, which hitherto has been considered to be an absolute *datum*, must be sought in this psychical aspect of the atoms, and is to be found in the analogies of our own psyche.[3]

[1] Comp. my writings: "Truth and Error in Darwinism," sect. vii. ("Mechanism and Teleology"); and J. H. v. Kirchmann's "Realistic Theory of Cognition," Nos. 15-22.

[2] Comp. among others, A. Zöllner, "Ueber die Natur der Kometen" (Leipzig, 1872), pp. 320-327.

[3] Zöllner says (pp. 326, 327): "As one sees, by this assumption, *all* local changes of matter, whether they take place in the inorganic or organic bodies of nature, are subject to the following law, which was already substantially expressed above (p. 217): "All the

The law of the conservation of energy signifies in metaphysical reference only the unchangeableness of the actual world-will on the side of its intensity; this law is, however, purely formal, and only teaches us: *if* this quantum of mechanical energy is converted into another form, *e.g.*, into heat, *then* it will furnish such and such a quantum of heat. But *whether* this mechanical energy is in the given case converted into *heat* or any *other* form, or whether it is transformed into tension by removal from its centre, or whether it is for the nonce not converted at all, on these points the abstract formal law of the conservation of energy says nothing. On the decision of *these* questions in every single instance depends, however, *the whole content of the world-process;* therefore all that determines the *content* of the cosmic process, *i.e.*, the whole sphere of the logical IDEA, is *not affected* by the law of the conservation of energy. Accordingly the law of the conservation of energy only proves to be the abstract formal *framework, within which* the logical necessity of the material content is manifested, and the qualitative determination of things, by means of causality and teleology obtains scope for display. The law of the immutability of the absolute quantum of force accordingly requires to be supplemented by other natural laws which determine the "*How*" of the force at every point of the unchangeable total; and only in these latter laws can, nay, *must* the teleological character of the metaphysical substance of the atoms attain expression: their striving after satisfaction of their special will and their instinctive warding off of pain (which springs from repression of this will). As, metaphysically speaking, the cosmic process is compounded of Will and unconscious-logical IDEA, of which two moments the former determines the "That,"

activities of natural existences are determined by the *sensations* of pleasure and pain; and are indeed such that the movements within a confined sphere of phenomena look as if they followed the *unconscious purpose* of reducing the total of painful sensations to a *minimum*."

the latter the "What and How" at every instant of the process: so, scientifically speaking, the world-process is compounded of the unchangeable cosmic quantum of energy and of the laws determining the conversion of energy in the particular cases, and this exact parallelism of the two ways of regarding the cosmic process may pass for a new proof that the metaphysical distinction of the moments Will and IDEA should be called anything but arbitrary, but is deeply founded in the essence of things, and is precisely adapted to enlighten natural science on the deeper significance of *its* first principles.

There is a further question whether the teleological laws of Nature that materially determine the conversion of force in respect to the mechanics of the atom are also sufficient to explain the uniform teleological behaviour of the ganglion-cell, or whether with this union of atoms and molecules into an organic-psychical individual of a higher order new laws must be supposed to come into play, which point to a specific difference between the unconscious individual aim of a ganglion-cell and the combined unconscious ends of the atoms and molecules that constitute it. From such a varying unconscious purpose, coincident with a variously constituted individual will or individual character, varying laws of motivation would then at once follow, inasmuch as a differently constituted unconscious individual will is compelled to feel pain and pleasure by different external circumstances.— An imperfect example may make this clear. In chemistry, the law holds good that if several substances are brought together in a condition capable of reaction, the molecular displacements are such that the algebraic sum of the positive and negative amounts of heat thereby developed to become a maximum. To this law the actions in the cell of the spinal cord poisoned with strychnine or in the cerebral cell of the maniac seems to correspond, where the chemical processes tend to the squandering of the stored-up potential energy. The influences in the healthy ganglionic cell, on the other hand, running counter to this conversion, which we have called the inhibitory potencies, *and in which the specific fitness of the function of the ganglia is first manifested*, seem to point to a *new* law of a higher order limiting the play of the chemical molecular laws. However, this is to be considered as merely an illustrative example, and must not be taken for more than it is worth.

If now it should turn out that the teleological-uniform mechanics of the ganglion-cell rests on natural laws which do not result from the mere combination of the mechanical laws of the atom, the atoms also could no longer be looked upon as the substrata of such laws of a higher order, because one and the same individual subject cannot be substrate of opposite mutually limiting natural laws. A metaphysical substratum must then be introduced for the additional laws of a higher order, which, together with the material atoms composing the cell, would *in combination* constitute the *entire* individual of this ganglion-cell.

From the side on which we have entered upon this investigation, it might perhaps appear premature to attempt to give a definitive decision on this question. But as we have already seen that this ultimate substratum would coincide with the organising principle which directs the teleological perfecting of the ganglion-cell as an integral element of the perfection of the collective organic type, and as this organising principle, as metaphysical support of the universal organic law of development, must necessarily be conceived as something superadded to the material atoms, we shall from this side likewise venture to decide our foregoing alternative in favour of an additional metaphysical agent, which connects the manifold of the outer and inner atomic functions in the ganglion cell into an external-teleological as well as into an internal-psychical unity, and thus exalts the cell into an internally as well as externally indivisible *organic-psychical individual.*

To be sure, whoever either denies the teleological character of molecular mechanics in the ganglion-cell (as the older Materialism), or ignores it as an intrinsically insoluble transcendent problem having no point of contact with science (as Maudsley), or, lastly, admits it indeed as fact, but thinks to explain it from blindly necessary and accidental causes (as Darwinism and Wundt), such an one will only act consistently when he declines at the outset every metaphysical or unconscious-psychical principle in addition to the atoms, and conceives the conscious as well as the unconscious psychical phenomena in the ganglion-cell as simply phenomenal combinations of the psychical functions of the atoms concerned.[1] He, on the other hand, who regards the teleology of material mechanics as of consciousness as parallel emanations of the unconsciously logical and teleological nature of the metaphysical substance (underlying both aspects of the phenomenon), will (even apart from the necessity of an organising principle as supporter of the law of organic development) rather incline to the other side of the alternative, and expect that the (as compared with the laws of the mechanics of the atom) higher forms of manifestation of teleology which come to light in the ganglion-cell, and the internal and external unity which exalts the ganglion-cell to the rank of individuality, spring from superadded functions of the metaphysical substance, which subordinate the isolated atomic functions to the single unconscious individual purpose of a higher order.

A play of innumerable atoms, acknowledging no superior but the One substance to whom they owe their being, must be more congenial to the democratic, levelling,

[1] Comp. the anonymous work, "The Unconscious from the Standpoint of Physiology and the Theory of Descent" (Berlin, 1872), chaps. iv. and v.

disorganising tendency of the Romance nations, which however cannot dispense with the sway of one all-powerful Cæsar if universal anarchy is not to prevail. An organic construction of the cosmos, in which the atomic forces or individuals of the first order only play the part of the simplest and lowest building-stones, and in each individual of a higher order are held together by an inner tie for a concrete purpose, in order again on their part to serve as building material for still higher individual aims, such a gradual construction will be more agreeable to the Germanic mind which knows that wherever a *living* architectonic work of art is to be brought to pass, levelling must be foregone, and submission be willingly given to the higher purpose.

6. *The Four Chief Grades of Nerve-Centres.*—"In dealing with the function of the nervous system in man, it is, then, most necessary to distinguish different nervous centres:—

"1. The *primary* centres, or *ideational* centres, constituted by the grey matter of the convolutions of the hemispheres. They are superordinate to

"2. The *secondary* nervous centres, or *sensory* centres, constituted by the collections of grey matter that lie between the decussation of the pyramids and the floors of the lateral ventricles. These are subordinate to the primary and superordinate to

"3. The *tertiary* nervous centres, or centres of *reflex* action, constituted mainly by the grey matter of the spinal cord; which again are superordinate to

"4. The *organic* nervous centres, as we might call them, belonging to the sympathetic system. They consist of a set of ganglionic bodies distributed mainly over the viscera, and connected with one another and with the spinal centres by internuntiant cords.

"Each distinct centre is subordinated to the centre immediately above it, but is at the same time capable of determining and maintaining certain movements of its own without the intervention of its supreme centre. For example, the rhythmical contractions of the heart are kept up by the ganglia distributed through its substance, and accordingly continue for a time after the removal of the organ from the body. But these local powers are not left uncontrolled: terminal branches of the vagus nerve, or rather branches of a motor nerve called the spinal accessory, which go with the vagus to the heart, are connected in some way with the ganglia; and when the vagus is irritated the ganglia are controlled and cease to act upon the heart, which comes to a standstill in a relaxed condition. The organisation of the entire nervous system is such that a due independent local action is compatible with the proper control of a superior central authority. The ganglionic cells of the sympathetic co-ordinate the energy of the separate elements of the tissue in which they are placed, and thus represent the simplest form of a principle of *individuation.* Through the cells of the spinal centre the functions of the different organic centres are so co-ordinated as to have their subordinate but essential place in the movements of animal life; and herein is witnessed a further and higher individuation. The spinal centres are similarly controlled by the sensory centres; and these, in their turn, are subordinate to the controlling action of the cerebral hemispheres, and especially to the action which, revealing itself in consciousness as will, represents the most complete co-ordination of the functions of the hemispheres, and is the highest display of the principle of *individuation*" (Maudsley, p. 109–110).

Two remarks may be made on the above division: in the first place, that a preferable succession would be an inverse one, and the denomination "primary centres" would better suit the "organic" ganglia; and, secondly, that the designation of spinal centres as *reflex* centres is misleading, since even the "organic" centres and sensory and ideational centres are only reflectorially active, as already discussed. Moreover, it must be held as settled that the differences between the ganglion-cells of the different centre are only gradational, which have only been formed by differentiation from the common structure of the ganglion-cell in the succession of animal life, and that this universal foundation of each single ganglion-cell—in spite of any partial elaboration in a particular direction—has been preserved. There are in the ganglion-cells, just as in the nerve-fibres, specific energies in the sense of impregnated dispositions to definite functions; but here, as there, this specification is only *relative*, not absolute, and everywhere it works in the frames previously indicated by the general nature of the ganglion-cell: stimulus and reaction, perception and will.

Corresponding to the relativity of the specific energies of the ganglion-cells, the transition from the centres of one kind to those of another is also rather gradual than abrupt. If the ganglia of an excised frog's heart incite the latter to beat for hours, and react on a stimulus with a rhythmical contraction, the different position in the body more than the specific reflex energy serves to differentiate these ganglia from the lower centres of the spinal cord. The *medulla oblongata* forms a kind of transition between the spinal cord and the sensory ganglia of the brain, and, so far as its historic evolution is concerned, certainly belongs to the brain, but functionally stands far closer to the spinal cord. The increasing extent of the sphere of motor innervation as we ascend the spinal cord is especially noticeable in the medulla oblongata. The latter is also, moreover, distinguished from the other reflexes of the spinal cord by a more ingenious combination of numerous movements for obtaining definite effects, "so that the mode of combination is often brought about by a self-regulation which is founded in the reciprocal relation of several reflex mechanisms" (Wundt, p. 178). In the spinal cord the ganglion cells at the different levels are tolerably uniformly ordered in the four columns of the grey medulla. Only in the medulla oblongata is this symmetrical distribution interrupted, in that larger groups of ganglion-cells are fused into compact distinctly isolated nuclei, which are united with one another, as with the parts above and below, by means of conducting fibres. Such nuclei then serve definite groups of complicated processes of movement, that partly, like the regulation of the heart-beat and inspiration, are persistent rhythmical functions which approximate to those of the vegetative ganglia (*e.g.*, movement of the intestines, tone of the vessels). By the union of two or several reflex centres with one another an alternating action is made possible, *e.g.*, between a centre of inspiration and another of exspiration (p. 181); the former (like most of the so-called automatic functions of lower centres) is set agoing by the stimulus of insufficiently aerated blood, the latter by the sensation of the inflation of the lungs mediated by the sensory nerves (p. 177). Similarly Wundt assumes special centres in the medulla oblongata for the acceleration of the beating of the heart and for its slowing and inhibition, for the distension of the vessels and for their contraction (p. 185), for vomiting, for the act of swallowing, and, lastly, for coughing and sneezing, which pass over into the mimic reflexes of laughing, crying, sobbing, &c. (pp. 176, 178). In the latter, reflexes of the sensory ganglia already co-operate with those of the medulla oblongata to produce a combined indivisible action.

Those centres which Maudsley comprehends under the name of sensory centres (although this name will not altogether fit the cerebellum, which is included among them) form in many lower animals, in which the Fore-brain (or cerebrum) essentially acts only as olfactory ganglion, the highest stage of development of their central nervous system, and is quite sufficient for their vital purposes. These animals move about with pretty much the same security and adjust their actions with the same appropriateness to the sensibly perceived external circumstances as a human somnambulist whose cerebral functions are completely suspended (M., p. 252). "Trousseau mentions a young amateur musician subject to epileptic vertigo who sometimes had a fit lasting for ten or fifteen seconds whilst playing the violin. Though he was perfectly unconscious of everything around him, and neither heard nor saw those whom he was accompanying, he still went on playing in time during the attack" (M., p. 151).

Similarly is it with the capability of certain idiots to master certain difficult feats of skill with long-continued training, which they at last perform with astonishing adroitness (M.) If one removes from a rat the cerebral hemispheres along with the corpora striata and optic thalami, on every repetition of a loud and abrupt noise, such as cats are wont to make, it makes a spring to escape (M.) Mammals or birds from which all the parts of the brain lying above the corpora quadrigemina are removed follow the movements of a burning taper with their head, thus still perceive the impression of light; and likewise "frogs [under operation], which are constrained to make movements of escape by cutaneous irritation, avoid an obstacle placed before them" (W., p. 194).

All this proves that, besides the perception of sense-impressions through the consciousness of the cerebral hemispheres, there must be an additional perception through a special consciousness of the sensory ganglia not included within the former, which Maudsley expressly acknowledges and very decidedly emphasises. One must only distinguish between a perception in the sphere of self-conscious intelligence and one in the sphere of (merely) conscious sense-activity (M.) But just in the same way we must also assume a *will* in the sensori-motor sphere, which for the rest does not need to be like the perception of the sense-impression serving as a motive to a conscious one. When Maudsley assumes a "sensorial madness" arising through disease of the sensory ganglia (p. 248), in which hallucinations of sense or morbid reaction lead to a pathological condition, with the cerebral consciousness either suspended or persisting, but incapable of resisting the sensori-motor will, the action of the ganglia motived by sense-perception, entering into conflict with the cerebral will and emerging victorious from this struggle, must necessarily be itself designated will.[1]

We arrive at the same result when we compare this sensori-motor sphere in man and the higher animals with the psychical life of those animals whose nervous system has not yet at all risen beyond the stage of sensory centres: as little as we can deny these animals a will, so little can we refuse it to the functions of the human sensory ganglia. The same holds good of the *fitness* of the sensori-motor reflexes. In those animals where the presence of conscious perception and will is beyond dispute, the purposive character of their relations to the external world is too evident for us to doubt the existence of an *intelligence* which it is true has not yet reached so far as the formation of abstract ideas or even to self-consciousness, but yet is a preliminary step to this cerebral intelligence of the higher animals.

Here, too, the parallelism with the well-known performances of the sleep-walker, indicative in part of highly developed intelligence, forms a good illustration. In both there occurs an adhesion of impressions, *i.e.*, a *memory*; but the stage of reflection, which is indispensable for a recognition, is wanting in them, *i.e.*, a conscious *recollection*, and the memory therefore manifests itself not so much on the side of representation as on that of will, *i.e.*, consists

[1] In such a case one may often say that the madman was perfectly conscious of the difference between good and evil: that however, despite of it, he was not in a position to keep back his diseased will from pathological excesses, thus also cannot be made responsible for actions committed in this way. The legislation of different states would then need a rectification in respect to the question of accountability.

essentially only in the ease of the connection between perception and voluntary reaction. This memory therefore furthers the elaboration of the instinctive facility and accuracy with which the most frequent and most important vital actions are performed by animals and man. Even in somnambulists who periodically lapse into their spontaneously somnambulistic condition, a certain memory is unmistakable. For example, they continue tasks which were left unfinished on the last attack at the right point, and the finished work shows that the intellectual bond with what went before had been unbroken. But at the same time, of course, the consciousness of the cerebral hemispheres can have no memory of that which the intelligence of their cerebral ganglia wrought in the somnambulistic state, just because it was *suppressed* during that activity, and could consequently receive no impression for revival.

In the psychical functions of the sensory centres, also, just as in those of the centres of the spinal cord, there is exhibited the interweaving of conscious and unconscious psychical activity. I need only mention the circumstance that most of the animal instincts fall into the department of sensori-motor action, *e.g.*, all building instincts. To whom would not occur the comparison of the singing-bird, which monotonously repeats the melodic-rhythmical period of its species, with the epileptic violin-player who plays the once-learned piece during his attack? Save that the singing-bird is at once aware of and enjoys his song with his cerebral consciousness, which was not possible for the epileptic.

It will not be necessary to repeat at this place the argumentation of the preceding section, which here only acquires still greater force. The ganglionic cells of the sensory centres also act reflectorially and mechanically, not therefore less purposively however, but only the more so, as their sphere of motor innervation and their inner faculty of elaborating perceptions is greater than in the case of the spinal cord. In the sensory centres, likewise, the psychical subjectivity goes hand in hand with the external mechanism of the molecular motions, and their consciousness is so much richer and clearer as the impressions conducted from the higher sense-nerves are more numerous and precise than those which the centres of the spinal cord receive from the general nerves of the body, and as their faculty of elaborating perceptions is greater than that of the latter. This higher development of the purposive external mechanics and of the intelligence is, however, merely the two-sided phenomenal expression of a higher (unconscious) purpose, which determines the individual life of the organ in question. Here, as there, the reaction of the will on a motive, the mental elaboration of impressions by the co-operation of many cells, and the purposive modification of function, by whose repetition the purposive disposition of the organ is perfected, go on *altogether unconsciously*. These three highest performances of the organic-psychical individual, which are fundamentally only one and the same function looked at from different sides, make up, however, the inmost core of the individuality of the organ. It might be called the actuality of its individual purpose, which is the same thing as the teleological function of the metaphysical substance, whose accidents or modes are the inner psychical and external material phenomenon of the individualised organ.

It would be a great error to try to see in this preponderating importance of the *unconscious* psychical function in the sensory centres any difference in kind from the functions of the cerebrum. What is added in the cerebrum is in essence only the degree of the elaboration of the perceptions, or, to speak in physiological language, the path within the organ which the stimulus traverses from its first entrance till the discharge into motor reaction. While this stimulus in passing from one cell to another liberates afresh in each a reflexion (perception and reaction), it unfolds into a successive chain of conscious ideas, forming the discursive reflexion which is intercalated between sense-perception and visible reaction, and determines the nature of the latter. But in this increase of the *absolute* number of conscious moments, the *proportion* of this number to that of the co-operating unconscious acts is by no means increased; for *every* progression of a stimulus from one cell to another is a reflex act, which is *per se* unconsciously performed; and the same holds good of the reception of the stimulus by the cell in question and its conversion into conscious perception. All *advance* in discursive reflection is unconscious, and it is as it were only the footsteps of this advance which attain to consciousness. But it is rarely that several such footsteps stand so near one another that we can follow the individual steps; for the most part, their relation to one another points to more or fewer great *leaps* of unconscious psychical function, in which the links of the logical chain are only *implicitly* contained between the conscious extremes.

The development which these thoughts have received above in Section B. has been so frequently misconstrued from the scientific side as speculative mysticism, that it is a peculiar satisfaction to me to be able to cite in confirmation the opinion which the English empiricist Maudsley has formed through his own medical treatment of mental disease and psychological observation. The testimony will be the less carped at by naturalists, as Maudsley himself inclines to Materialism, and tries to go as far as he can with a materialistic interpretation of his psychological observations. He certainly does not everywhere succeed, even in his own opinion, and least of all at the critical points, as we have already seen in one instance.

The existence of an "unconscious life of the mind" Maudsley declares to be established beyond a doubt, and says: "It is a truth which cannot be too distinctly borne in mind, that consciousness is not co-extensive with mind" (p. 25); and adds, that "the most important part of mental action, the essential process on which thinking depends, is unconscious mental activity" (p. 34). "He whose brain makes him conscious that he has a brain is not well, but ill; and thought that is conscious of itself is not natural and healthy thought" (p. 41). "An active consciousness is always detrimental to the best and most successful thought; the thinker who is actively attentive to the succession of his ideas is thinking to little purpose. What the successful thinker observes is that he is conscious of the words which he is uttering or writing, while the thought, unconsciously elaborated by the functional action of the brain, flows from unpenetrated depths into consciousness. . . . *Reflection* is then, in reality, the reflex action of the cells in their relation to the cerebral ganglia; it is the reaction of one cell to a stimulus from a neighbouring cell, and the sequent transference of its energy to another cell—the reflection of it" (p. 308). "The brain not only receives impressions unconsciously,[1] registers impressions without the co-operation of consciousness, elaborates material unconsciously, calls latent residua again into activity without consciousness, but it responds also as an organ of organic life to the internal stimuli which it receives unconsciously from other organs of the body" (p. 35). "Not only is the actual process of the association of our ideas independent of consciousness, but that assimilation or blending of similar ideas, or of the like in different ideas, by which general ideas are formed, is in no way under the control or cognisance of consciousness" (p. 30). "In composition the writer's consciousness is engaged chiefly with his pen and with the sentences which he is forming; while the results of the brain's unconscious working, matured by an insensible gestation, emerge from

[1] This only means here that such impressions can lie below the threshold of the collective consciousness of the cerebral hemispheres; if, however, they are to do something, they must lie above the threshold of the particular cell-consciousness. This distinction is lacking in Maudsley, because he does not firmly hold that a stimulus cannot be at all perceived without either being perceived by a *consciousness* or *producing* such a one.

unknown depths into consciousness, and are by its help embodied in appropriate words" (p. 30). "When the individual brain is a well-constituted one, and has been duly cultivated, the results of its latent activity rising into consciousness suddenly sometimes seem like intuitions; they are strange and startling, as the products of a dream ofttimes are, to the person who has actually produced them" (p. 32). "The best thoughts of an author are always the unwilled thoughts which surprise himself; and the poet under the inspiration of creative activity is, so far as consciousness is concerned, being dictated to. If we reflect, we shall see that it must be so; the products of creative activity, in so far as they transcend the hitherto experienced, are unknown to the creator himself before they come forth, and cannot therefore be the result of a definite act of his will; for to an act of will a conception of the result is necessary" (p. 33). "Therefore it comes to pass at times that, in the investigation of a new order of events by an intellect which is in genial sympathy with Nature, the law of them explicitly declares itself as by a flash of intuition after comparatively few observations. The imagination successfully anticipates the slow results of patient and systematic research, flooding the darkness with the light of a true interpretation, and thus illuminating the obscure relations and intricate connections. Therein a well-endowed and well-cultivated mind manifests its unconscious harmony with Nature. The brightest flashes of genius come unconsciously and without effort; growth is not a voluntary act, although the gathering of food is" (p. 531). "As in the child there is no consciousness of the *ego*, so in the highest development of humanity, as represented by these our greatest, a similar unconsciousness of the *ego* seems to have been reached; and the individual, in intimate and congenial sympathy with Nature, carries forward in organic evolution with a child-like unconsciousness and a child-like success" (p. 61). "Rules and systems are necessary for the ordinarily endowed mortals, whose business it is to gather together and arrange the materials; the genius, who is the architect, has, like Nature, an unconscious system of his own. It is the fate of its nature, and no demerit, that the caterpillar must crawl: it is the fate of its nature, and no merit, that the butterfly must fly" (p. 64). "It is not by introspective prying and torture of its own self-consciousness that mankind evolves the genius; the mature result of its unconscious development flows at due time into consciousness with a grateful surprise, and from time to time the slumbering centuries are thus awakened" (p. 66).[1]

If such a genius suddenly emerges at the right time as fruit of an unconscious development in unconscious harmony with all Nature, which has been nourished on a material blindly prepared by others, such an unconscious psychical process must be looked upon as in the highest sense a *teleological* event, for the explanation of which Maudsley probably would only refer to the unsearchable councils of the Creator. Otherwise expressed, the insufficiency of all materialistic explanations in the unconscious-psychical processes is evident the more we rise to an ever more highly organised centre (whether within one and the same organism or among the many differently constituted individuals of the human race). But since the differences are not of a fundamental kind, but only depend on a difference of the stage of development of the common primitive foundations of the ganglionic cell, this result must also reflect its light upon the con-

[1] "Not unamusing, though somewhat saddening, is it, however, to witness the painful surprise of the man of observation, his jealous indignation and clamorous outcry, when the result at which he and his fellow-labourers have been so patiently, though blindly, working, when the genius-product of the century which he has helped to create, starts into life—when the metamorphosis is completed, and the caterpillar has become a butterfly: amusing, because the patient worker is supremely astonished at a result which, though preparing, he nowise foresaw; saddening, because individually he is annihilated, and all the toil in which he spent his strength is swallowed up in the product which, gathering up the different lines of investigation and thought, and giving to them a unity of development, now by epigenesis ensues" (p. 67).

ception of the simplest reflex processes in the ganglion cell.

7. *The Morphological Significance of the Parts of the Brain.*—The morphological interpretation of the different parts of the brain has only been founded on reliable principles since embryology has come to the aid of comparative anatomy, the importance of which was first clearly recognised by Baer. In the lower orders of worms, *e.g.*, the Turbellaria, the entire central nervous system consists of the bilobed supra-œsophageal ganglion, from which nerve-threads radiate to the different parts of the body. In the Annelida and Articulata this supra-œsophageal ganglion has expanded into an œsophageal ring, and this is continued into the ventral cord; in the larvæ of the Ascidians, in the Amphioxus, and the Vertebrata, on the contrary, the supra-œsophageal ganglion has been prolonged into the spinal cord. In the larva of the Ascidians and the Amphioxus the spinal cord is still a simple uniform strand, which seems to terminate in precisely the same way before and behind, and only with more exact observation can there be perceived in front a slight rounded extremity. In the Cyclostome fishes (Myxine and Petromyzon), at a further stage of embryonic development, this vesicle becomes a pyriform swelling, and thus forms the primitive basis of the vertebrate brain; but then it is differentiated by cross constrictions into several vesicles which lie behind one another in a straight line, and this process of constriction recurs in the embryonic development of all the vertebrata without exception.

At the outset there are formed three sections—Fore-brain, middle brain, and hind-brain; the first might be designated the olfactory ganglion, the second the optic ganglion, the third the auditory ganglion. But soon there appears a further differentiation, the Intermediate-brain being detached from the Fore-brain, and the After-brain from the Hind-brain; the former, might be termed the finer organ for the perceptions of the sense of touch, the latter the centre for the automatic regulation of complicated organic functions subservient to life. In the Cyclostome fishes these five divisions lying in a straight line behind one another and tolerably equal in value, are preserved without essential change of form; in the cartilaginous fishes Middle-brain and After-brain are prominently developed; in the higher vertebrata, on the other hand, Fore-brain and Hind-brain, so that the former overlaps the Intermediate and Middle brain, the latter the After-brain. A distinction of a similar kind again occurs between the reptilia and birds, on the one hand, and the mammalia on the other. In the former, the Middle-brain and the middle part of the cerebellum undergo a relatively important development; in the latter, the Fore-brain more and more overshadows all the other parts, so that at last in monkeys and man it even overlaps the Hind-brain.[1]

In the human brain there belong to the Fore-brain the two *cerebral hemispheres*, corpora striata, corpus callosum and fornix; to the Intermediate-brain the *optic thalami* and the other parts which surround the so-called third ventricle, together with the infundibulum and pineal body; to the Middle-brain the *corpora quadrigemina* and the aqueduct of Sylvius; to the Hind-brain the *hemispheres of the cerebellum* and the middle lobe; to the after-brain the *medulla oblongata*, together with the fourth ventricle, the pyramids, olivary bodies, &c. The original functions of the five parts have been preserved unchanged for the intermediate-brain, middle-brain and after-brain; on the other hand, the Hind-brain or cerebellum has its functional sphere already considerably enlarged in the Amphibia and lower mammalia, and the Fore-brain or cerebrum has in the higher mammalia attained such general importance for all the functions of perception,

[1] Comp. Häckel's Anthropogenie, p. 514-529.

that its original destination as olfactory centre only claims an inconsiderable part of the organ.

According to experiments by Gudden, the brain of new-born birds, whose eyes had been extirpated, remained undeveloped, whilst in rabbits the development of the brain was not thereby impeded (Wundt, p. 194); this proves how much more important a part the function of the corpora quadrigemina, excited by the visual sense, plays in the mental life of birds than in that of mammals. If, on the other hand, the olfactory nerve of new-born dogs be divided, they are no longer capable of any intellectual and emotional development, and give the impression of unsympathetic and feeble-minded individuals. This proves how much the mental life of these mammals depends on the sense of smell.

Now, if we consider that the intelligence displayed by the Middle-brain and Fore-brain, as we saw in the preceding section, is only different in degree, it might appear almost a matter of accident that just the Fore-brain or the olfactory ganglion, and not the tactile, visual, or auditory ganglion, has, in the higher vertebrata, attained so enormous a development, that the groups of ganglion-cells adjunct to the original olfactory ganglion have become a kind of universal centre, in which, in addition to the olfactory organ, the other sense-organs also, nay, even all the parts of the body and the lower centres, obtain a central representation. The importance to life of the olfactory organ taken alone would hardly afford sufficient explanation of this; more pertinent seems the consideration that the Fore-brain occupies a position of polar antagonism to the spinal cord and medulla oblongata, that it lies *peripherally* in respect to the centre or centres of gravity of the central nervous system. This sounds perhaps paradoxical, but has all the deeper significance. As the whole nervous system arises phylogenetically and embryologically from the skin-sense lamina, *i.e.*, from the extreme periphery of the organism, that part of the central nervous system also, which leads to the mental centre of self-consciousness, must have a peripheral importance for the organism as such and its organic life.

For the organism as such the centre of gravity of the central nervous system lies neither in the too little efficient spinal cord, nor in the cerebral hemispheres, whose conscious - spiritual purposive activity already appears as something transcending the immediate ends of organic life, but in the parts interposed between Fore-brain and spinal cord, which guide the universal reflex processes of the organism and adapt its vital actions to the external circumstances mirrored in sense-perception. This relation finds also an anatomical expression in the circumstance that the groups of ganglion-cells in the stem of the brain and the spinal cord aggregate into central medullary masses, which send out conducting fibres towards the periphery; in the hemispheres, however, the grey matter forms an *external cortical layer* to which tend the diverging conducting paths of the trunk of the brain. This contrast is not yet clearly developed in the more solid or less hollow cerebrum of fishes and amphibia; here the whole mass of the hemispheres is traversed by grey matter in an irregular fashion, so that we have before us a transitional stage from the formation of the nucleus to the cortex. The cerebellar hemispheres, on the other hand, exhibit already in fishes a clearer severance of the cortical layer from the nucleus (comp. W., p. 55-56, note), and this development of the cerebellum in excess of the cerebrum proves that the former has in these animals also to perform functions of a higher order.

Having already briefly discussed in the foregoing section the functions of the after-brain or medulla oblongata, we now proceed to the consideration in detail of the four other parts of the brain.

8. *The Centres of the Space-Senses.*—Of all the parts of

the brain, the function of the Middle-brain or of the corpora quadrigemina (called bigemina in lower vertebrata) has been longest and most certainly known. The parallel development of the corpora quadrigemina with the acuteness of the sense of sight in the animal kingdom leaves us to infer that this centre has the office of working up the visual impressions, and of reflectorially calling forth those movements which are in relation with visual impressions. Destruction of the corpora quadrigemina produces not only blindness, but also paralysis of the movement of the eye and accommodation. One must therefore assume that the cerebral hemispheres only receive the visual perceptions in the form prepared by the corpora quadrigemina, and that only those movements which are caused by a co-operation of visual and other sense-impressions proceed from the hemispheres, but that such movements or modifications of continuous movements, which are exclusively determined by impressions of sight, are independently cared for mainly by the corpora quadrigemina. The accommodation of the eyes is governed by the posterior, the ocular movements by the anterior tubercles of the corpora quadrigemina; and according to Adamük, stimulation of the anterior tubercles on the right side produces movements of both eyes to the left, on the left side movements to the right. The stimulation of the front of the anterior tubercles causes the visual axes to assume a horizontal direction; that of the middle part raises and renders them convergent; that of the hindermost part leads to a downward movement, with still stronger convergence (Wundt, p. 147).

Not quite so well established is the significance of the (improperly named) optic thalami or of the intermediate-brain. Wundt (p. 198) probably correctly regards them as the *tactile centre*, according to the analogy of the just-mentioned visual centre, *i.e.*, as the organ which mediates "the functional union of locomotion with the sensations of touch" (perhaps also with the muscular sense or specific feeling of muscular movement). The optic thalami also act independently of the will of the cerebral hemispheres as primary regulators, whereby certainly the will of the hemispheres is not precluded from employing them, in order to enable more complicated movements to be executed by them on a given command. At all events, they must in all bodily movements, even though initiated by the will of the hemispheres, co-operate as *regulators*, without which the *estimation* of the movement as a whole and in all its parts would be wanting. We are, namely, always compelled to estimate the *degree* of our several muscular contractions according to the *position* which the particular muscles assume at any moment in relation *to the other* parts of the body; but this position is ascertained by the sense of touch. If the service of the latter is interrupted, the visual sense can in an extreme case act vicariously for the sense of touch, as in the case of a person suffering from *Tabes dorsualis* of the spinal cord, whose tactile feeling in the lower limbs had been lost; or in the instance of a woman with anaesthesia of one arm, who always let her child fall when she averted her gaze from it. The compensation of the visual sense is here always imperfect, and never attains the direct certainty of reflex action like the regulation by the sense of touch executed by the optic thalami. If the optic thalamus be injured on one side, this reflex regulation is destroyed for one-half of the body. Whilst now the muscles of one-half the body act correctly, those of the other are smitten by a sudden helplessness, which looks astonishingly like paralysis, without indeed being paralysis; and the result is an unsymmetrical locomotion, which is called, on account of the tendency to rotation of the head, "circus movement" (Wundt, p. 196–199). That there is no actual paralysis is evident from this, that the disturbance comes to an end in course of time by the will of the hemispheres learning to correct the faulty movements. The purposive movements to escape made by rabbits or frogs after removal of their hemispheres and corpora striata sequent on *cutaneous irritation* may be referred to the optic thalami as their centre. A confirmation of this hypothesis is the circumstance that such a frog, after injury of one optic thalamus, carries out its attempts to flee in the form of circus movement.

The close juxtaposition of the corpora quadrigemina and optic thalami, the demonstrable paths of communication between them, and the circumstance that in lower vertebrata (*e.g.*, frogs) the optic thalami are insignificant, and their functions partially performed by the corpora quadrigemina, seems to point to a closer connection of the two centres, which would correspond to the close affinity of the senses of sight and touch. These two are the *only spatial* senses which we possess—senses, *i.e.*, which spread out their sensations in space; and the supposition does not seem to me unfounded that the ideal fusion of the tactile and visual space into the indivisible space-perception which we are wont unconsciously to effect must have here a similar physiological foundation, as the blending of the visual space of the right eye with that of the left eye into an indivisible visual space possesses in the chiasma of the optic nerve. In the same way it is not improbable that the union of the corpora quadrigemina with the optic thalami can independently introduce certain movements, which may be termed reflexes to such space-perceptions, as are combined of sensations of sight and touch.

These assumptions will hardly meet with opposition when we remember that the left half of the corpora quadrigemina only contains the left half of the binocular visual image, the right half only the corresponding right one, so that both halves of the image can *only* be brought to blend into a single and whole image *by the co-operation of both halves of the organ.* Finally, these suppositions also find support in this, that for the regulation of the position of the several bodily parts in space there is yet a second organ, the posterior brain or cerebellum, which, it is true, is influenced also by the other sense-organs (especially the senses of hearing and equilibrium and sense of sight), but likewise is especially determined in its functions by the sense of touch. One may comprehend from this development of the Hind-brain exceeding its original purpose as auditory ganglion that the intermediate-brain, or the optic thalami, may lag behind in their development in most animals, without prejudice to the organism; it would, however, not harmonise with our views on the purposive economy of the organism if *two* organs existed to fulfil a single purpose. We shall rather have to assume that the perceptions of the sense of touch which take place in the optic thalami and those which occur in the cerebellum are *made use of* in an altogether different way. Whilst in the cerebellum the impressions of touch are pre-eminently combined with those of the sense of equilibrium, so as to gain as perfect a *total perception* as possible of the position of the whole body and of its several parts in space, the intuition of the tactile space seems to be prepared in the optic thalami for the perception of the cerebral hemispheres, in like manner as that of visual space in the corpora quadrigemina, and to be fused into the indivisible tactile-visual space even before the entrance into the hemispheres. If this mode of conceiving the matter is correct, it also explains why the consciousness of the hemispheres feels itself unable to dissolve again the fusion of tactile and visual space, although in abstract reflection it perceives the heterogeneity and duality of the two spaces to be beyond a doubt. If this fusion were only a product of the activity of the hemispheres, there would probably be no particular difficulty in producing again the whole element in intuition also. The like holds of the impossibility of decomposing the superficial extension of the visual perception into its non-spatial elements of sensation; whilst, on the other hand, the possibility of this process with the third dimension of space or that of depth is an argument in favour of the supposition that the chief part of the genesis of the perception of depth only appertains to the hemispheres.

9. *The Cerebellum.*—The theory of the functions of the cerebellum is still open to considerable doubt. It is certain that the opinion of Gall of a close relation of the same to the sexual functions is incorrect; the centre for the latter is rather still to be sought in the medulla oblongata.[1] On the other hand, the parallelism in the development of the muscling of the body and of the cerebellum which runs through the whole vertebrate kingdom shows that this organ must be of importance for an energetic innervation of the muscles, and that the muscles under normal circumstances draw a considerable part of their impulse of innervation from the cerebellum. This, however, does not entitle us to designate with Luys the cerebellum the *source of energy of all* motor innervation, since even after destruction of the cerebellum any energetic movements may be called forth by all the other centres, and these latter can, to a certain extent, compensate for the loss of the cerebellum.

What we know with the utmost certainty of the cerebellum, because we do not demonstrate it by vivisection, but by the most numerous experiments in the living man, is the fact that it is the organ of *dizziness* in all its forms. Dizziness may be produced by unilateral injuries of the organ, by one-sided pressure on the same, by cross conduction of a galvanic current, finally by the visual perceptions of moving objects, nay, even by merely imaginary ideas of possible movements, which are connected with certain visual perceptions. As is well known, dizziness is a phenomenon not subject to caprice, *i.e.*, to the will of the cerebral hemispheres, and exhibits itself as disturbance of the involuntary regulation of the bodily movements. As partial disturbance of the function of the cerebellum produces partial disturbance of sensation in both eyes (here too the decussation is a partial one in the same sense as in the corpora quadrigemina), it produces an altered idea of the situation of the eyeball, and thereby an apparent motion

[1] Longet, Anatomy and Physiology of the Nervous System; I. 615.

of objects, to which there is added with greater degrees of dizziness an obscuration of the field of vision. Since the organ continues to be functional, and endeavours to adapt the deportment to the sensations, if the sensations are pathologically perverted, this adaptation must lead to objectively distorted muscular movements, and these are the *rotatory movements*, which accompany every dizziness, although in the weakest degrees of giddiness the particular impulses of innervation of the cerebellum are paralysed by opposite ones on the part of the cerebrum (W., p. 207–221).

If we now ask how, of all the central organs subserving the regulation of the bodily movements with respect to their situation in space, it is precisely the *auditory* ganglion that has come to be the most important, the key to this enigma must lie herein, that the specific sense of equilibrium is in the closest connection with the organ of hearing, and therefore has also been assigned for its central representation in the first degree to the same ganglion as the sense of hearing. This sense of equilibrium is located in the three semi-circular canals, which must be termed a manometer for the inner hydrostatic pressure variously exerted in the direction of the three axes situated at right angles to one another, and whose injury calls forth the same phenomena of giddiness and rotatory movements as those of the cerebellum itself. This organ of equilibrium ascertains the right position of the *head* in respect of the line of gravity, and as the attitude of the body in relation to the head is determined by sensations of touch, indirectly the position of the body as a whole. It is clear that this sense of equilibrium could only be developed *pari passu* with the evolution of the corresponding centre, and that this correlative development of the cerebellum must consist in the unfolding of reflex tendencies with a view to the regulation of the deportment according to the sensation of equilibrium. Thus the development of the centre for the sense of equilibrium soon outstripped that of the centre for the sense of hearing in the Hind-brain, and whilst the sense of hearing probably found pretty early a second central representation in the Fore-brain, the centre of equilibrium set itself with other subsidiary aids to fulfil its own task, in the first place, in alliance with the nervous bundles of the sense of touch of the whole body, in the second place, in conjunction with the sense of sight.

From this connection there also results an explanation of the circumstance that among vertebrate animals living in water and air the development of the cerebellum is, on the whole, more considerable than in animals living on the surface of the earth. For in creeping and walking the sense of touch aided by the horizontal surface of the ground already affords a tolerable support, which makes the regulation according to the sense of equilibrium to appear less urgent, but in flying, and quite specially in swimming in deep water, the sense of equilibrium affords the chief, if not the sole, foundation of regulation.

In man the original connection of cerebellum and sense of hearing is, strictly speaking, only displayed in two points—firstly, in that the nervous constitution of the organ of hearing is developed in the embryo from the vesicle of the Hind-brain; and, secondly, in that the musical rhythm received through the ear involuntarily impels to rhythmical movements. We shall not go far wrong if we designate the cerebellum the *centre for dancing*, and the fact that a weary troop marches on with fresh elasticity with the striking up of military music is explained by the fact that, instead of the fatigued cerebrum, corpora striata, and optic thalami, now the cerebellum as fresh organ especially undertakes the innervation of the muscles. Although almost all the senses seem to possess a tolerably perfect central representation in the cerebellum, yet on its destruction the sense-perception of the cerebral hemispheres is not affected. This is proved by the latter receiving no class of sense-perceptions (not even those of hearing) through the medium of the cerebellum in the sense in which they receive the visual perceptions through the medium of the corpora quadrigemina.

The hemispheres of the cerebellum are, with the exception of the hemispheres of the cerebrum, the sole centre, which has developed a cortical layer of grey matter, and this circumstance points to the fact that the passage from the compact nuclear formation to that of a superficial distribution serves in both cases the same end. This end can only be the reflexion of the provinces of the body in provinces of the grey cortical layer. A compact nucleus is more adapted to the collection of impressions streaming in from the periphery into an indivisible whole. Where, however, the point in question is how to act on any single province of the whole body apart from the rest, a superficial distribution of the acting layer will be a more suitable formation for the distinct separation of the motor innervation of different provinces than a compact nucleus affording no facilities for the separation of the several parts. Although the attempt to prove the mirroring of the provinces of the body in the cortical layer of the cerebellum has not as yet succeeded, we shall still be obliged to assume it, relying on the analogy of the cortical layer of the cerebrum, where this proof has recently been forthcoming for the several parts.

Whether the functions of the cerebellum are really exhausted with the performances of which we have spoken must be considered as at least doubtful. In any case, it is in the vertebrate animal kingdom the *first* centre to be developed, and even in man the most *highly* developed centre next to the Fore-brain, and it would certainly be rash to assert that our knowledge had at present exhausted the purpose of this organ.

10. *The Fore-Brain.*—By the experiments of Fritsch and Hitzig definite centres of innervation have been proved to exist in the grey cortical layer of the cerebral hemispheres for particular groups of muscles (*e.g.*, for the extensors of the fore-leg, the flexors of the fore-leg, the muscles of the neck, the muscles of the hind-leg, &c.),

lying together in a limited part of the anterior and lateral surface (W., p. 168). The places in question have already reacted on weak galvanic currents, and if the stimulation of other parts has not hitherto been followed by motor or sensory effects, that perhaps lies partly in an unsuitable intensity and quality of the stimuli applied, partly in the rapid blunting of the irritability in consequence of the exposure of the brain. Extirpation of the motor centre alluded to causes disturbance of the movements in question of some duration, but, in course of time, a normal state of things recurs.

Another part of the anterior lobes has long been known by pathological observations as a centre of language. Speechlessness or aphasia is divided into an *ataetic* and an *amnesic* kind; in the former the patient will not succeed in giving the conception which floats before his mind its linguistic sign; in the latter, different words are confused with one another. Perhaps this difference points to two different centres, which must co-operate in the function of language (W., p. 230).—Further supports for the exact determination of the distribution of the central seat of perception and innervation are still entirely wanting, and the assertions of phrenology rest on weak foundations.[1]

[1] From recent experiments on monkeys, in which single parts of the brain were electrically irritated and then made inactive by destruction, David Ferrier asserts that he has obtained results which, if they are confirmed, would again represent an appreciable progress in our knowledge of the physiology of the brain (comp. "Proceedings of the Royal Society," vol. xxiii., No. 162). He first asserts that removal of the frontal regions and posterior lobes impairs neither the power of feeling nor the capacity of moving; but that the former disturbs intelligence and attentive observation, and the latter calls forth a state of depression of common feeling even to refusal of food. Further, according to him, the various senses have the following central representation in the cerebrum: vision in the "angulargyrus," hearing in the upper half of the superior temporo-sphenoidal convolutions, common sensation (tactile sense) in the "Hippocampus major" and the uncinate convolutions, smell in the "subiculum of Ammon" or the "uncinate convolution," taste in the lower part of the "temporo-sphenoidal lobe." All these central representations correspond to the sense-organ of the opposite half of the body, with the exception of the olfactory centres, which correspond to the nostrils of the same side.

In the large hemispheres more than in any other part of the brain the several groups of ganglia can act vicariously for one another, and therefore injuries and disturbances, which do not at the same time affect the corpora striata or the peduncle of the cerebrum, disappear more easily and completely than in any other centre whatsoever. Considerable losses of substance of both hemispheres, or one-sided loss of a whole hemisphere, are sustained by pigeons without permanent change in their behaviour, and by rabbits and dogs with a certain loss of intelligence. Even in man total destruction of a cerebral lobe without palpable disturbance has often been observed, although here more widespread injuries of both sides are always sure to be accompanied by motor disturbances, more rarely by those of the senses or of the psychical functions (W., p. 222).

These facts prove that, although specific tendencies to definite functions are found in the cortical layer of the cerebrum at certain places, these specific energies have here still only a relative, not an absolute, importance; that here, too, they are only a consequence of habituation to a certain kind of action continued for generations, whose nature again is conditioned by the commissural connections and the stimuli conveyed by the same (W., p. 231). If these connections and the relations to the rest of the nervous system depending thereon change, in spite of the (partly innate, partly individually acquired) dispositions in a short time other specific functions are exercised by the parts concerned, so that no break occurs in the psychical and organic functions as a whole.

This substitution is favoured partly by the anatomically uniform nature of the grey cortical substance in all parts of the hemispheres, partly by the extraordinarily rich and numerous connections of the several parts with one another. These connections, if we disregard the fibres of the Corona forming the continuation of the ascending path, are of three kinds: (1) the callosal fibres which form commissures between similarly situated parts of both hemispheres; (2) the arcuate fibres which unite the cortical surface of neighbouring sinuses; and (3) the longitudinal commisures which put remote parts of each single hemisphere into communication with one another (W., p. 157).

It is only the abundance and excellence of these paths which makes possible such a facile psychical communication of all the ganglionic cells of the anterior brain with one another, that their more vivid perceptions flow together into a single consciousness by the act of communication and comparison, which, *e.g.*, does not obtain between the perceptions of the cerebellum and those of the fore-brain. Now, as that consciousness which philosophises and writes books is the consciousness of the cerebral hemispheres, it is evident that it cannot know anything directly of a consciousness of the cerebellum; it is an ignoring of the impossibility of gazing directly into the consciousness of the cerebellum with the philosophising consciousness, when Wundt and others think they can from this fact deny a consciousness of the cerebellum and of the sensory centres (W., p. 713–715). Undoubtedly there exist paths of communication between all the other nerve-centres and the cerebral hemispheres, so that not merely all peripheral provinces of the body, but also all subordinate central organs obtain representation in them; but these connections must, for *teleological* considerations, *be rendered difficult* in order that the whole advantage of the division of labour among independent centres, and the disburdening from common work thereby effected, and the concentration on mental interests, *may not be lost again* for the fore-brain. Either, therefore, the existing paths will serve only for transmitting commands to the executive sub-officers, or (as on the part of the corpora quadrigemina) to conduct the synthetically prepared material of sensation, or only specially powerful and strong impressions are telegraphed to the fore-brain. In all cases, however, the large hemispheres are conscious of the stimuli conducted from other centres (just as those directly received from sense organs) only as their own stimulations, for what is perceived is only the modification of one's own condition by the stimulus. Reciprocal action is wanting *in the same sense* in which it takes place among the ganglion-cells of the hemispheres, and from which the compound phenomenon of a consciousness of a higher stage of individuality results through the comparison of both perceptions in both cells. In lower animals, *e.g.*, the Cyclostome fishes (Myxine and Petromyzon), where no one of the five parts of the brain has attained decided predominance, but all five regulate their affairs separately, such co-ordination as there is being due to simple superposition, although the parts are not without organic connection, there can be just as little talk about an indivisible consciousness as representative of the organic unity of the individual as in a tapeworm, a piece of coral, or an oak tree, although in these instances the relations between the different consciousnesses become ever looser. The Myxine has not one but *five* brain-consciousnesses, which only in their totality, along with the numerous consciousnesses of the spinal cord and other cells, represent the *whole* psychical life of the animal. Man is altogether in the same case; one of those five, however, the consciousness of his cerebral hemispheres, has been so uniquely developed in advance of all the others, and has acquired such a predominance over the latter, that it includes in itself not only qualitatively and quantitatively the *chief part* of the psychical life of the individual man, but also has become, by taking the lead in the government of the motor muscles, the psychical counterpart of the organic unity of the human individuality. Wundt altogether mistakes these relations when he lays down the false proposition that the consciousness of a coherent nervous system must always be a single one, and that *therefore* within a nervous system different co- or sub-ordinate kinds of consciousness may be assumed to be impossible (714 above, 715 below).

It was mentioned above that the fore-brain is originally

an olfactory ganglion; in the human embryo the development of the nervous foundation of the organ of smell still proceeds from the most anterior vesicle of the brain. Even in the cartilaginous fishes the olfactory organ is prominently developed, and the anterior part of the Fore-brain is prolonged into two "olfactory lobes" which in many higher vertebrata unite to form an "olfactory bulb." In man, where not only the hemispheres have attained an extraordinary size as organs of ideational activity, but also the sense of smell falls into the background as compared with the other senses, the olfactory centre is also of moderate size, and is tolerably concealed in the basal part of the head of the corpora striata. The circumstance that fibres of the olfactory nerve as well as bundles of motor-fibres of the peduncle of the cerebrum meet here leads us to conclude, that from this spot those reflexes are effected which are initiated by odorous impressions (W., p. 202).

The remaining mass of the corpora striata, together with the nucleus lenticularis, is to be regarded as an intermediary for the conduction of the impulses of the will from the lobes of the hemispheres to the muscles (W., p. 203). This is confirmed both by vivisection and in the case of man by pathological evidence, as also by the parallelism of the development of the hemispheres and corpora striata in the animal kingdom. The disturbances of movement of the nature of paralysis after apoplectic fits spring very frequently from apoplectic inhibitions of function in the corpora striata, and in man the result of disease of the corpora striata and of the motor parts of the hemispheres is pretty much alike, save that in the latter case recovery takes place much more easily. The corpora striata are accordingly (apart from the olfactory centre) to be designated *centres for the co-ordination of voluntary movements* (initiated by the hemispheres). They execute on a single voluntary impulse combined movements, whose mode of combination may be partly innate, partly acquired by practice, but which are still always felt as *voluntary* movements so far as the hemispheres are conscious of their impulse of innervation, and merely not conscious of the intermediary functions concerned in the execution of the mandate.

11. *The Co-operation and Subordination of the Nerve-centres.*—Having in the preceding sections examined the functions of the different parts of the nervous system, we are in a position to render an account to ourselves of the purposive connection of the whole.

Whoever should approach the organism of the higher vertebrata with the preconceived opinion that in it, as in the plant, everything is accomplished by democratic co-operation of cell-individuals with equal rights, would, when he considered the intensive concentration of the sway of the higher over the lower elements and of the cerebral hemispheres over the whole, be convinced that he was possessed by prejudice. Whoever, on the other hand, from the standpoint of a one-sided psychology should bring with him the opposite opinion that a single central organ guides and governs all, that nothing happens without its order, and everything happens only as it has been prescribed even to the smallest detail, would again have to be taught by the facts that, in spite of a rigid centralisation for the common interests of the collective organism, and in spite of a certain sovereignty of the supreme authority, this latter is yet relieved of all pettifogging details, because the principle of the *self-government* of subordinate spheres is thoroughly carried out in a remarkable manner. The whole organism is only developed and preserved by the continual self-activity of all the single individual cells, as the state only by the self-activity of all the citizens; but the social activity of these individuals is not, as in the simple form of a small democratic republic, uniformly distributed, but graduated in many ways.

The individuals arrange themselves in groups or families

of the most diverse form, each of which represents a higher stage of individuality, and endeavours to fulfil a higher individual aim; the groups likewise coalesce into circles, and these into provinces, and the provinces obtain a government of their own through special functionaries. As such a province we may understand the sum of those parts of the organism which are traversed and innervated by one and the same nerve. The magistracy of the provincial government of such a province would be the first centre in the spinal cord (or in the brain) with which the particular nerve comes in contact, *i.e.*, into which it enters or from which it springs. These provincial governments now have further governing-bodies, which however are only distinguished partially by *local* demarcation from the sub-offices pertaining to them, in another part by *qualitative* separation of their departments like the various ministries within the same central government. Lastly, over these different provinces is enthroned the chief of the executive, who, however, has at the same time reserved to himself a province of his own for independent work. The various ministers here, however, form no council, but each rules independently over his own sphere; and although between related provinces direct communication takes place to facilitate common functions, yet the establishment of complete unanimity is not left to their collective agreement, but is assured by the direction which they collectively receive from the highest power in the state.

This supreme governor occupies, then, pretty much the position of a gifted monarch who performs the part of his own prime minister without thereby limiting the spontaneous action of any minister in his own department, or of the president of a republic who disdains being, like a constitutional prince, merely the dot upon the *i*, and not only reigns, but also actually governs. Thus the organism, as model of an artistic union of guiding-head, independent provincial government, local self-government, and individual self-activity, keeps the right mean between democratic anarchy and centralised autocracy.[1] What this organisation of Nature has least affinity with is the constitutional system with its parliamentary machinery and the ideal brutality of its government by majorities. However, it would perhaps be hazardous to reproach Nature that it also has not followed this doctrinaire model, which, until quite recently, passed pretty generally as the ideal of political organisation. It were rather worth considering whether, conversely, our modern political wisdom might not derive a stimulus to fresh revision of its doctrines from the study of the arrangement of the natural organism.

Through the provinces being in great part not demarcated from one another by localisation of the sphere of government, but by the qualitative difference of offices, there results the peculiar phenomenon that each province of the body is represented *in more than one* brain-centre, and according to the nature of the stimulus or motive can derive its impulses of innervation now from this, now from that centre. This result is one of the most important achievements of modern nerve-physiology, and thoroughly disposes of the popular prejudice that for every province of the body *a single* corresponding centre has to be sought in the brain. Undoubtedly the brain forms in a certain sense a reflected image of the whole body according to its provinces of innervation. It is also correct that this reflected image is in one respect simpler than the original, namely, so far as a physiological element in the centre corresponds to a sphere of motor innervation of relatively considerable extent, whose joint action is effected by the former by means of a single impulse. But in another direction the reflected image is more complete

[1] "The cells are individuals, and as in the state, so here, there are individuals of higher dignity and of lower dignity; but the well-being and power of the higher individuals are entirely dependent upon the well-being and contentment of the humble workers in the spinal cord, which do so great a part of the daily work of life" (M. 180.)

than the original, because it does not offer a single, but (like the image of a mirror cut with facettes) a repeated reflection (W., p. 227–228). In this way, *e.g.*, all the provinces of the body are represented both in the cortex of the cerebrum and in that of the cerebellum, and, moreover, even in the optic thalami and in the corpora striata, and, lastly, by far the largest part once again in the spinal cord, including the medulla oblongata. One and the same movement of a bodily province, namely, can be innervated by a reflexion from the spinal cord or medulla oblongata, or be excited by the optic thalami on occasion of tactile sensations, or be called forth by the cerebellum to preserve one's balance, or spring from the corpora striata, which have received their impulse from the cerebral hemispheres, or, lastly, perhaps be also produced directly by the latter (with evasion of all the other centres except the spinal cord).

Now every one of the centres which have been named (with the exception of the cerebral hemispheres) can again send the same motor impulse downwards on *two sorts* of occasions, or in each of these centres the stored-up energies can be set free in one of the directions pre-designated by the existing tendencies by means of stimuli of two different kinds: firstly, through such as are conducted *from below*, and secondly, to such as are conducted from a *superior* centre. The former are the perceptions conveyed by sensory nerves, the latter are the result of the direct action of the higher governing bodies; in both cases the centre in question reacts independently, conformably to its individual purpose, on the received stimulation; in both cases we have therefore to do with a *reflex act*, which reveals the inner teleology of the independent mode of action of the centre (W., p. 830).

Marshall Hall had based his reflex theory on the assumption of separate paths for reflexes on the one hand, and for the sensory and motor excitements leading to and coming from the brain on the other. This assumption can, however, be established neither physiologically nor anatomically; on the contrary, everything favours the identity of both paths in the sense just explained. In the more simply constructed spinal cord of fishes anatomical inquiry renders it directly probable "that the same ganglion cells which give off motor fibres to the nerve-roots effect by ascending processes a union with the more highly situated motor centres, and by others running backwards with the sensory parts" (W., p. 121–122).

It is clear that an arrangement of the sensory and motor paths making possible the mode of action laid down, must correspond to the repeated reflexion of all or very many provinces of the body by means of the different centres. We may connect with this what was remarked above in Section 3 on conduction in the spinal cord. We there saw how the possibility of the reflexes of the spinal cord was bound up with the further conduction of the stimuli of sensation to higher centres. In the uppermost part of the spinal cord or in the medulla oblongata all the motor and all the sensory fibres unite into a motor and a sensory main path, each of which again divides in the medulla oblongata into several branches. The main motor path first divides into two main branches, of which one leads through the peduncle of the cerebrum to the fore-brain, and the other to the parts of the middle-brain. The former remains purely motor, the latter enters in the centres, where it terminates, into direct connection with parts of the sensory path. The former divides into two sub-divisions, of which one directly leads to the motor part of the cortex of the cerebral hemispheres, whilst the other terminates in the corpora striata and nucleus lenticularis; the latter main branch, on the other hand, divides into three subdivisions. Of these, the one leads through the laqueus to the corpora quadrigemina, the others through the tegmentum to the optic thalami, and the third finally to the cerebellum (W., p. 165).

Thus we see how each of the different centres has its

share in the main conduction which leads downwards to the provinces of the body. That, for the rest, each of these ramifications not merely represents a part of the corporeal provinces, but all taken together, is only made possible by this, that all the conducting fibres are interrupted both on their entrance into the spinal cord, and also further above by ganglion-cells, so that an association of many conducting fibres coming from below repeatedly takes place by means of the grey matter, and a carrying forward of the conduction in an upward direction through several co-ordinate fibres, each of which has now the same significance for all the conducting fibres below in connection with it.

The course of the chief sensory path is in this distinguished from that of the motor path, that only a *small* part of it leads directly to the cortex of the cerebrum; a second branch turns here too to the cortex of the cerebellum, and a third in several subdivisions to the anterior and middle ganglia of the brain (W., p. 165–166). The latter branch offers here, at all events, a partial compensation for the small size of the branch leading direct to the cortex of the cerebrum, because it is to be assumed that the consciousness of the hemispheres receives the chief part of its sense-perceptions (with perhaps the sole exception of the perceptions of hearing) only through the intervention of the sensory ganglia, which work up the stimuli of the sensory nerves independently into orderly and complete perceptions. The sensory paths to the great hemispheres, whether direct or through the sensory ganglia, seem to find their central ending in such districts of the cortex as lie *behind* the fissure of Sylvius, so that thus in general the anterior parts of the cortical layer are to be regarded more as motor, the posterior more as sensory, central parts (W., p. 167), and would stand in a similar relation to one another as the anterior and posterior columns of the grey matter of the cord.

The varied manner whereby one and the same movement may be set up, and the variety of the intermediate stages which a motor impulse issuing from the cerebral hemisphere can traverse, afford a clear insight into the relative facility with which, on the functions of a centre being disturbed, an adjustment can take place by the vicarious action of other centres. One can, of course, here not leave out of sight the fact that pathological processes for the most part acquire in course of time a wider distribution, and thereby frequently again destroy the adjustment which has already taken place. That, however, even in those cases where only a single centre loses its functions there occurs a strong disturbance of all motor phenomena, is an argument in favour of the view that in normal circumstances the path for any complex movement innervated by the hemispheres is that which is best exercised and usually employed.

Complete incapability of motion or paralysis is therefore only induced by arrest of the function of several chief centres, or by interruption of the chief motor path from the brain to the body. An incomplete paralysis, however, presents an entirely different picture, according as the disturbance of function or arrest of conduction relates to the Fore-brain or to the Intermediate, Middle, and Hind brains. In both cases the execution of all movements is still possible; but in the former case it occurs only as involuntary movement of reflexion or regulation; in the latter case only as voluntary movement. If the arrest of function concerns the Fore-brain or the *crus cerebri*, the influence of conscious will (innervation of the hemispheres) is impaired, but the involuntary movements remain untouched by it (*paresia*). On the other hand, if the arrest of function concerns the middle parts of the brain or the paths leading thereto (*laqueus* and *tegmentum*), the conscious will (after overcoming the first disturbance) retains, it is true, its sway over every single province of innervation, but the regulation and involuntary combination of movements is wanting (*ataxy*). In the former case, the sick person has to make great efforts to overcome the arrest of function by the innervation of the hemispheres, and his movements become truly troublesome and difficult, his gait dragging. In the latter case, the will of the hemispheres must see to all the detail of movement, for which, in other cases, the subordinate centres would make far better provision, and the movements thereby become unsure (even perhaps trembling), the gait hesitating (W., p. 205–206).

A question which must not be left undiscussed is the following:—On what does it depend whether a stimulus affecting the periphery of the body liberates at once a reflex reaction in the particular spinal centre, or only in some one of the higher centres? The mere strength of the stimulus alone cannot here be decisive; for it is indeed true that a stimulus propagates with certainty its excitation to a greater height the stronger it is, and that no centre remains closed to the strongest stimuli; but, on the other side, we also know that the weakest of all stimuli are able to reach the cerebral hemispheres, and that in the normal state of waking life reflexes of the subordinate centres can only be set up in consequence of a relatively very small part of all the stimuli affecting the organism. This state of things is explained by the general law that, as the ganglion-cell exerts on the nerve-fibre an influence, so every higher centre on those subject to it, which simultaneously *lowers* the *reflex irritability* of the lower centres, and diminishes the *resistance* in conducting to the higher centre. This centrifugal current of innervation, *inhibitory* in respect of the spontaneity of the lower centres but helpful for the perception of the higher centre, exists, in the first place, as a persisting tone in the whole nervous system; secondly, it is reflectorially called forth in a more intense degree on the preliminary announcement of stimuli; and, thirdly, it can be voluntarily sent out from the cerebral hemispheres as result of a conscious reflex process. The latter case gives us the psychological interpretation of the inner nature of this current of innervation, which now appears on its negative side as *inhibiting will*, on its positive side as *attention*.

It is well known that the involuntary inclination to reflex movements (*e.g.*, to shrink on being tickled, or to dance with expressive dance-music) may be suppressed by the conscious will, which must have different degrees of energy according to the strength of the reflex tendency. This however means, in physiological language, that the cerebral hemispheres may innervate the reflex centres in question in such a way that their reflex irritability is momentarily lowered, or that their tendency to reflexion is paralysed by negative impulses. To the same series of phenomena belongs the fact that the conscious will in the healthy waking state keeps in check the instinctive impulses which are rooted in lower central organs (*e.g.*, food- and sex-instinct), but that in dreams, when the activity of the cerebral hemispheres is enfeebled, or on morbid disturbance of the same, these impulses press forward in ruthless and shameless fashion, and in madmen, *e.g.*, often enough seek their satisfaction without restraint in the crudest fashion. It is teleologically of the highest importance that the reflex actions of the lower centres only display their unchecked activity precisely when the cerebrum is deprived of power by sleep, or is claimed by another direction of the attention; it is just the same as in political life, where the governor of a province only acts without reserve on his own initiative, when the prince is not present to take his supreme resolves, or if he be otherwise occupied, and cannot therefore concern himself at the moment with the affairs of a province.

I have (comp. vol. i. p. 131–132, 174–176, 275–276, and vol. ii. p. 105–108) represented attention as a centrifugal current of innervation facilitating conduction, which may be caused partly by reflex ideation, partly by ingoing stimuli, and this often-impugned conception is confirmed in all the main points by the thoroughgoing investigations of Wundt (W., p. 717-725).

Suppose some one is reading a book, and a person present in the room puts a question to him; undoubtedly the subject of the question will not immediately affect the consciousness of his hemispheres, but yet the latter have been stimulated. It is, as it were, a notice-signal, such as the telegraphist sends before forwarding a dispatch. This stimulus suffices to turn reflectorially the current of innervation of attention in this particular direction, and the result is, that the consciousness of the hemispheres *after an interval* takes notice of the question perceived in the auditory centre, and not yet obliterated there. Here appears the importance of highly developed independent sensory ganglia, which perceive the impressions as ordered perceptions before the consciousness of the hemispheres notes anything of the occurrence of a perception.

In the same way as the cerebral hemispheres send forth the innervation-current of attention and of the arrest of the will to the sensory ganglia and sensori-motor centres as reflexion on the stimulus provisionally conducted thither, in the same way must we conceive such currents as radiating from the middle parts of the brain to the sensory nerves and to the medulla oblongata and spinal cord, and from every superior part of the medulla oblongata and spinal cord to every lower part of the same, partly as persisting tone, partly as momentary reflectorial strengthenings of this tone. On the persisting tone of this inhibitory current depends the balance of chemical composition and decomposition in the lower centres, *i.e.*, their nutrition (M., p. 179), in like fashion as that of the nerve-fibre on the inhibitory current of the ganglion-cell from which it springs (comp. above, Section 2). "The increased irregular activity" (in comparison with the co-ordination effected by higher centres) "of the lower centres that have escaped from control betokens degeneration: it is like the turbulent, aimless action of a democracy without a head" (M., p. 179). This must never be forgotten in the consideration of the appropriateness of the reflexes of the lower nerve-centres, that they only fulfil their normal, proper, and most frequently proposed task on the supposition of the presence of higher guides, to whose orders they readily submit; that the reflex action on commands coming *from above* is the *usual* case, and reflexion on a peripheral stimulus in the absence of higher instructions only the rarer *exception*.

The influence of the inhibitory current coming from above is experimentally demonstrable, and that too in a twofold way. Namely, if a part of the nervous system be separated from its higher centres, the inhibitory current is interrupted, and this interruption comes immediately to manifestation in the considerably increased irritability of the part isolated above. If, on the other hand, the connection of the parts remains unaffected, but higher centres be stimulated (*e.g.*, the upper part of the spinal cord) by stimuli conducted thither, their heightened activity makes itself also manifest in a *strengthening* of the inhibitory current, *i.e.*, the irritability of the lower centres is now found *to be reduced below* the normal state (W., pp. 174 and 118). The enhancement of the irritability of the lower centres in the first case is also demonstrable by slicing away the hemispheres and adjoining parts from above downwards. These experiments, in conjunction with preliminary psychical observations, are quite decisive, and unambiguously prove the artistic and purposive organisation of the nervous system, in which the lower energies are kept, it is true, prepared and always ready for action, but, at the same time, are held in check by the superior authorities, as a squadron of skilful riders and snorting steeds by the will of the leader, until the moment seems to have arrived for unchaining these energies by a nod.

12. *Organism and Soul.*—After the foregoing expositions it can hardly be necessary to point out that, in the present state of nerve-physiology, the old question as to "the seat of the soul," which in philosophical reference could only have been raised by an erroneous metaphysic, is now deprived of all significance on the physiological side also.

The older philosophy could only propose this question so long as it, in the first place, looked on the soul as a metaphysical individual, independently existing apart from the organism belonging to it (monad); and, secondly, as subjected to objective-spatial determinations, being, *e.g.*, of punctual magnitude and locally fixed. Now, one may indeed look upon the soul as psychical substance *per se*, but as such it is not individual (not monad). One may also regard it as psychical individual; as such, however, it is not to be conceived as freed from the body, by which alone it can be individualised. Further, one may conceive it in objective-spatial relations, but only in and through the organism, in the unity through which it alone becomes individual; abstracted from body it is non-spatial in respect to the objective real space, and can merely copy in its *idea* a subjective-ideal space according to the former. The soul conceived in its *separation* from the body is thus not individual and *non-spatial*, and there can be no talk of a place or *seat* of the same; the soul understood as organic-psychical *individual* is just as long, thick, and broad *as the body* or living organism, and cannot have any seat *in* it.

Physiology and physiological psychology, namely, teach us that we have to assume perception and will (and as mediator between both the unconscious-teleological uniformity of the metaphysical substance) wherever a reflexion takes place. This happens, however, not only in every ganglion-cell, but even in the axis cylinder of every stimulated nerve-fibre. For we have seen above, in Section 2, that even in the conducting fibre the stimulus lights upon inhibiting agencies which wholly or partially absorb it, and on stored-up tension, which, in consequence of this absorption (psychically: perception) of the stimulus, becomes free (psychically: will). The same relation, however, recurs in the protoplasmic content of every living cell in the body (comp. C. Chap. iv. 2). Now, as the organism as such only reaches as far as the *life* of its parts, as this life consists in reflexion, whose inner psychical side cannot be entirely wanting, the individual soul also reaches as far as the organism in the narrower sense, and both only end where the living organism is bounded by dead excretions of its earlier vital processes.

Accordingly, so far as the soul is conceived as unit and individual, its objectively spatial determination coincides with that of the organism; but this does not prevent our recognising the inner organization and the different value of the organs just as much on the psychical as on the material side of the phenomenon. Psychical functions are connected with all the organic vital functions of the cells in the body, but in the economy of the psychical individuality the psychical functions of the different cells have an importance at least as distinct as their organic functions for the economy of the organic individuality; nay, the difference is far greater still on the psychical side.

We have seen how the psychical functions rise in gradual succession from muscular fibres to nerve-fibres, from these to the vegetative ganglion-cell, and from this, lastly, to the cells of the spinal cord, medulla oblongata, sensory centres, and cerebral hemispheres. The gradual character of this step-by-step advance of functions, which is unambiguously illustrated in the parallel scale of the animal kingdom, leaves no room for doubt that the *same* principle is exhibited at *all* stages, and that it is a serious error to try to seek *the soul only in the highest link* of this long chain, namely, exclusively in the cerebral hemispheres of man (and at any rate of the highest mammals). This older conception, in which Wundt is still in the main entangled, whilst Maudsley has positively surmounted it, lapses into the old error of the localisation of the mind, in that it designates a part of the Fore-brain (the cerebral hemispheres) as sole "seat" of the soul. We must break definitively with this error. Only *particular* psychical functions are assigned to particular parts of the nervous system. Soul in general is *everywhere and nowhere*, according as one understands the term. The individual soul, however (as unconscious unitary totality of the psychical functions of the organically psychical individual), is, *per se*, nowhere, and, referred to the external phenomenal side of the organically psychical individual, it reaches as far as the organism.

As concerns the relation between the internal and external phenomenon, one must hold fast to this, that the immediate content of consciousness is never able to explain the processes of the material phenomenon in the organism, but that *the converse also holds good*, as must at length be granted by all sober men of science. If one is not inclined absolutely to forego all explanation, and to confess to the ignorabimus of Du Bois-Reymond, one must admit that only *one* way remains open by which an explanation can at least not be called impossible. That way, however, consists in this, that we derive the inner uniformity of the conscious mental functions and the outer uniformity of the counterpart of the material forces from a *common source*, and, moreover, not from such a one as formerly might have arranged by a single act the harmony of both uniformities for all time (by pre-established harmony), but from a source which is *immanent* with its essence in all the inner and outer phenomena, and in living activity constantly brings its *essence* to two-sided *manifestation* (comp. above, Section 5). This source of the inner and outer uniformity can accordingly be no other than the nature of the metaphysical substance itself, which is the indivisible essence of both sides of the phenomenon, as well for each single individual of higher or lower order, as also for the individual of the highest and lowest rank, *i.e.*, for the world as a whole.

Without going back to the mysterious *bond* which closely unites the outer organic individuality with the inner psychical, it is impossible to grasp the organic-psychical individuality as real living and concrete *unity*; it is, in other words, impossible to study *physiological psychology*. This bond, however, can by no means be sought in the sphere of the *phenomenon*, whether external material or inner conscious-mental, since we indeed started with the perception that each side of the phenomenon, even taken in its totality, is *unable* to explain the other side. Consequently this bond can only be sought *beyond matter, as beyond consciousness*, *i.e.*, physiological psychology is forced by its *own definition* to pass over into the sphere of *metaphysics*. When this irrefragable truth first becomes generally and clearly perceived, the day of reconciliation between Physical Science and Philosophy, which so long (and not without teleological warrant) have shunned one another, will begin to break with beaming splendour, and a new era of science begin.

The *bond*, however, which unites organism and consciousness into the indivisible organic-psychical individuality—the living *spring* whence issues the uniformity of the material and conscious-mental order in ever-renewed harmony—this *essence*, which is revealed in both aspects of the phenomenon, is the *Unconscious*, or the Unconscious Spirit in its twofold character of energetic *Will* and logical (therefore also purposive) *Idea*, and this All-One Unconscious it is which is designated in its functional individuation "unconscious soul."

ADDENDA.

ADDENDA.

VOL. I.

P. 7, note, last l.—Comp. also my "Erläuterungen zur Metaphysik des Unbewussten" (Berlin, Carl Duncker, 1874). p. 8-11.

P. 20, l. 24.—The second enlarged edition of "Das Ding an Sich" appeared in 1875, with the title "Kritische Grundlegung des transcendentalen Realismus" (Berlin, Carl Duncker).

P. 23, l. 17.—A thorough investigation of the part which the Unconscious, in the sense of an unconscious-logical mental function, plays in the whole Kantian philosophy, but quite specially in the Critique of Judgment, and next to that in the Critique of Pure Reason, has been undertaken by Johannes Volkelt in his dissertation "Kant's Stellung zum unbewusst Logischen" (Phil. Monatshefte, 1873, Bd. ix. Heft 2 and 3), and in his work "Das Unbewusste und der Pessimismus" (Berlin, F. Henschel, 1873), p. 44-62. He shows in both places "that the deepening of the Kantian philosophy must always of necessity lead further into the realm of the Unconscious," since in all departments of Kantian inquiry there appear contradictions in the solutions given by Kant, which call for removal, and can only be eliminated by the introduction of the conception of the Unconscious. Kant has, therefore, also in this respect, as in so many others, laboured and performed less for the progress of philosophy by his *solution* than by his *statement* of problems; and, at the same time, has also more truly paved the way for the recognition of the Unconscious than many a one who had far more distinctly grasped the Unconscious as an isolated conception.

P. 28, l. 25.—Likewise in regard to the Hegelian philosophy J. Volkelt makes some excellent remarks in his book "The Unconscious and Pessimism" (p. 62–78), where it is made clear "that the unconsciously logical must form its *vital element*" (p. 62), and that "Hegelianism pre-eminently possesses the inherent tendency to develop the principle of the Unconscious in its whole extent" (p. 76). If with Kant the Unconscious occupies somewhat the position of an *unsuspected* presupposition, which a thinker hardly ventures to own to himself, with Hegel the unconsciousness of the IDEA in its being *per se* forms a self-evident presupposition, which, by very reason of its self-evidence, he does not further discuss; whereas exposed, as it is, to most misunderstanding and hostility, it is precisely the point which needed the most unequivocal articulation and thorough proof. Accordingly the Unconscious appears in Hegel also an Unconscious in the literal sense of the term, although intrinsically and substantially it pervades and determines the whole content of his philosophy.

P. 28, l. 32.—For the rest, there may be found in Hegel's works a sufficient number of passages to prove to the incredulous that the conception of Hegelianism just indicated was really that of the master himself, and these have been skilfully collected by Volkelt. The expression "objective thought" Hegel finds "unsuitable, because *thought* is usually too much employed as *appertaining* only to mind, to *consciousness*" (Encyclop., § 24). If the inner side of the world be designated Thought, *nothing of the nature of consciousness* should thereby be attributed to it. The logical in the world should rather form a system of thought *devoid of consciousness* (*ibid.*, Appendix, p. 45 ff.) Hegel declares the office of Logic to be to elevate the categories originally only *instinctively* active in the form of impulses to the stage of consciousness (Works, iii. p. 18–19). Instinct, however, he calls *purposive activity* acting in *an unconscious* fashion (Encyclop., § 360). In his "Æsthetics" he says (2d ed., i. p. 53): "Fancy has a mode of production that is at the same time *of the nature of instinct*, in that the essentially symbolical and sensuous character of art-work must possess a subjective existence in the artist as native tendency and natural impulse, and as *unconscious* action be also the expression of the man on his natural side."

P. 29, l. 36.—The *essence* of the Unconscious remains altogether indefinite in the following observation, which for the rest proves that Schopenhauer had a correct feeling of the *importance* which a profound analysis of the Unconscious must acquire at least for psychology and æsthetics: "All that is *original*, and therefore *all that is genuine* in man, acts as such *unconsciously*, like the forces of Nature. What has passed through consciousness has thereby become a representation. Accordingly *all genuine and sterling* qualities of the *character* and of the *mind* are originally *unconscious*, and only as such do they make a deep impression. Everything of the kind that is conscious has been already touched up, and is intentional, easily passes therefore into *affectation, i.e.*, deceit. What man performs unconsciously costs him *no trouble*, can, however, also *not be accomplished by any* trouble. Of this kind is the formation of original conceptions, as they underlie and form the core of all genuine achievements. Therefore only the innate is genuine and will stand its test, and every one who desires to achieve anything must in every case, in *action*, in *writing*, in *culture*, *follow rules without being aware of them*" (Parerga, vol. ii. § 352).

P. 32.—According to Herder, "Nature thinks better than man." Haym declares (Preuss. Jahr., Bd. xxxi., 1873.

Heft 1, p. 43) that he is speaking of the unerring Unconscious, which "includes in itself a kind of omniscience and omnipotence, of the one organic Principium of Nature, of the organic Omnipotence distributed everywhere, supporting or restoring life," from which he might just as well deduce the growth of crystals or the instincts of animals, or, lastly, the life, endeavour, and fate of man. On the preceding page Haym quotes a sentence from a letter of Jacobi to the Princess of Galizin: "Our consciousness develops from something *that as yet had not consciousness*, our thought from something which has not yet thought, our reflection from something which has not yet reflected, our will from something which has not willed, our rational mind from something which was never rational soul. A mechanical lever—which need not therefore be quite void of sense—was everywhere the first."

P. 39, l. 3.—An excellent account of the services of the philosophical physiologists may be found in Volkelt, "The Unconscious and Pessimism," p. 78–86. Why Carus could not become the standard-bearer of a new school, of a band of adherents collected round the flag of the Unconscious, is there shown on p. 83–86 (comp. also A. Taubert, "Der Pessimismus und seine Gegner," p. 160).

P. 40, l. 12.—The somewhat modified position which Wundt takes up in his most recent work with regard to the notion of the Unconscious is noticed in the Appendix, "On the Physiology of the Nerve-Centres" (comp. above, p. 208–210).

P. 41, l. 14.—For the rest, the sentence quoted has been anticipated by George Christopher Lichtenberg, in whom is found the following passage: "We become conscious of certain ideas which do not depend on ourselves; others—so at least we believe—depend on ourselves; where is the boundary? We only know of the existence of our own sensations, ideas, and thoughts. *It thinks*, one ought to say, just as one says, *It lightens*. To say *cogito* is already too much, as soon as one translates by *I think*. To assume, to postulate, the ego, is a *practical* necessity."

P. 42.—In a manner independent, as it would seem, of the Continental evolution, the conception of the Unconscious has gained a place in *English* literature in the last decennia; it is a philosopher, a historian, and a physician in whom it has found its clearest expression. Hamilton has inferred the existence of unconscious ideas chiefly from the circumstance (comp. "Lect. on Metaph.," i. p. 352 ff.) that on the revival of a former train of thought sometimes a whole series of intermediate links seems to be overleapt—an argument certainly of little value in this form. The best clue to Carlyle's position in respect to the conception of the Unconscious is afforded by the essay entitled "Characteristics" (which first appeared in the *Edinburgh Review*, No. cviii., and was afterwards reprinted in his collected essays). Of all English authors Maudsley has most decidedly and most thoroughly grasped and defended the conception of the Unconscious, except that he seeks to interpret the Unconscious as far as possible materialistically. The Appendix is sufficiently occupied with Maudsley's views (comp. above p. 253–256) to render it unnecessary to characterise them further here. Lastly, Lewes ought to be cited as an English author who has admitted the notion of the Unconscious in a certain direction.

However defective and incomplete may be the notices here collected, they may yet suffice for the purpose of showing that the principle of the Unconscious, as everything historically important, has been arrived at by a *gradual* process of formation and growth; that all phases and schools of philosophy, from the oldest times to the present day, more or less strive after this principle (comp. J. Volkelt, "Das Unbew. u. d. Pess.," the first part, "History of the Unconscious"), and that in the present work I have only more plainly asserted and shown the deep significance of this principle, as well as most completely established it, but have by no means aired it as a brand-new discovery (or, as it has been more maliciously called, "invention").

P. 46, note, last l.—That it is in general *lawful*, nay, even *imperative*, to introduce into *philosophical* inquiries the notion of *probability*, which in modern natural philosophy is already universally acknowledged to be the sole foundation of all human knowledge; and that even in philosophy, when discussing problems which admit of various solutions, an effort must be made to determine the probability of the assumption of different conceivable hypotheses as far as seems possible, can only be disputed by two parties, namely, on the one side, by that school which regards the problem of philosophy *exclusively* as the ascertainment of an *absolute certainty*, and declares all other knowledge save a supposed absolute one to be essentially *unphilosophical*; and, on the other hand, from the opposite quarter of an absolute scepticism, which questions the possibility of all knowledge, not only absolute, but also relative, and denies to man the capability of establishing any distinction between truth and untruth. Almost all past philosophy has oscillated between these two extremes. When the pretension to absolute knowledge has once more justly become ridiculous for a time, scepticism regains the upperhand, and it is then set up as the sole problem of philosophy to show that philosophising is nonsense. In fact, it is hardly comprehensible how to-day, after so many failures of systems giving themselves out to be absolute truth, after such clear disclosures of the gradual attainment of truth, after such distinct perception of the insufficiency of the instruments of human knowledge in presence of the overwhelming extensive and intensive magnitude of the universe, there can still always be found ingenuous people who declare the problem of philosophy to be that of absolute knowledge, and venture to assert all knowledge to be unphilosophical which renounces the claim to absolute certainty. That certain knowledge is and must remain the *ideal* of our cognitive efforts is not to be doubted; but one might at the present day sufficiently know that ideals are *just* what are *not* to be found in actuality; that they rather only form the asymptote, which the curve of historical development more and more approaches without ever meeting. But equally mistaken is it on the other side, when the impossibility of realising the ideal as such is perceived, straightway to reject the ideal as a phantom without any real significance, or to declare real and ideal to be *infinitely* wide apart, and therefore *incommensurable.* Were scepticism right, *all* our supposed knowledge would be *equally wide* of the truth (for if it once touched it by accident, we could indeed know nothing of this concidence); accordingly all possibility of an historical evolution of knowledge, all possibility of science, all perceivable or declarable distinction between knowledge, faith, and crazy imagination would be abolished. One only needs to become conscious of these consequences of a thoroughgoing sceptical principle to see how insupportable it is for the human mind; and so it comes to pass that humanity ever again relapses from scepticism into the dogma of the attainability of absolute knowledge, only, after a little time, once more to exhibit its utter untenability. We are saved from this barren circle only by the open acknowledgment of the relative truth and relative untruth of the two extremes. The dogma of absolute knowledge is right in setting up its ideal, and in the belief that the endeavour after this ideal is not fruitless. Scepticism is right in denying the complete attainability of this ideal to be ever humanly possible. But the former is wrong when it misapprehends the distinction between ideal and reality, and denies off-hand validity to everything, which cannot claim to be *faultless* realisation of the ideal; the latter is wrong when it abolishes the possibility of distinguishing in human knowledge *different degrees* of approximation to the ideal or remoteness therefrom. It must be strenuously maintained that a different *dignity* appertains to different degrees of cognition, because without this even practical life becomes a senseless hurly-burly. If, however, one chooses to ascribe to scientific knowledge a higher dignity than to unscientific imagining and thinking, to the knowledge conscious of its material proof a higher worth than to the groundless conviction of a faith which rests merely on postulates of feeling, or on the personal authority of him who transmits it, or maybe on morbid fixed ideas, then there is no other means available but to *quantitatively* determine the *degrees* of the approximation of knowledge to the cognitive ideal of certainty, whether this determination be made in numerical form or in the less distinct shape of an emotional estimate of quantity without numerical expression. If Leibniz was right, that there is no assertion, however false, in which there does not lie a grain of truth, and no truth, however sublime, with which there is not some untruth mingled by reason of its expression in language, then there is also no thinking, believing, or knowing in which an unclear feeling does not point to the intermixture of true and untrue elements. It behoves us to scientifically purify this feeling, and to determine the proportion of true and untrue elements, in order precisely to define the degree of approximation of our knowledge to certainty. If one wished to express the dignity of our knowledge by the proportion of its true and false elements, as happens in a wager about the truth of an assertion, one would have a proportion between two variables, which would render difficult the comparison between several such proportions. It is better therefore to express the worth of the knowledge by the ratio between the true elements contained therein and the totality of the elements supposed to be true, or, in other words, one takes the constant cognitive ideal of certainty as standard of worth, as 1, and expresses the degree of the approximation of knowledge to certainty by the degree of approximation of a proper fraction to unity. Whoever has once made himself familiar with this mathematical mode of expression will soon feel its natural fitness, and easily get accustomed to fix his indefinite emotional estimate of the worth of a cognition by means of a coefficient of probability, whose magnitude may always be conceived as fluctuating between a least and a greatest limit, and accordingly as affected with a probable error.

P. 51.—Objections have been raised from various sides against this employment of the calculus of probabilities, which, however, have betrayed for the most part far too considerable a defect of comprehension for it to be rewarding to occupy ourselves more closely with them, and which one and all do *not* enter upon the point, which I have already indicated (vol. i. p. 48, note) as that, where the concrete applicability of the argumentative processes in question may most easily miscarry.

I will only mention here one opponent, partly because his *fallacious* objections possess a certain plausibility, partly because he has called my attention to the necessity of a *supplement* to my argumentation for the benefit of readers slow of comprehension or ill-disposed, which I had thought I might leave as superfluous to the intelligence of the reader himself. Albert Lange, in his "History of Materialism" (2d ed., vol. ii. p. 280–283, and p. 307–309), disputes the applicability of the entire inferential process to the problems of Nature, so far as concerns regressive inferences from phenomena to their causes, and that on the ground that the actual as a special case of very many possibilities must always appear extremely improbable *a priori*, a circumstance, however, which would not affect its reality, as the fraction of probability means nothing more than the degree of our subjective uncertainty (p. 282 l. 15–11 fr. b., p. 283 l. 3–6 fr. a.) He supports this denial on the ground that the whole theory of probability presupposes an *abstraction* of the efficient causes, of which we are entirely ignorant, whereas certain general conditions are known to us on which we base our calculation (p. 282 l. 11–7 fr. b.) Were the latter assertion correct there would be no reply to the suggested inference therefrom; but in fact it requires an important modification. If, namely, the co-operating causes which we abstract were absolutely unknown *in all respects*, there could be no talk of probability at all; the calculus of probability is, on the other hand, only possible on the supposition that the co-operating causes of which abstraction is made are *accidental* causes. But by accidental causes in the sense of the calculus of probabilities are to be understood such as are *not in this form* indispensable to the occurrence of the phenomenon in question, therefore also are not constantly met with in the same, but so change that their influence is more completely *compensated* the more frequently the occurrence is repeated. The estimate afforded by the calculus of probabilities rests on the supposition of a *complete* compensation of the accidental co-operating causes in infinitely numerous repetitions. Such accidental causes are, *e.g.*, in inorganic nature the causes which condition the falling of the die on this or that side, in organic nature those which give rise to monstrosities and arrested developments.

Only by leaving out of sight this fundamental assumption of the calculus of probabilities can Lange deny the admissibility of a regressive inference from perceived effects to the nature of the causes. If, *e.g.*, I approach a game of *rouge et noir*, in which I see red appear twenty times in succession, there is certainly no doubt that this event may be produced by a *mere combination of accidental causes*; but little as this possibility is to be doubted, yet the extraordinary small probability of the same gives me the right to conceive also the other possibility, that a *constant* cause is present which favours red. Lange will certainly charge no one with drawing a wrong conclusion, who should hesitate to risk his money in such a game, because the suspicion (*i.e.*, the inference of probability) at once occurs that the play is contrived with a view to deception, although the possibility is always conceded that this suspicion may be erroneous. But if Lange admits the validity of such an inference, he cannot refuse the like to my examples; he must then be able to prove *a priori* that the class of constant causes which I suppose is impossible. His objection, totally devoid of all proof, in fact amounts to this. The inferential process he cannot by rights impugn, but he only tries to question, from the prejudiced standpoint of a materialistic-mechanical view of the world, the admissibility of the hypothetical goal to which it is applied. From the point of view of the calculus of probabilities, such a procedure would only be legitimate if from the first such an enormous probability were assigned to the mechanical view of the world, forbidding the resort to metaphysical principles (not merely to mythological personal spirits), that even the counter-instances of the highest probability had no power to shake that probability. Were this the case, all philosophy and metaphysics, as Lange thinks, would be impossible; whether it be so is first to be determined by my investigation, and in the meantime it appears to me an unscientific prejudice, a mere *petitio principii*, whose untruth will become more and more apparent.

Lange tries to strengthen his protest against the resort to metaphysical principles by a simile, when he asserts that by the same method upon the frequent recurrence of good luck in games of chance one might prove with equal probability the co-operation of a Fortuna or a *spiritus familiaris*. In the first place, there is here wanting the elimination of constant material causes presupposed by me in my discussion, *i.e.*, before such inference to a Fortuna an exact investigation must be made whether the dice or the arrangement of the game of *rouge et noir* is not affected by errors which act as constant causes. But suppose this inquiry were carried out with extreme precision, and had yielded a negative result, nothing, in fact, could be alleged against the inference to a Fortuna as constant cause save the circumstance, that the non-existence of such a mythological personage has on other grounds a considerably greater probability than the evidence for its existence furnished by the game. That this is actually the case it will not be necessary to prove; but precisely on that account the example can prove nothing against the introduction of impersonal metaphysical principles for the explanation of the processes of organic formation, since for the non-existence of these such an overpowering probability is by no means established. Lange has, therefore, by no means, as he purposed, pointed out a methodological error in my explanation, but he has only revealed the blinding power of the materialistic prejudice by which he is possessed.

But now it is further to be considered that the parallel drawn between a man winning ten times in succession and the origin of organic fitness in Nature proves nothing for an altogether different reason, in that, namely, Lange speaks only of *one* man who gains in a single case ten times in succession, whereas the marvellous conjunction of the conditions of organic adaptation is repeated in *innumerable* cases simultaneously and successively. That this particular man is favoured by a Fortuna would only be a conclusion analogous to that of a purpose in organic Nature, if this man not only gained in *one* game ten or twenty times on doubling his stakes, but had this unheard-of luck his whole life long on all the gaming-tables of the world, and if a failure of this unheard-of luck belonged in his case as much to the class of exceptions as abortions to the exceptions of purposive organic formation. Conversely Lange would only then be right that the reality of the *a priori* improbable in organic Nature does not summarily compel the regressive inference to a constant cause, if the occurrence of this *a priori* improbable harmonious fitness were as rare an exception among innumerable unsuccessful malformations and deformities as the ten or twenty times successive gain is a rare exceptional case in games of chance (altogether corresponding in the degree of its rareness to the *a priori* theory of probability). This colossal difference is so evident as to make its oversight by Lange very surprising; it would by itself suffice to render impotent all the attacks of Lange upon my exposition.

P. 71, last l.—These remarks must suffice as a justification that no other term than "Will" has been selected for the designation of the single principle undoubtedly underlying all the manifestations of the volitional sphere. This term, rightly hit upon by Schopenhauer, only met with such violent opposition in the philosophy of the schools, because the psychology of the latter was entirely confined to the department of *conscious* psychical activity, and aimed at detaching this as something specifically higher and alien from its unconscious natural basis, so that the extension of a term chiefly borrowed from conscious mental life to unconscious psychical functions appeared to it a crime against the majesty of the mind already artificially disengaged from Nature. The more the doctrine of the essential identity of the conscious mind with unconscious Nature has gained acceptance, the more admirers and imitators Schopenhauer's use of the expression "Will" has found. (Comp. Göring, "System der Kritischen Philosophie," Leipzig, Voit & Co., 1874, part i. chap. iii., especially p. 68–71, where various objections to the conception of unconscious will are refuted.)

P. 74, l. 34.—If recent investigations have shown that in certain parts of the cerebral hemispheres there are also found motor nerve-endings, yet the following sufficiently weighty arguments taken by themselves are not thereby affected.

P. 77, l. 2.—In order that a movement may ensue correctly, *i.e.*, in the right proportion of the intensity of all its components, a clear perception of the position of the particular bodily parts must not only be present at the beginning of the movement, but also during the successive moments of execution; it is, however, requisite for this that both the sense of touch as well as the muscular sense (or muscular feeling) be correctly functional. Only when the right feeling of the position of the parts is given (for the rest, this feeling need not take place in the cerebrum, but will usually have its material substratum only in the cerebellum, optic thalami, or corpora striata), only then can the degree of motor innervation be rightly estimated, and be controlled by a comparison of the perceived feeling of muscular movement during the nearly completed movement with the muscular feeling anticipated by the idea, *i.e.*, be strengthened, or hindered, or modified during action. Thus undoubtedly the muscular feeling anticipated by the idea (but only through the controlling comparison with the muscular feeling perceived before and during movement) can serve as *regulator* of movement, but the regulator is something different from the producing or impelling factor, and from that which directs the impulse of innervation to definite nerve-endings and determines the quality of the movement. Maudsley calls the latter element "*motor intuition or percept*," distinguishing it (Physiol. of Mind, p. 465) just as much from the conscious representation of the intended movement as from the muscular feeling, and assumes that the receptive muscular feeling is indeed necessary for its origin and elaboration (in man perhaps, certainly not in animals), but that it is necessary neither for the latent existence nor for the active function of the motor intuition, inasmuch as the necessary regulation by the muscular sense may be provided for by another sense, *e.g.*, the visual sense (comp. above in the Appendix, p. 261–262). Maudsley holds the intervention of the intuitions of movement to be just as indispensable in the reflex action following on a sense-perception as in voluntary movement after a conscious idea, and regards it as self-evident that these motor intuitions are *unconscious* ("Phys. and

Path. of Mind," pp. 177 and 187). By the latter, however, he understands only molecular predispositions, that are functional without consciousness, at least without coming into the consciousness of the cerebral hemispheres. That such predispositions co-operate in the production of voluntary movements at the most diverse places of the central organs of the nervous system is, of course, not to be disputed. Indeed, in the complicated action of lifting the finger, every nerve-fibre and every ganglion-cell which is irrigated by the current of innervation issuing from the cerebrum displays its special inherited or acquired molecular powers, and only by such participation of the subordinate nerve-centres does it become possible also in voluntary movements for a *single* impulse of innervation issuing from the cerebrum to bring about so complex a result of aptly compounded muscular actions. The main difficulty still remains, how the ideational cells in the cerebral hemispheres are to send forth, conformably to the ideal content of the particular ideas, impulses of innervation, which are distinguished not only by the intensity and quality of the innervation, but also by the different *direction* of the emission, so far, namely, as the terminations of the fibres to be in each case affected are to be sought at different places of the cerebrum. It is the translation of the ideal matter of representation (the words, "little finger" or "fore-finger") into mechanical action, which will for ever render futile all mere mechanical explanations.

P. 80, l. 14.—In a depreciatory criticism in "Ausland," 1872, No. 40, in which J. H. Klein, from the standpoint of natural science, breaks his staff over the Philosophy of the Unconscious, the foregoing passage is particularly cited as a *glaring proof* of the frivolous superficiality and worthlessness of my work (p. 939), and Darwin's exact method of investigation held up to me as a model (p. 943). Here Herr Klein has only made the little mistake of overlooking that, precisely in the point attacked, not only Darwin entirely agrees with me, but also the most important of the examples quoted (as well as those on p. 81) are borrowed directly from Darwin's "Origin of Species." Herr Klein further warns every one against a philosopher who so far contradicts himself as to assert at the beginning of a chapter that *different* instincts appear with a like bodily constitution *in* DIFFERENT *species*, and at its close tries to prove why *within* THE SAME *species like* instincts must follow from like bodily constitutions (p. 941). "May God protect exact science from such superficiality!" (p. 939).

P. 102, l. 18.—The garden spider goes into the rain-corner of its web a day before change of weather, and begins a day before the return of fine weather, perhaps already in the midst of rain, to examine its web. "Fine weather, however, does not then last long. Sometimes the spider pulls its web to pieces, and then builds an entirely new one. This is a sure sign of fine weather. With more exact observation it may be discovered that the web is not always similar; its meshes are now wider, now narrower. If they are wide, it is a sign that fine weather will at the most last five days, but if they are close, one may safely reckon on eight fine days" ("Ausland," 1875, No. 18, p. 360). One easily sees that for the catching of flies the closer web is certainly the more advantageous, but that in consideration of the destruction of the web by rain and wind there is necessary for the spider a certain frugality in the employment of the productive power of its spinning glands, which is estimated according to the future state of the weather.

P. 131, l. 27.—The sensation of black is, namely, the sensation of that process of chemical restitution or recomposition of nervous matter which is opposed to the process of consumption or decomposition appearing in consciousness as sensation of white (according to Hering's physiological theory of light and colour, comp. "Naturalist," 1875, No. 9). The chemical recomposition of all nervous matter (and especially of the conducting fibres) is, however, stimulated and guided by centrifugal currents of innervation from the particular centres, and we become partially conscious of this current of innervation in sense-nerves terminating in the cerebrum as attention (comp. above, p. 282–284). It is thus one and the same thing whether we say: In nerve-fibres without terminal organs of visual perception, or in the parts of the retinal image represented by no primitive nervous fibres the corresponding recomposition is wanting, because the external occasions to decomposition are wanting; or whether we say: When centrifugal sense-stimuli are never conducted, no centrifugal current of innervation can come to pass, which, indeed, must first arise reflectorially.

P. 139.—I can now no longer look upon the example quoted as stringent proof of what should be proved at this place; for in fact, even in the normal state, besides the one main path of reflexion (which leads by the shortest route from the place of insertion of the sensory to that of the motor nerve in the grey matter of the spinal cord), there exist a number of side-paths of greater or less resistance, which are brought into requisition according to the varying amount of the stimulus and the irritability. If, now, the main path is destroyed, the branch paths become functional, when either the applied stimulus is adequate or the irritability of the spinal cord sufficiently increased. (The latter takes place partly by means of strychnine, partly by the separation of the spinal cord from the brain and its inhibitory influences.) But it is noticeable that the side-paths pass through more central places of grey matter the more circuits they make, and that every passage of the excitation through grey matter (on account of the inhibitory influences and specific stores of energy ready for liberation contained in the ganglion-cells) is no longer simple conduction, but itself again a reflexion.

The greater circuit, therefore, a stimulus makes before it again emerges as motor reaction, the more complicated becomes the composition of the total reflexion from a whole series of simple reflexes, in each of which the problem of the inner psychical aspect and purposiveness of the reflex is repeated. Consequently, if the above example does not directly prove what it ought to prove, it yet tells far less for the opposite purely mechanical conception, but leaves the problem recurring at every moment always open. But this problem is hereby resolved, that the purposiveness of the reflex mechanisms has itself been gradually brought about, and is teleologically modifiable; that the existing dispositions or accessory mechanisms have themselves only arisen through a sum of purposive functions, which were possible *without* these mechanisms; and that they continue to readjust themselves by suitable modification of the functions, which with frequent repetition produce a modification in the existing molecular dispositions.

P. 142, last l.—Compare this chapter with the Appendix, especially Sections 3, 4, 5, 6, and 11.

P. 157, l. 6.—The conspicuous statements are taken from Burdach's "Physiology." If in the given form they do not appear altogether tenable before the tribunal of the physiology of the day, this does not alter the general fact under discussion. It is precisely modern physiology which sees itself more and more driven to the recognition of vicarious functions, and biology finds in the theory of descent and the gradual differentiation of the various organs from original homogeneous tissues the key to the possibility of those occurrences, which appear from this point of view as a kind of ancestral reminiscence on the part of the tissue of a phylogenetic period of development, when the division of labour in the organism had not yet progressed so far.

P. 161, l. 2.—The preceding passage, which already appeared in the first edition of this work, is the clearest proof how little they have understood the purport of my theory who imagine I desire in any case *to supersede* or *set aside* physico-chemical explanation employing efficient material causes by metaphysical explanations. Nothing is further from me than an undertaking so senseless and so inconsistent with the spirit of modern science. On the contrary, *no* speculative philosopher has *ever* so readily acknowledged the independent claims of Physical science and rated their value as highly *as I* myself, who hold it to be the undoubted and hopeful task of physical science to investigate the efficient material causes of material phenomena, and who esteem it the "*duty*" of the investigator of Nature, as such, not to be led astray in this search after efficient material causes by the intermixture of metaphysical, teleological, or other principles of explanation. This recognition of physical science in the department of material phenomena and their causal connection cannot, however, blind me (like some "modern" philosophers) to the perception that neither do material phenomena *exhaust* the phenomenon of cosmic existence, nor the causal connection, as such, the cognition of the material phenomena in their property of uniformity; that thus *beyond* natural science and its solutions *yet other problems* await solution. Now so far as a natural philosopher claims to be at the same time "*homo sapiens*," *i.e.*, a cultured and thoughtful man, one *must* require of him that he be conscious of the *limits* of his special science and their *non-coincidence* with the limits of human knowledge in general, and foster even a certain general human interest for more general philosophical efforts. On the other hand, it is not to be required of any man who does not claim to be a scientific specialist that, in occupying himself with certain problems, he should especially aim at extending the present field of natural scientific knowledge, *i.e.*, search after a causal explanation of material phenomena by material causes beyond the measure of the enlightenment afforded by contemporary science. He will leave *this side* of the scientific physical problem of humanity to the specialists, and be by no means hindered by this renunciation, but rather placed in a better position to devote his full powers in a fruitful way to the other side of the problem, which just as little allows of neglect. But when natural philosophers so much mistake the state of affairs, that they account any application of philosophical principles of explanation and every personal renunciation of independent investigation in the sphere of natural science as a kind of sin against the Holy Ghost, one can only as much lament such a professional limitation of the field of view as the terrorism which many champions of this school exert on public opinion, not without a certain success in confusing the public mind as to what really constitutes the genuine "scientific spirit." It seems high time to openly protest against this terrorism, and to point out earnestly and emphatically to the credulous victims of popular scientific lectures and journals, that physical science and its strict inquiry into material causes is always only *one* aspect (and that, too, *sub*ordinate to the mental sciences) of science in general. Otherwise there is danger lest physical science may in our own time strive after an autocracy just as unjustifiable, and, if possible, still more dangerous, than that actually possessed by theology in the Middle Ages.

P. 181.—Maudsley says in his "Physiology of the Mind," p. 118, "The idea that vomiting must take place when a qualmish feeling exists will certainly hasten vomiting, and there is a very remarkable instance in the *Philosophical Transactions* of a man who could for a time stop the motion of his heart by composing himself, and then either conceiving vividly or directly willing what was to happen. There are examples of the influence of ideas upon the involuntary muscles, and they accord with what has been previously said of the subordination of the organic nerve-centres to the cerebro-spinal system. Some people even are able, through a vivid idea of shuddering or of something creeping over their skin, to produce a *cutis anserina* or goose's skin. The immediate effect of the idea in this case, however, is probably to excite the appropriate sensation, which thereupon gives rise to the sequent phenomena.

"Examples of the action of ideas upon our voluntary muscles are witnessed in every hour of our waking life. Very few, in fact, of the familiar acts of a day call the will into action: when not sensori-motor, they are usually prompted by ideas."

The unconscious influence of fancy in dreams is very clearly manifested even in those persons who are not sufficiently nervous in the waking state to collect decided experiences in this respect in their own person, where, *e.g.*, the dream-idea of being injured or wounded at particular parts of the body can excite clear local sensation of pain, which disappears on waking.

Although I think I am able to give a thoroughly natural explanation of cutaneous bleedings by the influence of fancy, yet in presence of the religious vertigo which has recently again manifested itself in connection with this subject, truth requires the admission, that, according to my more exact information, no case has hitherto been established where the phenomena in a stigmatic have been scrutinised and pronounced spontaneous bleeding by physicians unprejudiced (*i.e.*, inaccessible to Catholic sacerdotal influence) and of the first scientific rank. On the contrary, several cases have been made public where such an inquiry has proved the object of religious superstition to be the result of an illusion (comp. "Deutsche Klinik," 1875, No. 1–3; "Louise Lateau's Three Predecessors in Westphalia," by Dr. Brück, Member of the Sanitary Board). It is at the same time by no means necessary to imagine deceit in the ordinary sense, although its possibility is not excluded. The persons of whom such bleedings have been related are almost without exception hysterical women, with thoroughly ruined nervous systems and more or less deranged mental constitutions, who are swayed by perverted impulses, and in regard to the usual significance of their actions cannot be called accountable. The instinctive cunning and love of dissimulation in the female character, which in such individuals is for the most part abnormally developed previous to their illness, is in the condition of hysteria directed to apparently quite senseless objects, and often calls forth an astonishing ingenuity in order to deceive in a perfectly purposeless way even the nearest. It is quite common for the natural feminine vanity to throw itself in such cases upon the morbid condition itself, in order to arouse interest through the unusualness of its phenomena, and not rarely is united with this the perverted impulse of self-injury and physical self-torture, in order to revel and luxuriate in the imagination of an imposed martyrdom. Even the soberest and calmest spectators are usually almost impotent in presence of such hysterical derangement; one may imagine how easily a sympathetic environment may strengthen the whims of the patient, and convert them into real fixed ideas. Over and above this, there is usually found in a family where such a morbid character arises an hereditary disposition, which appears in less degree also in other members of the family. If, then, a mother or sister gives herself up to admiring and fostering the perversities of the sick person, she not only confirms her in her delusions, but probably helps the realisation of her hysterical tendencies, *i.e.*, becomes an accomplice in the eventual delusion. Now as madness in the female sex—both real and hysterical madness—for the most part gravitates only in two directions, in the sexual or in the religious (or in both simultaneously), it is evident that nothing must be more suited to strengthen and to guide into special channels such perverted tendencies than a religious exaltation, and specially the amalgamation artfully nourished by the Catholic Church of sexual excitement, delight in cruelty, and religious ecstasy, caused by the ardent absorption of the phantasy in the tortures of the heavenly bridegroom. Add the priest, who supports the unfortunate one in her delusion, and probably declares the self-inflicted injuries, into which the spiritual revelling in martyr-agonies explodes in the state of over-strain, to be symbolic signs of divine grace, then the sick person readily enough believes she is following a direct divine behest by frequently evoking these symbolic marks, and may very easily, in spite of her objective fraud, have the firm subjective conviction of being a selected instrument of divine grace when she sees the religious effects which she exerts on the credulous who flock to her. Everywhere where priests are behind the scenes one may assume it probable at the outset that this is the true state of the case, and the probability of an objective delusion becomes certainty if, beside the stigmatisation, other phenomena are related which contradict the laws of organic life (*e.g.*, the year-long abstinence from food in the waking state). But it is not these unfortunates who should be relegated as impostors to the house of correction, where several of them have been incarcerated, but the priests, to whose shameless love of domination even the morbid obscuration of the human mind serves as a welcome means to more surely befool the masses they have cunningly stupefied.—For the rest, these remarks are not to be taken as deliverances on the possibility of spontaneous cutaneous exudations, but only to protect myself from being quoted as sponsor for ultramontane sacerdotal craft.

P. 182, last l.—Many cures are only seemingly sympathetic, inasmuch as remedies are applied whose medicinal effect is not known, either merely by the parties concerned or even by the faculty of medicine of the day. Such co-operating causes are excluded in sympathetic cures by mere conjuration. The best accredited and most striking effects of conjuration may well consist in the stopping of bleedings (contraction of the veins and capillaries by the nervous agitation of the charmed person) and in the assuaging of pain caused by burns.

P. 200, l. 35.—Comp. Ernst Häckel's "Anthropogenie, oder Entwickelungsgeschichte des Menschen," Leipzig, Engelmann, 1876.

P. 202.—With regard to the critical objection that in this chapter the clues afforded by Darwinism with respect to the origin of purposive adaptations in organisms are left unnoticed, the following is to be observed. Darwinism, even if it were right in all its assertions, offers *at the most* an explanation why the fertilised ovum brings with it this or that constitution for its ontogenetic course of development; this individual development itself, however, *it does not discuss at all*, but assumes it as a physiologically given fact, that such an organism unfolds from such a germ. There is in this, however, nothing but a lack of philosophical wonderment, an incapacity to apprehend the problem. For all phylogenetic development is compounded of a series of ontogenetic developments, and therefore the former can never explain the latter but rather presupposes it, although it is correct that a definite individual development is conditioned in the mode and manner of its course by the phylogenetic development which has preceded it. But the *first* question always is to comprehend how an individual development is *at all* possible; and this problem is altogether independent of the explanation of phylogenetic evolution, which is indeed only compounded of individual developments, as the building of bricks or the plant of cells. Wherefore, also, an independent investigation of the problem of individual organic development is philosophically as much authorised as demanded, quite apart from the question whether Darwinism is right.

Undoubtedly this inquiry must be completed by testing the solution which Darwinism offers of the problem of phylogenetic evolution. This is done in Chap. x. C., and still more thoroughly in my memoir, "Truth and Error in

Darwinism." The result is that all Darwin's principles of explanation are only tenable and available for any sort of explanation of natural phenomena on the *foundation* of a tacitly presupposed but openly rejected "organising principle." At bottom this is nothing more than the confirmation of the *a priori* and self-evident proposition regressively gained by criticism, that all phylogenetic development is only compounded of a series of ontogenetic processes of evolution, and that the ontogenetic development as such is accordingly not explicable from a phylogenetic evolution, but only by an organising principle which guides and secures the purposive (isolated and correlative) variation and transmission.

P. 200, l. 21.—Without question it may be very attractive to analyse psychologically, to classify, and to investigate in their causal relations all the numerous veils and disguises in which the longing after sexual union conceals itself according to the character and the circumstances (as has also been frequently attempted, especially by the French); but even if such a psychology of love succeeded in giving an intelligent account of the whole inexhaustible variety of the forms which love can assume, yet nothing would be thereby gained for the understanding of love so long as the fundamental problem were not made perfectly precise and satisfactorily solved. This fundamental problem of love must, however, of course, turn on that which is not diverse but common, and this common element in the apparently heterogeneous expressions of the one passion is manifestly nothing else but the longing for sexual union. What is problematical in this point is, however, this: how the corporeal or mental, æsthetic or emotional, *pleasure* which one finds in a person can lead to the altogether heterogeneous wish for sexual union with the same, and can increase this wish to a passion? This, and nothing else, is the fundamental problem of love; and whoever does not *perceive* the problem, or whoever does not find anything at all wonderful or *problematical* therein, will least of all be enabled to *solve* it, and all the psychological studies of such a one concerning love can only be a more or less clever prattle on *side issues*. We can only hope for a solution of the problem when the *essence* of sexual love has been rightly apprehended as the longing veiled by more or fewer accessories for sexual union with a particular individual.

P. 242, last l.—Comp. here A. Taubert, "Der Pessimismus und seine Gegner," Berlin, C. Duncker, 1873, No. 4, "Die Liebe."

P. 249, l. 2.—The usual division into sensuous and intellectual feelings and impulses is doubtless warranted, if thereby the different nature and worth of the spheres is sought to be indicated to which the particular feelings and impulses are related through the ideas with which they are connected, but it becomes an unauthorised distinction when it imports more than this qualitative difference of the particular spheres of representation, and is employed to impeach the homogeneity of the will in itself and its satisfaction or non-satisfaction. (Comp. here Göring, "System of Crit. Phil.," part i. chap. vi., "The division of the impulses and feelings into sensuous and intellectual," p. 107 ff.; also chap. iv., "The falsity of the distinction between lower and higher will," p. 78–87.)

P. 249, l. 15.—The more opposition this proposition has encountered, which is so simple, but appears so surprising and almost paradoxical to thinkers unaccustomed to abstracting from the simply concomitant representations of feelings, the more do I rejoice that on this point I can appeal to no less an authority than Kant. He says in the "Crit. of Pract. Reason" (Werke, viii. 131): "The *representations* of objects may be ever so *heterogeneous*; they may be ideas of the understanding, even of the reason, in contrast to ideas of sense; yet the *feeling of pleasure* by whose instrumentality they properly come to be the determining ground of the will (the expected agreeableness, satisfaction, which incites to the production of the object) is not only of *the same kind*, inasmuch as it can always only be empirically known, but also in that it affects *one and the same* vital energy, which is manifested in the *faculty of desire*, and in this respect *can differ in nothing but degree* from every other determining ground" (that is, from every feeling called forth by another determining reason). "How otherwise should we be able to institute a quantitative *comparison* between two determining grounds altogether different in their intellectual clothing, so as to give the preference to that one which most affects the faculty of desire?"

P. 250, note, last l.—That desire is more original than the state of feeling whose production is desired is shown in numerous cases when violent desire already enters into consciousness in the stage of tormenting unrest, whilst its content or its aim is still completely unconscious. Maudsley says in his "Phys. of Mind," p. 355–356: "In the child, as in the idiot, we frequently witness a vague restlessness, evincing an undefined want of or desire for something of which itself is unconscious, but which, when obtained, presently produces quiet and satisfaction: the organic life speaks out with an as yet inarticulate utterance. Most striking and instructive is that example of the evolution of organic life into consciousness which is observed at the time of puberty, when new organs come into action and exert their physiological influence upon the brain; vague and ill-understood desires give rise to obscure impulses that have no defined" (rather: conscious) "aim, and produce a restlessness which, when misapplied, is often mischievous. The amorous appetite thus first declares its existence. But to prove how clearly antecedent to individual experience it is, and how little it is indebted to the consciousness which is a natural subsequent development, it is only necessary to reflect that even in man the desire sometimes attains to a knowledge of its aim, and to a sort of satisfaction, in dreams, before it does so in real life. . . . These simple reflections might of themselves suffice to teach psychologists, if they would condescend to them, how far more fundamental than any conscious mental state is the unconscious mental or cerebral life."

The relation of will and feeling and the reasons for the assumption that the latter is to be conceived as a consequence of the former, *and not conversely*, is discussed by Göring, together with a refutation of the contrary opinions, in his "System of Crit. Phil.," vol. i. pp. 50, 60–65, and 89–95. (Comp. also in the same, chap. v., "The separation of the emotional faculty.")

P. 276, l. 3.—In dreams this creative activity is well known to us all. We all possess it, as our dreams prove; but its degree is usually so low that it cannot assert itself in the waking state against the twofold competition of the impressions of perception and of the abstract associations of thought. Accordingly the study of the creations of dream-fancies affords a serviceable preparation and excellent aid to the comprehension of the creations of artistic fancy, although the difference between a thoughtless dreaming and a sober creative fancy must not be overlooked. I refer for these things to the memoir of Johannes Volkelt, "Die Traum-Phantasie" (Stuttgart, 1875), which combines in an equal degree critical sobriety and speculative penetration, and works up everything hitherto achieved in this department (comp. in particular, No. 15, "The Unconscious in Dream-Fancy").

P. 280, note.—What Schiller thought of the Unconscious in artistic production in a *scientific* form appears from his letter to Goethe on the 27th March 1801. He there says: "A few days ago I attacked Schelling for an assertion in his 'Transcendental Philosophy' that 'in Nature a primal Unconscious is to be elevated to consciousness; in Art, on the contrary, the procession is from consciousness to the unconscious.' It is true he is dealing here only with the *contrast* between the products of *Nature* and of *Art*, and *so far* he is quite right.

I fear, however, that 'Messieurs les Idealistes' are so absorbed in their IDEAS as to take all too little notice of experience, and as experience shows the poet likewise begins *with the Unconscious,* nay, may think himself lucky if he only gets so far through the clearest consciousness of his operations as to *re-discover undimmed* in his completed labour *the first obscure whole-idea* of his work. Without such an obscure but powerful whole-idea, which is antecedent to everything technical, *no poetic work can come into being,* and poetry, methinks, just consists in this, in being able *to utter and impart* that Unconscious, *i.e.,* to *translate* it into an *object.* The non-poet may just as well as the poet be affected by a poetic idea, but he cannot *body* it *forth;* he cannot *represent* it with the force of necessity; just as the non-poet as well as the bard may produce a product consciously and with necessity, but such a work does not take its rise in the Unconscious, and does not end there. It remains only a work of reflection. The Unconscious, *combined* with reflection, makes the poetic artist." The "obscure whole-idea" is not to be confused with the unconscious idea, but is already a conscious reflexion of the latter, and not even the first which emerges in consciousness, but is brought about by a vague moody sensation. Schiller was well aware of this also, and expresses it in his letter to Goethe of the 18th March 1796: "In me the feeling is at first without definite and clear object; this is formed only later. A certain musical word comes first, and with me the poetical idea only follows this." He writes to Körner on the 1st December 1788: "Ye critics, or however ye may be called, be abashed or tremble in presence of the instantaneous transitory *frenzy* which is found *in all true creators,* and whose *longer* or shorter duration distinguishes the thinking *artist* from the dreamer. Hence your lamentations over infertility, because ye *too early reject* and too strictly select (*scil.* from among the ideas streaming in *pêle-mêle*)." But not merely the *beginning,* but also the *continuation* of artistic production appears to him conditioned by the Unconscious, and at the close of the twentieth of his letters on the æsthetic education of mankind he declares "that the mind in the æsthetic condition certainly acts freely, and free in the highest degree from all *compulsion*, but by no means free from *laws*, and that *this æsthetic freedom is only distinguished* from *logical necessity* in thought, and from moral necessity in volition, through the laws according to which the mind proceeds *not being represented*, and because they meet with no resistance, not appearing as necessitation." Whoever in this way draws his poetical ideas from unconscious inspiration, and artistically shapes them according to laws acting unconsciously in him, is a genius. "When the genius has by his products *furnished* the rule, science can *collect* these rules, compare them, and try whether they are to be brought under one more general, and finally under a single principle. But since it proceeds from experience, it has only the limited authority of empirical science. It can merely lead to a *rational imitation* of given cases, but never to a positive extension. All *progress* in art must come from *genius*, *criticism* merely leads to *faultlessness*" (Letter to Körner of the 3d February 1794). These unambiguous testimonies to the truth of the Unconscious are the more valuable as they spring from the self-observation of a great poet, who did not, like Goethe, for instance, draw without effort from the fountain of the Unconscious, but earnestly strove after clearness and thoughtfulness, and wrestled with the artistic form in earnest critical labour, which might not unnaturally have tended to the over-estimate of his reflective industry.

P. 314, l. 29.—It is in ethno-psychological respects extremely characteristic that the treatment of geometry among the Greeks aims at a rigorous discursive mode of proof, and sedulously ignores the most obvious intuitive demonstrations; whereas that of the Hindoos, in spite of an endowment for arithmetic far surpassing the Greeks, is yet entirely based on direct intuition, and is usually confined to an artificial construction in support of intuition, to which the one word "see!" is appended. The Greeks always aim at strictly proving the smallest step in thought, and often employ ingenious trains of discursive reasoning in proof of the simplest proposition, in order not to be obliged to have recourse to direct intuition, which does not rank with them as proof. Accordingly they have constructed an imposing system of geometry, which at the same time contains a methodical guide to the solution of all problems not admitting of direct treatment. Among the Hindoos, on the other hand, every proof of a geometrical proposition is a happy flash of intelligence, and the various propositions are placed in juxtaposition without any connection; therefore, in spite of their luxuriant fancy and intuitional power, and in spite of their achievements in arithmetic and algebra, far out-stripping those of the Greeks, they never got far in geometry, and have attained only a very imperfect insight into its elements. It must, however, be styled wonderful that Schopenhauer, who had no knowledge of these historical facts, was led by his peculiar kinship with the Indian mind to make demands in reference to the treatment of geometry which must be termed a reawakening of the Indian mode of thought. As our whole modern mathematics has grown out of a synthesis of the Euclidian geometry with the Arabian algebra borrowed from the Hindoos, so at the present time the necessity of taking account in geometry of the Indian element of intuition is becoming more and more recognised on the part of pedagogical science. But although much may thereby be rendered simpler, easier, and clearer, yet the proposal of Schopenhauer to base geometry altogether upon intuition is essentially impracticable, and discursive proof will always have to go hand in hand with this to control intuition.

P. 315.—As an example of what has been said with respect to the Indian mode of treating geometry, we may give the Indian proof of the Pythagorean theorem, of which the figure of Schopenhauer is only a special case. This proof depends on the circumstance that the square of the hypothenuse as well as the sum of the squares of the other sides is equal to a third magnitude, namely, the quadrupled triangle plus the square on the difference of the other two sides.

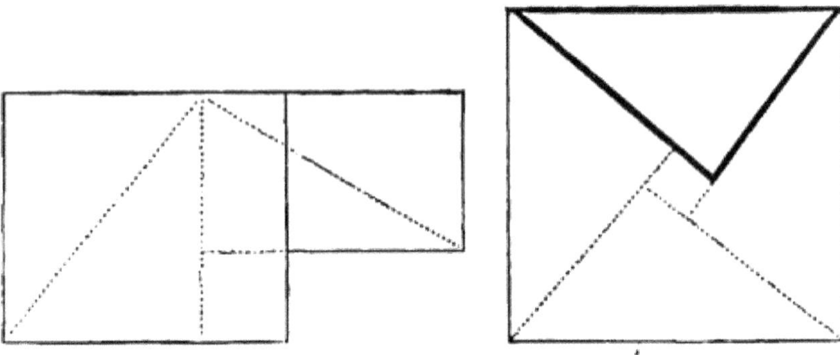

As in the equilateral triangle the latter is equal to zero, the general proof takes the form of that for the equilateral triangle (comp. Hankel, "Zur Geschichte der Mathematik im Alterthum und Mittelalter," Leipzig, 1874, p. 209). Without doubt this oldest of all the numerous proofs which have been subsequently attempted is by far the best, because it is the most evident, simple, and instructive. But that it rests on *immediate* intuition will hardly be asserted by any one speaking precisely, since the equality of the two magnitudes in question which is to be proved must always be first *concluded* from their perceived equality with a third, which latter, moreover, is differently presented *to intuition* in the two figures, and is *only* identical *in conception*.

P. 331, l. 11.—To be sure, Schopenhauer submitted to these realistic concessions only in his later period. In the earlier period of his productivity, when he subscribes to a more consistent idealism, he most decidedly denies all causal influence of things in themselves on our faculty of representation (W. as W. and I., 3d ed., i. 516, 581), and thereby logically arrives at a conception of the subjective phenomenal world of waking life, which is distinguished from that of the dream by no essential mark, but only by the accidental one, that a continuity of connected memory exists between the divisions of the day of the waking life, which is entirely wanting between the nocturnal segments of the dream-life (*ibid.*, i. 21, and Volkelt's "Dream-Phantasy," p. 194–203). In fact, if the transcendent causality of things in themselves on our presentative faculty be denied, all assignable distinction between the objects of the dream and those of waking perception ceases; for the difference of the two kinds of subjective appearance only consists in this, that the instinctive necessitation to the transcendental reference of the matter of consciousness to an existence independent on consciousness is in the *dream* a deceptive *illusion*, in the waking state, however, an instinctive *truth*, which has its real correlate in the transcendent causal action on perception of that which exists *per se* so far as the quality of the objects of perception is conditioned by the nature of that which exists *per se*.

P. 332, l. 5.—Modern Physical Science acknowledges very decidedly a view of the world in which the forms of existence and of movement, Space and Time, have transcendent validity. It assumes (just as Kant and Schopenhauer in his later period) that our sense-perception is certainly in general subjectively conditioned, but that in the special concrete case its occurrence and constitution is determined by the causal action of things, whose existence is supposed to be independent of our perception of the same, *i.e.*, of things in themselves in the Kantian sense. Physical Science knows that all our sense-qualities (Light, Colour, Sound, Heat, Odour, Sweetness, &c.) only come to pass through the co-operation of these things acting on us and our subjectivity; that thus these cannot appertain to the world of things in themselves; nevertheless it asserts that the mode and manner of our concrete sensation may be dependent on the mode of the arrangement of the constituent elements of things in themselves and the forms of their motion. This hypothesis, which in Physical Science does not pass for hypothesis, but as certainty, however involves the assumption that Space and Time are the forms of existence of this world of things in themselves transcending consciousness. For a definite order or grouping of atoms presupposes the existence-form of *Space;* causal action on the sense-organ at a definite point of time of the subjective flow of ideas the form of *Time* as transcendent real form of the action of things in themselves; and the forms of (mechanical and molecular) *motion*, from which arises the grouping of the atoms at any point of time, and on which depends the mode of action of the complex of atoms on our sense-organs, can manifestly only be conceived as real processes transcending consciousness if the forms of which they are compounded, *i.e.*, Space and Time, have transcendent validity. Thus the scientific world of the self-moving atoms, on the one hand, is, in fact, a world of things in themselves in the Kantian sense, and, on the other hand, a world in the forms of Space and Time. It is not a subjective phenomenal world, for atoms have never manifested themselves to any physicist. It is *intelligible* in the Kantian sense, so far as it lies *beyond* the possibility of all experience, and is a world existing *in and for itself*, whose existence and inner movement is assumed to be thoroughly *independent* of any representation of a consciousness. It is thus in *every* respect only to be styled a world of *things in themselves*, and as such it can indeed *only* be justified if the object of its supposition be to *explain* the transcendental objectivity of our phenomenal objects and the transcendent conditionality of our perception. But, nevertheless, it is a world *of space and time*, and can only be such if *anything* is to be at all *explained* by its assumption. Let the atom be denuded of its materiality and deprived of extension, thus be spiritualised into the immaterial monad, it yet always retains its punctual *place* in relation to other atoms, its distance from them, its direction and velocity in approximation and removal from them, thus purely spatial and temporal determinations. Should Physical Science try to make the attempt to denude the atoms of these determinations also, all possibility of an explanation of subjective phenomena would be *cut away*, thus the hypothesis of a real world of atoms would have *all scientific ground withdrawn from under its feet.* A spaceless and timeless world of spiritual monads would *ab initio* render any Physical Science impossible, and all scientific explanations based on the opposite assumption would then not only be valueless, but even *vicious in principle.* In fact, a world of spiritual monads without Space and Time (or vicarious forms of existence and motion) is also metaphysically impossible, since the Absolute Spirit before its outward *action* in Space and Time is unfolded neither *actually* nor *plurally.* Space and Time are the forms in which the All-Spirit *realises itself* in manifold existence from its essential unity and ideality; they are the forms of its self-individualising manifestation, in which its essence is revealed or appears.

It is accordingly no wonder that the investigators of Nature themselves, with their confused perception of the problems of the theory of cognition, should regard the scientific view of the world now in a realistic, now in an idealistic sense. If one starts with the view that the transcendent real world is devoid of light, colourless, soundless, &c., nay, even non-material, and consists merely in a magical play of imaginary points, one may well be inclined with Kant to seek reality in empirical perception as subjective phenomenon, and to regard things in themselves as a transcendent province of intelligible things of thought and properly unapproachable. Conversely, if one starts from this, that the predicate of reality can only be assigned to a thing existing in and for itself, *i.e.*, independently of every consciousness representing it, there is no doubt that *not* the ever-shifting *subjective* phenomenal world of consciousness, but the world of the complex of atoms existing of themselves or the world of the *objective* phenomenon of the world-essence is to be styled real, the more so as it (just as the subjective phenomenal world) subsists in the forms of space and time, and the phenomenal objects of consciousness only receive a real objectivity by being transcendentally referred to the immediately real things in themselves, and have a practical and epistemological meaning for consciousness simply as representatives of these latter. Thus the scientific cosmic theory, when looked at more closely, wears indeed the air of a *transcendental realism*, which has as much risen above *subjective idealism* (which in strictness declares the thing in itself to be a mere negative limiting notion, an indestructible illusion of our waking as of our dreaming consciousness) as *naïve realism* (which converts uncritically the objects of the subjective phenomenal world into absolute things in themselves). *The same consequence* of a transcendental realism results from a critical development of the philosophical theory of cognition, as I have shown in my writings, "Kritische Grundlegung des transcendentalen Realismus," and "J. H. v. Kirchmann's erkenntnisstheoretischer Realismus," so that in this department also the full agreement and union of Philosophy and Physical Science, here too so long at variance, is now restored.

P. 341, l. 36.—Compare with this statement and that on p. 309, l. 13, vol. i., the similar view of Lotze on the *a priori* in his "Logik," book iii. chap. 3, particularly p. 520.

VOL. II.

P. 50, l. 23.—(Comp. also vol. i. pp. 98 and 133.) Time, as we saw, vol. i. p. 346, first enters into the psychical processes through the continuance of the molecular vibrations. When, *e.g.*, a stimulus is propagated by a sensory nerve to some point in a centre, there felt, translated into will and propagated as motor impulse by motor paths to the muscles, the time of conduction in the sensory nerve as in the motor nerve is to be deducted from the total duration of the reflex process. There still remains the time which is required in the ganglion-cells of the centre, first, to extinguish the conveyed stimulus by the inhibitory influences (period of latent stimulation), and, secondly, to allow the exciting forces to increase until they have reached a degree sufficient to innervate the motor nerves (this degree might be termed the threshold of motor innervation). The sum of the two latter times constitutes in physiological language the central period of reaction. It is considerably augmented by the circumstance that a single ganglion-cell does not suffice for a reflexion, but several always participate, so that in each extinction of the stimulus and discharge of the stored-up energies is repeated. The reaction-time becomes a minimum when the places of insertion of the sensory and motor nerve (as in the spinal reflexes) lie very close to one another; it is augmented in proportion as more ganglion-cells are traversed by the stimulus before the same is outwardly discharged as motor impulse. The latter retardation attains its maximum in the cerebral hemispheres and their elaboration of the conveyed impressions by conscious reflexion. The fluctuating, hesitating, and doubting is of longer duration the more cells are drawn into action, *i.e.*, the further the reflexion is spun out before the resolution to act is taken. But with all that, each single action of the Unconscious woven into this process is *timeless*, *i.e.*, in each single cell there is no time to be interposed *between* sensation and will, although both, in consequence of the repeated molecular undulations, possess a certain *temporal extent*, which may in part be coincident (as the duration of every cause coincides with that of the effect to the merest fraction).

P. 86, l. 5.—Comp. the preceding addendum to p. 50, l. 23.

P. 89, l. 5.—If we enter more minutely into the physiological aspect of the question, in place of the atom, the ganglionic cell, as indivisible nerve-element with an indivisible consciousness, is the order of individuals to be particularly taken account of. The ganglion-cell possesses a certain individual force or individual will, which, through its individual character (or, in physiological language, through its inherited or acquired specific energies), is led to manifest itself in certain favoured directions. The satisfaction of this individual will can, as we shall soon see, only be felt as pleasure by reflective comparison with the pain of non-satisfaction; the repression of the same, or the suppression and enforced inhibition of its manifestation makes itself, on the contrary, immediately perceptible as a painful feeling (qualitatively coloured by unconscious representations). Now we know from the Appendix that the satisfaction of the individual will of a ganglion-cell, or, in physiological language, the actualising of its predispositions in specific energies, consists chemically in a *decomposition*, *i.e.*, that the discharge of force or transformation of tension into *vis viva* is effected by a decomposition of complex chemical compounds into simpler ones. Chemical combination, whereby the tension or store of work is accumulated as a normal process of nutrition, proceeds in the state of repose so slowly in comparison with the suddenness of the discharge, that at each single moment without doubt the threshold of consciousness (at least for the collective consciousness of the ganglion-cell) is not overstepped. It is otherwise if an external stimulus is conveyed to the cell through the immerging fibres. In this case the stimulus is mainly extinguished by the inhibitory influences, and only secondarily after an interval, during which the stimulus has become latent, does the cell answer by an active discharge of force The stimulus consists in a current of innervation, *i.e.*, in a series of impulses of vital force. That this *vis viva* is extinguished or absorbed by the inhibitory influences of the cell physically only admits of the interpretation that it is transformed into tension, and this transformation is compressed into a space of time sufficiently confined to be felt as contrast to the natural direction of the individual will, *i.e.*, as pain. The qualitatively coloured pain thus felt acts now as motive to the manifestation of will, and the reaction of will is, as it were, the attempt to free oneself from the pain of the imposed constraint. This second phase of the reflex process in the ganglion-cell does not, in the first place, enter into consciousness by itself, but only so far as the painful feeling is paralysed and disappears from consciousness through the satisfaction of the manifestation of will or discharge of force. The matter of consciousness is thus essentially composed of sensations, which arise through the extinction of inflowing stimuli in ganglion-cells by means of their inhibitory influences.

On the other hand, the mere process of *conduction*, so far as it is understood as mechanical propagation of the received stimulation without absorption and active regeneration of living force, cannot lead to the genesis of sensation,[1] at least not of sensation in nerve-elements, but at the most in the atoms constituting them (where the absorption and regeneration of *vis viva* is to be traced in each single vibration). Accordingly, it might seem as if the nerve-fibre, as such, were incapable of sensation, because it only mechanically conveys the peripheral or central energies of stimulation. But we have already seen in the Appendix that the nerve-fibre also possesses a store of force of its own, which it sets free as the result of stimulation, and that in its course

[1] Maudsley says, *op. cit.*, p. 305: "When the whole energy of an idea passes immediately outwards in ideo-motor action, then there is scarce any, or there may be no, consciousness of it; in order that there may be consciousness of the idea, it is necessary not only that its excitation reach a certain intensity, but that the whole force of it do not pass immediately outwards in the reaction. . . . The persistence for a time of a certain degree of intensity of energy in the ideational circuit would certainly appear to be the condition of consciousness." This is, however, only possible if the energy of the stimulus is absorbed by the cell *i.e.*, converted into tension.

a part of the stimulus is absorbed. Only the tendency to decomposition is in the fibre far greater than in the cell, and at the same time the store of active force and the inhibitory influences far less than in the latter. On the other side, it would be an extravagant idea if we believed that in the ganglion-cell the *whole* living force of every stimulus is annihilated, and the reactive innervation generated afresh exclusively from the existing store of force; rather is this only an extreme case for a cell destined solely for central functions. But at the same time all ganglion-cells are also more or less predisposed for direct conduction (*e.g.*, all bodily pains are conducted through the grey strands of the spinal cord to the brain, whilst the white strands only conduct the painless sensations of the tactile and muscular sense). The oftener a ganglion-cell has conveyed a stimulus in a particular direction, the more is it accustomed to this path, and with the less expenditure of its own energy does it perform its work, *i.e.*, a so much larger part of the received energy of stimulation it propagates unabsorbed, and a so much smaller part of the energy of stimulation it absorbs, to replace it from its own resources. The less, however, the absorbed part of the energy of stimulation becomes, the weaker becomes the sensation, *i.e.*, the sensation is the more enfeebled in the passage of the stimulus through a cell, the more the cell is exercised in conducting in this particular direction, and sinks with a certain degree of exercise below the threshold of consciousness. This exercise is, however, always related only to a particular kind (form of vibration) of stimulus, and must be acquired anew for a newly occurring unwonted kind of stimuli. Thus then is it also possible that the absorbed part of the energy of stimulation in the nerve-fibres remains for the ordinary kinds of stimuli under normal circumstances below the threshold, whilst the nerve-fibre may again bring into use its capacity to feel, either if unusual stimuli are conveyed to it, or if it is placed under abnormal circumstances (*e.g.*, through the enhancement of its irritability in consequence of separation from its centre).

The physiological mode of looking at the matter, therefore, altogether confirms the above supposition that it is the collision of two wills opposed in their content from which consciousness springs. The individual will of the nerve-element is disturbed in its equilibrium by the will of the stimulus invading its repose; the elastic interception of this disturbance is the absorption of the stimulus by conversion of its *vis viva* into tension, a self-preserving process on the part of the cell that is diametrically opposed to its tendency to will-manifestation, *i.e.*, to the discharge of its tension into living force. The conflict with the individual will, the forcing of the same from its position of equilibrium into the direction opposed to its own tendency, is felt as pain, and the restitution, or the second act of the self-preserving process of the nerve-element, is the discharge of the reaction, which at first aims only at the restoration of the state of equilibrium; but, the opportunity for the manifestation of will once being given, goes beyond the state induced by the stimulus, namely, discharges an excess of tension accumulated by nutrition.

P. 93, l. 18.—Comp. on this section my "Erläut. zur Met. d. Unb.," p. 42–49.

P. 118, last l.—Comp. my "Erläut. zur Met. d. Unb.," p. 49–51.

P. 148, l. 23.—According to recent investigations by Kleinenberg ("Hydra," Leipzig, 1872), the differentiation of the protoplasm into nerves and muscular fibre already begins with the Hydra or the fresh-water polypes, but in such wise, that it is the *same cell* whose peripheral rotund form plays the part of a sensitive cutaneous cell, whilst its central fibrous processes serve as the contractile element, *i.e.*, as prototype of the muscle-cell, in that they are excited to contract by the external part. Kleinenberg has called these cells "neuro-muscular cells." They exhibit the transition from the more lowly organisms, in which all parts of the protoplasm of a cell *uniformly* act as nervous and muscular elements, to the higher ones, where the functions are not merely distributed to different parts of the same cell, but the different functioning elements have become differentiated into separate cell-layers.

P. 155, note, last l.—An attempt to eliminate the concept of force from molecular physics has recently been made by Alexander Wiesner ("Das Atom," Leipzig, 1874); as, however, in this writer philosophical acumen and mathematical aptitude are alike wanting, and his explanations, regarded even from a purely physical point of view, appear but little tenable and plausible, the development of molecular physics is hardly likely to be furthered by this attempt. Although Wiesner is perfectly clear as to the necessity of removing the idea of matter from the atom, yet a certain remnant thereof remains clinging to his atom, because with the reduction of all force to energy of motion there would otherwise remain no subject of the motor function. The attempt to regard the corporeal atoms as the converging, the ether as the sphere of the parallel atoms, can hardly claim serious consideration, especially as all coercive force is wanting to the united atoms.—Another and far more important memoir by A. Pfeilsticker bears the title "Das Kinetsystem, oder Elimination der Repulsivkräfte und überhaupt des Kraftbegriffs aus der Molecular-Physik" (Stuttgart, 1873). Here, however, the author would be misunderstood if the title were thought to imply that the writer denies the concept of force altogether. The author's intention is only the perfectly proper one, to take the idea of force out of the sphere of mathematical physics as such, simply to hand it over to metaphysics, and in the mechanics of the atom, *in place* of force, to be satisfied with its most direct expression, acceleration. The work performed by a force is most directly measured by the magnitude of the acceleration called forth by it in other atoms; mechanics, therefore, needs the *standard* for the *magnitude* of the force as *surrogate* of the idea of force itself. In this, as we know, there is nothing new, and Pfeilsticker merely makes use of a certain modification in the meaning of certain expressions and formulæ in order to make more complete the agreement between the metaphysical idea of force and its mathematical surrogate. It does not, however, occur to him to deny that the "property" of an atom "to cause changes of movement according to certain laws" in other atoms (p. 14) must be philosophically retained as metaphysical cause of these uniform changes of motion, *i.e.*, as *force* behind acceleration.

P. 158, l. 15.—It used to be assumed that the ether alone filled up the space between the celestial bodies. This view is, at the present time, more and more receding before the other, that the permanent gases in a state of extreme attenuation occupy this intermediate space. That the intervals between the planets are filled with permanent gases may at the present time be assumed as tolerably certain, but that also between the several suns of our world-lens the corporeal molecules of the gases are not wanting can now likewise be regarded as probable. Accordingly, if the ether has lost its importance as a hypothetical medium for the filling up of cosmic space, it has in compensation continually gained in recent times in significance as an hypothesis for the explanation of the constitution of matter. Edlund's remarkable "Theory of Electricity," for which I venture to prophesy an important future, rests on the assumption that the non-electric state of a body is the condition of static equilibrium between the ether-atoms contained in it and the whole of the ether outside it, whilst positive or negative disturbances of this state of equilibrium represent the two species of electricity (cp. "Naturforscher," 1872, Nos. 21 and 23; 1873, Nos. 24, 39, 41). The propagation of the light-vibrations, whose transversal direction must pass for strictly proved, is with this state of things only mathematically intelligible if the atoms which are its substrates essentially follow other laws than the body-atoms subject to the laws of gravitation. Experiments on interference seem to show that the ether as medium of the light-vibrations is to be regarded as at rest in relation to the motion of the earth, so that to our apprehension it seems to stream through the pores of our atmosphere with a velocity which is approximately equal, but opposed to, that of the earth in the mundane space. Recently Maxwell has set up an "electro-magnetic theory of light," which proceeds from the fundamental thought that the medium of electricity and that of light is one and the same medium, namely, the ether (Naturf., vi. p. 159). He has in a theoretical way, as a consequence of his hypothesis, developed the condition that the square root of the di-electric constant must be equal to the refractive power of light; and the empirical confirmation of this law, both for various substances (Naturf., vi. p. 247), and also for different axes of a crystal, by the experiments of Boltzmann is well calculated to give a strong support to the theory of Maxwell. But even apart from electricity and light, the hypothesis of the ether is indispensable for the constitution of the solid, rigid bodies, which can never be explained by merely attracting, but always only by the mutual action of attracting and repelling forces. This has hitherto been recognised by all mathematical physicists; the first interesting attempt to constitute solid bodies merely from attractive forces, and to eliminate the repulsive or ether-atoms from this part of mathematical physics, is that by Pfeilsticker in his memoir "Das Kinetsystem" (Stuttgart, 1873). Unfortunately, however, the suppositions there made (infinity of matter) are of so doubtful a kind, and the indications afforded so scanty and provisional (the memoir is only to be the precursor of a detailed "Kinetology"), that no opinion on the alleged solubility of the problem can be formed. On the whole, therefore, so far the hypothesis of the repulsive ether-atoms will have to pass for just as well-founded as that of the attractive corporeal atoms.

P. 158, l. 24.—If one recognises the mutual penetrability of the atoms (cp. p. 170), it undoubtedly follows from the consideration of freely mobile corporeal atoms, that they must vibrate through one another without hindrance (because the velocity with which they travel will be infinitely great as the attraction at an infinitely little distance), and after the backward swing must return to their point of departure to begin their play over again (Pfeilsticker's "Kinetsystem," sects. ii. and vi.) A gradual diminution of the amplitude of body-atoms vibrating through one another and final reduction to zero would only be possible with a sort of frictional resistance, which is excluded in the case of freely movable atoms. But the case appears to be different when the empirical fact of relatively rigid combinations of atomic groups is taken note of, however it be explained; for in it there is then given such an arrest of the free movement of the atoms as must finally induce their coming together. If, then, as Pfeilsticker maintains, the rigid corporeal atoms were explicable without repulsive forces, the gradual union of corporeal atoms into a point must also be conceivable, and therefore his assertion seems unjustified that several atoms can only be united in a point if they are originally created in this form. On the other hand, the other remark (p. 29) is excellent, that homogeneous atoms (no matter what their nature), if they are once united in a point, can no longer be separated by internal or external influence, even if they possess no attraction for one another; for every action would always affect both atoms *equally*, thus never be able to produce a different effect in both.

P. 170, l. 10.—My assertion of the perfect penetrability of the corporeal atoms has certainly appeared to many a physicist accustomed to the dogma of impenetrability a philosophical paradox, and it affords me therefore particular satisfaction to be able to point to an authority like Dr. Albert Pfeilsticker, all whose calculations in his "Kinetsystem" depend on the absolute penetrability of the atoms as on a self-evident supposition. When Dr. Alexander Wiesner in his memoir "Das Atom" (Leipzig, Thomas, 1874) controverts "Pfeilsticker's penetrability theory," he does this simply on the ground of a remnant of the old prejudice of matter that clings to him despite all his protestations, without which remnant nothing "movable" would remain for him, since, as above remarked, he desires thoroughly to eliminate the notion of force.

P. 171, l. 10.—An instructive instance of the fixity of sense-prejudices is afforded by Albert Lange, who, in his "History of Materialism," gives, in a special section, "Force and Matter" (Thomas's trans., vol. ii. p. 351–397, Eng. and For. Phil. Library), an instructive sketch of the historical development of the physical and chemical atomic theory, and of the present views of natural philosophers on the relation of force and matter. He there, so far as criticism is concerned, agrees substantially with my foregoing disquisition; remains, however, almost avowedly wavering between Scylla and Charybdis, because he sees the impossibility of retaining the concept Matter, and yet does not venture to take the only consistent step which successfully solves the problem. He blames Büchner because, from his lay point of view, he "cannot sufficiently free himself from the sensuous idea of compound, apparently compact, bodies, such as our touch and eye present them to us. The professed physicist, at least the mathematical physicist, cannot make the least step in his science without freeing himself from such ideas" (p. 370). The result of his historical exposition comes to this: "That the progress of the science has led us more and more to put force in the place of matter, and that the increasing exactness of research more and more resolves matter into force. The two ideas, therefore, do not stand so simply as abstractions beside each other; but the one is by abstraction and inquiry resolved into the other, yet so that there is always something left" (p. 379). Nothing could be objected to the last clause if it only meant that in the *previous* phases of molecular physics such an unresolved remainder of matter *has been* left; but it does not follow from that that the process of resolution in question must stop at a definite limit, and *must* for all time necessarily still retain a matter undefinable and valueless for explanation behind the forces alone of account for scientific purposes. On the contrary, the previous course of science undoubtedly demands the making a clean sweep of the last remnant of the sensuous prejudice blamed in the case of Büchner. If matter, as such, is resolved into forces, the substance supporting the force-effects demanded by the nature of our thinking can no longer be matter as such, which is constituted of these force-effects (p. 293, above); but still less can it be the abstract ghost of a matter remaining after the deduction of all forces, the only definition of which is limited to its being a substantial support of the dynamic effects. But if nothing remains of the union of force and matter but the union of force with the category required by thought of substantiality, the problem, insoluble according to Lange, is very easily solved by the simple recognition that it is force and *only* force to which the predicate of substantiality belongs. Herewith the "indispensable" support of the force-effects at once ceases to be "incomprehensible" (p. 395), and the "limit of natural knowledge" erected by sense-prejudice falls away as a mocking subjective phantom. If matter as such *can* not be hypostatised because it is proved to be result of force-effects, if the idea of stuff has been itself volatilised into the mere category of substance, it is, in fact, undiscoverable why it "never at all occurs" (p. 395) to Lange to connect the indispensable category of substantiality with the *only quality* which turns out, on the analysis of matter, to be its real core, namely, force, *i.e.*, to recognise this itself with Leibniz as the true and only substance. The only assignable reason for this is, that Lange imagines that he can in his philosophising retain, even in the last and highest principles, sensuous intuitiveness, and with the surrender of these must lose the scientific ground under his feet. This is, of course, a prejudice of the crudest sensualistic empiricism, which has no idea that all science just *begins* with the elevation of sense-intuition into conception. Hence it is but matter of course that his resistance to the surrender of intuitiveness occurs at this point much too late; for the category of substantiality, into which the concept of stuff is for him volatilised, is yet as abstract as possible; and of force, he himself confesses (p. 371) that it "cannot be at all adequately represented in forms of sense: we help ourselves by pictures, such as the lines of the figures in the doctrines of mathematics, without ever confounding these pictures with the notion of force." Had Lange consistently held fast to this simple truth, the false appearance of incomprehensibility arising from the perverse struggling for sensible intuitiveness in the highest principles would have disappeared of itself.

P. 200, l. 27.—Häckel still maintains in his "Anthropogenie" (p. 246) the morphological equivalence of the segments in the articulata and vertebrata, relying on the point that in the embryo of the vertebrate the rest of the vertebræ are ordinarily developed from the anterior vertebræ that are first to make their appearance, as the divisions of the annelids arise by *terminal gemmation.* But "Si duo faciunt idem, non est idem," *i.e.*, the morphological meaning of an ontogenetic metameros is only certainly to be perceived from the phylogenetic developmental history of the same. Here, however, on tracing the annelids to their origin, we find a *chain* of similar individual organisms, whilst the ancestors of the vertebrates nowhere exhibit such a chain, but always only a *single* organism (*e.g.*, Amphioxus), whose cord is ossified at a certain stage of development in order to attain a firmer skeleton, but at the same time is internally articulated for the sake of retaining greater mobility.

P. 219, l. 19.—Häckel asserts that the homogeneity of the mass in the non-nucleated protozoa is proved by the microscopic observation of the pigment-corpuscles, which have been offered the Moner "to devour," that move unimpeded and uniformly in all directions in the body of the protozoon. Of course, according to this, the truth of the following propositions must be admitted: "Every part may receive and digest food; every part is irritable and sensitive; every part may be moved independently; and every part is, lastly, also capable of propagation and regeneration" ("Anthropogenie," p. 381). Only we must understand by "part" a piece of an empirical size, and by no means a chemical molecule of the albumen in question; only on this supposition can we speak of a homogeneity of the Moneres in contrast to the nucleated Amœbæ, but by no means in the chemical signification of the word. For that even the lowest animals are not "structureless," as a solution of albumen, is manifestly shown by the distribution of the granules through the whole protoplasmic mass. The functions of nutrition, movement, and sensation are also performed in the nucleated cells; not by the nucleus, but by the nucleated protoplasm, and only the function of propagation, *i.e.*, the initiative to cell-division, is in the case of the latter centralised at the nucleus, whilst in the Moneres this also is still decentralised. What part in all these functions is played by the granules, on that point I will make no conjectures; at all events, they suffice to enable us to speak of a *morphological* structure *in addition to* the *chemical* structure of the protoplasm, and distinguish the *living* lumps of protoplasm specifically from all albuminous droplets externally resembling them. If the *chemical* structure of the proteid substances were alone sufficient to cause the vital phenomena of the protoplasm, it would at least be very surprising that all attempts to produce

Moneres from finely distributed albuminous droplets have hitherto remained without result.

P. 247, l. 11.—J. H. v. Kirchmann asserts in his memoir "On the Principle of Realism," p. 43: "In truth, then, the ideation of the Unconscious has all the determinations which make knowledge in man a conscious knowledge," and seeks to prove this assertion in the following manner: "Now we find in *conscious* knowledge (1.) that it has a content wholly in the form of *knowledge;* (2.) that it knows at the same time this form itself, or that knowledge knows, *besides* its content, at the same time *itself* as knowledge (is conscious *of itself*); (3.) that knowledge can embrace the many *dispersed* ideas received one after another and relate them to one another in the most varied manner, in virtue of the forms of relation inherent in it; and (4.) that knowledge, *in spite of* the plurality of its content and of its ideas being *separated in time*, still *knows* itself *as One.* Now of these determinations affecting the form of knowledge, the Unconscious thinking of the All-One possesses, according to the explanations of the author, unquestionably those under 1, 3, and likewise 4; for the rationality attributed to it, which is essentially expounded as relation of the single ideas in the form of means to others as ends, belongs indeed to the determination under 3, and the all-unity of the Unconscious leads also to the determination under 4. But even the determination under 2 cannot be denied to the thinking of the Unconscious, because only thereby is the *picking out* of the suitable means *from the whole mass of ideas* possible in the special cases of the auxiliary intervention of the Unconscious, and because the contrast of Volition and Ideation must be likewise contained in it as *known*, since the goal, the suppression of the Will by conscious thinking, can only thereby be represented by it at all."

On this the following is to be remarked. Nos. 3 and 4 concern the *union* of the scattered given empirical thought-material in consciousness, or the *connecting relations* of the content of thought, which is *cut up* both in space and time through the narrowness and discursiveness of perception. Unconscious thinking, however, does not need subsequently to collect the inner manifold of its content into a unity, because it is originally an indivisible totality, not an aggregate of scattered fragments. It need not at all become conscious of its own unity, because its internal plurality is not *given* to it, like conscious perception, but *posited* by it itself, and indeed is posited *in* an indissoluble unity. As little as the form of unity has to be subsequently applied to the matter of the unconscious Idea, so little have the relations in which the many moments and parts of this matter stand to one another and the whole. So far as these relations may be contained in intellectual intuition in general, so far do they lurk implicitly in the matter of unconscious perception, without the latter needing to become conscious of their presence in abstract explication; so far, however, as the relations of our conscious thinking depend on its discursiveness, so far can they in general find no entrance into unconscious ideation. The assertion of Kirchmann that his points Nos. 3 and 4 find application to unconscious thinking in my sense is then certainly erroneous. But as concerns the point No. 1, the expression made use of in the same, "form of knowledge," is altogether ambiguous. If it merely implies as much as "form of ideality" (in opposition to the form of reality or of existence), nothing more is posited by it than the community emphasised by me (and cited by Kirchmann shortly before) of an ideal content without any reality of its own for the unconscious and conscious presentation. If, however, "form of knowledge" means the same as "form of consciousness," then it is precisely the *point in dispute*, whether this determination belongs to unconscious perception, so that Kirchmann cannot render as a *reason* for its affirmation what is only the affirmation itself.

It is, according to this, clear that, of the four points mentioned by Kirchmann, *only the second* touches the core of the pending question, although he leaves something to be desired in clearness of expression. It is declared to be a characteristic form of conscious knowledge that consciousness not merely knows its own content, but that it knows it also as content in contrast to its form, *i.e.*, that it has it for object, wherewith at the same time the knowledge of itself is connected as subject. In truth, the *knowledge* of the form of consciousness as such, and of the opposition of the matter to the same, is only a result of a higher development of conscious intellect, but it remains, therefore, still correct that the actual *existence* of this contrast of form and matter of consciousness and the objectivity of the matter resulting from it is characteristic for conscious thinking. This is, however, only the case because for unconscious thinking this separation and this opposition of form and matter of knowledge, of subject and object of the thinking act, does *not* exist, because here subject and object are in direct identity, or rather still remain in indifference, have not yet stepped out of their original non-separation. This contrast first arises from the real conflict of opposing and mutually inhibiting individual wills. In the All-One, that has nothing outside itself, there is nought conceivable that could disturb the identity of the subject-object in the Unconscious Idea and lead to the separation of reflecting knowledge from thing known.—Kirchmann gives two reasons why unconscious knowledge must at the same time be knowledge of itself as knowledge, *i.e.*, consciousness (or, more precisely, self-consciousness), whose probative force, however, has not become very clear to me, even taken in the sense of its author. He asserts, namely, that, in the first place, the selection of the most suitable means from the whole multitude of ideas, and, secondly, the presentation of volition as contrast of the logical, is not possible without knowledge of knowledge. But now the suitable means are not deliberately set apart from a whole mass of actual inappropriate representations, but of all possible representations only those become efficient which are logically demanded (demanded, *e.g.*, as means to end). It is not obvious what influence the logical or teleological determination of the quality of the awakening Idea could have on the destruction of the indifference of subject and object or of form and matter in the Unconscious Idea. (Other objections to the unconsciousness of the Absolute Idea derived from the positing of purpose have been already discussed, vol. ii. p. 255 ff.) As little evident is it how from the circumstance that the willing must for the Idea be a *known* one, the other assertion is to be derived that the coming to knowledge of the Will through the Idea must be *conscious*, or that with this knowledge there must be reflection on the knowledge as such. Not, as Kirchmann thinks, as represented goal, but as starting-point, must volition in some way or other become conscious, in order that a process may at all come to pass (see further vol. ii. p. 256–258, and vol. iii. p. 163–169). However, this consciousness is one entirely undetermined in content, that only gives an impulse to the unfolding of the Idea, but does not enter into its content.—Thus, on closer investigation, disappears every semblance of probative force for the proof attempted by Kirchmann of his assertion that the ideation of the Unconscious has *all*, or even only *any one*, of the determinations which make knowledge in man *conscious* knowledge.

P. 271, l. 12.—Comp. here my memoir "Die Selbstzersetzung des Christenthums und die Religion der Zukunft," 2 Aufl., Berlin, C. Duncker, 1874, particularly chap. vii.: "Die historischen Bausteine zur Religion der Zukunft."

P. 271, l. 31.—On the appearance of the sixth edition of this work it was still unknown to me that the hope here expressed had already begun to receive its realisation in a "Christliche Dogmatik" that had appeared simultaneously with my first edition (Zurich, Orell &

Füssli, 1869). The author (A. E. Biedermann, Professor in Zürich) of this book, which I regard not merely as the most important theological, but also as one of the most distinguished speculative achievements of the last generation, may well claim a like position in the Protestant theology of the last third of this century to that of Schleiermacher in the first third, and stands in a similar relation to Hegel as Schleiermacher to Plato and Spinoza. In place of the nebulosity of Schleiermacher, he offers, however, a concentrated wealth of acute speculative thought, and stands on the shoulders of the historico-critical school, whose results he does not hush up like the compromising theology, but accepts in all their clear fulness, and turns to good account as negative transition to his own positive speculation, which is to unfold the proper thought-content of the representable elements in the historical dogmas now breaking up through their immanent contradictions. If the historical continuity of Christianity were in any wise to be saved, it would without doubt be in this way; to my mind, however, the harmony of the thought historically transmitted with that finally sifted out by speculation is so far-fetched, that in the end only the name is saved, concealing something altogether new. But what is pertinent here is the fact that speculative reforming tendencies are showing themselves in the circles of Protestant theology itself, which sooner or later must gather round their flag all who seek to retain a *living* Christianity, thus are averse to a rigid orthodoxy, and yet find themselves just as much repelled by the rationalistic, illuminated, and pale sentimental irreligiosity of liberal Protestantism as by the obscurity and hushing-up system of the theology of compromise. The speculative content of this new reformed theology as a purified Hegelianism is very closely allied to the principles advocated by me, although in some points it departs from it in substance, in others only in terminology (cp. especially the sections "Das Wesen Gottes," § 617–631; "Das Dasein Gottes,"

§ 632–640; and "Der Begriff des absoluten Geistes," § 696–717).

Biedermann too seeks for the higher synthetic unity of a view of the world, which conceives the Absolute only as the *vital force* poured out in the All and of one, which apprehends it as spiritual *personality*, and sees in both only partially true modes of thinking, which must be sublated in the higher conception of the *impersonal absolute Spirit* (p. 645). That he terms the former view the *pantheistic*, appears to be an unessential difference of expression; it seems to me that the etymology of the word "*pantheistic*" would not at all admit of the setting aside of the immaterial spiritualistic moment, and that a view which comprehends the Absolute only as unspiritual natural force can only receive the name of Naturalism or Naturalistic Monism, but not that of Pantheism. On the other hand, the latter term is properly covered by the principle of an impersonal Absolute Spirit, for which Biedermann has not missed the adequate expression. His attempted synthesis of Theism and Pantheism is therefore substantially quite the same as that which is aimed at in my synthesis of Naturalistic Monism and Theism, namely, Spiritualistic Monism or Pantheism.

Biedermann openly acknowledges that the understanding must necessarily be led to conceive the indivisible absolute ground of the inner purposiveness of the world as *impersonal* and immanent, and that every attempt to refer the immanent conformity to law and purpose to the wise will of a personal Creator not only denudes it of its absoluteness, but also brings the immanent purpose of the world into an insoluble antinomy with the personal aims of its Creator (§ 628). He declares that God is not merely immanent in the world in his *action*, and transcendent to it in his being, but that he is immanent to it as very ground of its existence, and that this groundedness of the world is *his being itself*, that does not lie as an otherness behind it (p. 629); that a transcendence of God in respect of the world can only be asserted so far as he remains unaffected by the forms of particular existence of the world (Spaceness and Timeness), *i.e.*, as he is indeed everywhere and always immanent to finite existence as its *ground*, but yet himself is in no place and in no time (*ibid.*) Nowhere have I found the arguments against the personality of the Absolute Spirit marshalled with such thoroughness, clearness, and acuteness as by Biedermann. He shows that all the proofs of the existence of God can only lead to the conception of an impersonal Absolute Spirit as ground of the natural and moral order, but that the mind only arrives by an illegitimate leap at the supposition of a personality of the Absolute Spirit (§ 632–640). He further maintains that every one of the attributes of God assumed on the part of theology, thought out in all its consequences, leads to an antinomy between the absoluteness and the personality of God, which can always only be regarded as a specialised expression of the general contradiction existing between these conceptions (§ 617–631). Lastly, he deals with this contradiction in its general form, and shows the untenability of all the attempts made from the most diverse sides to obscure or to overcome it (§ 716). To these demonstrations of Biedermann, which excellently supplement my own, I refer all readers who might not feel satisfied and convinced by my expositions, which could not possibly penetrate far into the theological domain within the limits of the present book.

When we consider that Biedermann's work was composed *before* the appearance of the first edition of the "Philosophy of the Unconscious," we should not be surprised that the author still holds to the Hegelian categories of the Being-in-self and Being-for-self of the Absolute Spirit; that he speaks of a reflection of the natural processes and of the acts of individual spirits in the pure Being-in-self of the Absolute Spirit (p. 638), and accordingly of a self-consciousness of the latter (p. 561). It is, however, easily discernible that, with Biedermann's metaphysical point of view, there is no longer any necessity at all for the assumption retained by him from the traditional Theism that *everything* ejected into natural actuality from the absolute Idea by the absolute Will notwithstanding that it does not cease to be comprehended in the creative Idea of the Absolute Spirit, is again superfluously *reflected* in the Absolute, and thus becomes *conscious* in the same. That in *certain* acts such a reflection takes place is true, but they are in comparison with the total action of the Absolute only *partial* reflections, and can therefore also only produce *partial* apperceptions, *i.e.*, finite individual consciousnesses, but not lead to an indivisible collective consciousness of the Absolute Spirit, to a divine self-consciousness. If there really were such an absolute self-consciousness, this would be the absolute Ego, *i.e.*, the absolute Personality, at least in intellectual reference, and Biedermann's argument against the personality of the Absolute would in this respect be adduced in vain. But since that assertion is only a theistic reminiscence, no longer fitting in with Biedermann's metaphysical Pantheism, it is to be hoped that the consistent following out of his perception of the untenability of the Personality of the Absolute Spirit will lead him likewise to abandon the self-consciousness and the consciousness, and therewith to come over in principle to our point of view. How near he stands to the latter, despite his apparently opposite mode of expression, even in his "Christliche Dogmatik," is best proved by § 627, dealing with the divine omniscience. We there read: "In order to comprehend the knowledge of God as *absolute*, as *omniscience*, the doctrine of the Church commands us to think away all the discursive elements of finite human knowledge (§ 409). But the more this is actually done, *the more disappears also all analogy with a personal knowing*, and there only remains *the impersonal spirituality of the immanent ground of the world*, in which everything that flows from it is of necessity (!) again reflected in it (!)." Apart from this "being reflected," by which the thought is disfigured, it is clear enough that "the pure spirituality of the essentially single ground of the whole world-process" (p. 566), which is to admit of no analogy with *personal* knowing, is intended to affirm precisely the same as my unconscious intuition of the absolute Idea, except that it is here not yet clearly elevated into scientific consciousness, that the form of human knowledge, which must be abstracted from absolute knowledge, is nothing more than the form of consciousness.

Before we quit Biedermann, another inconsequence must be pointed out, which likewise must be regarded as a concession to the traditional Theism, namely, he asserts that, although personality must be excluded from the *notion* of the Absolute Spirit, it is yet the only possible *image* through which the essential being of God can be brought home to us, although inadequately, and that the religious feeling cannot dispense with the imaginative realisation of God (p. 645–646). Granted that the unsuitable image of a spiritual personality is always a relatively truer representation than that of an unspiritual natural force, granted also that human thinking can never entirely extricate itself from the soil of sensuous perception, it yet by no means follows from these premises that the "absolute personality" is and *always* must remain the only possible kind of the representation of God. For there is no dualism of concept and percept in human thinking, but thinking is *itself* "*as pure thinking* only a scientific *elaboration* of our *perceptions*" (p. 646). If, accordingly, this process of elaboration has once reached such a point that the determination of personality is to be unconditionally *eliminated* from the idea of the Absolute Spirit, all relapse into a surmounted stage of this elaborative process of the ideas is to be unconditionally *avoided*, —notwithstanding the circumstance that even so there is still a residuum of *perceptional* elements in the concept of the Absolute Spirit,—and consequently without impairing religious feeling.

P. 286, l. 3.—Yeast still proved after cooling from – 113°

C. a vital stimulator of fermentation ("Naturforscher," 1874, No. 37, p. 351).

P. 287, l. 5.—As these scientific facts are among those cited in my book which have encountered the most opposition, it affords me the greater satisfaction to be able to point to the memoir of a modern exact naturalist (Prof. W. Preyer, "Ueber die Erforschung des Lebens," Jena, Mauke, 1873), who not only gives a connected history of the respective discoveries (from Leuwenhoek's discovery in the year 1701) (p. 25–31 and p. 49–64), but also entirely agrees with my view that the condition in question exhibits the *absolute cessation* of all life, in contrast to all states of vital function, however reduced. He says (p. 31): "And yet there are very many at the present day who would declare all the observations and experiments I have cited, even those instituted by myself, illusions. Since such experiments can, however, be easily instituted (I have demonstrated the facts in my own laboratory and auditorium very frequently for years), the doubts will certainly gradually disappear, and the old views of life be for ever abandoned."—I therefore beg every one who intends to dispute the statements in question first to make himself acquainted with the passages referred to of the above-mentioned brochure. Preyer can the less be objected to on the scientific side as surety as he is an avowed materialist, and even from the fact that life may for a long time completely cease in an organism and then re-awaken, hastily thinks to be able to draw capital for his materialism.

P. 291, l. 18.—A similar case to the stratified grains of Famintzin is presented by the interesting experiments of Moritz Traube ("Journal of the Meeting of Scientific Investigators in Breslau," 1874, p. 191), who by introducing drops of glue into diluted tartaric acid obtained the chemical precipitate of a colloid membrane. The imitation of an organic cell thus obtained showed by intussusception of water the analogue of organic growth. With a proper concentration of the two agents, the compression of the molecules in the membrane is such that the passage of the chemically different molecules is prevented; on the other hand, the endosmosis of aqueous molecules into the interior of the cell goes on unhindered. In consequence of this, the drop swells, and the membrane is stretched by the pressure from within like a soap-bubble. It would soon burst, if the still undissolved glue in the interior did not form a reservoir, whence it may be recruited. The water, namely, that has effected an entrance, dissolves some glue, and as soon as the interstices between the molecules of the membrane become by the stretching of the latter so great, that the molecules of the glue and of the tannic acid can communicate with one another through the same, new molecules are precipitated owing to this chemical contact, which arrange themselves in the tissue of the membrane, and thereby strengthen it. If the drop of glue is attached in hanging fashion to the glass rod supporting it, the concentration of the gelatinous solution is everywhere pretty much the same, and the increase therefore tolerably equal at all parts, so that the spherical shape is on the whole preserved with the augmentation. On the other hand, if the drop is attached lying or standing to the upper end of the glass rod, the solution of glue is arranged by the influence of gravity in horizontal layers, that become ever more diluted above (remote from the glue-reservoir). In consequence of this, the parts of the membrane at the top of the cell are more unfavourably situated as regards the nutritive material; they become thinner than the others, and therefore yield more to the equal hydrostatic pressure. The result is that at the apex of the cell the tension of the membrane is strongest, therefore also the opportunity of growth greatest, *i.e.*, that the cell stretches most in the direction opposed to gravity, thus grows into a horizontal sac.—These experiments are well adapted to explain the most elementary processes of organic cell-growth and the partial dependence of the favoured direction of growth on the direction of gravity, on the mechanical side, in that they set up analogous, but also certainly only analogous, relations. For the difference is at once evident that in the organic cell-growth the nutritive matter is received from without, whilst here it is given to the cell as an internal store of gelatinous material, and the cell swells only through the absorption of water. The living cell contains the phases of youth, age, and death morphologically preformed in itself; the glue-cell is simply limited in its growth to the quantity of its given store of food; it does not die of decrepitude, but because it has emptied its food-reservoir (in case the membrane holds out so long). The organic cell lives by morphological and chemical moulting, *i.e.*, by change of matter; for that there is required, however, not merely reception of matter, but also excretion of matter. The glue-cell has no excretion of matter, and therefore no change of matter, *i.e.*, no life; there takes place in it no chemical, and still less a morphological moulting process. The only chemical reaction that takes place in it is the first precipitate and the subsequent gradual strengthening of the membrane; this process belongs, however, in the organic cells to the vital process only so far as secretion belongs to the vital process of an organism, and the secretion as such can just as little be called living as the shell of the snail, the web of the spider, or the urine of man are called a living part of these organisms. Like the Moneres, most cells pass their youth, when they are most alive and perform the chief part of their functions, without precipitating a membrane, and with the secretion of such an encysting-stage already begins, in which the living intercourse with the outer world is limited or entirely abolished. This excluding precipitated membrane is therefore as little as the calcareous capsule of the gargol or trichine to be considered a living part of the organism, but at the most as a *caput mortuum* of past vital action. That vital action was secretion; but secretion can only be considered a vital function when it occurs as result of the change of matter or of the moulting of a living organism, and we can never reason backwards from the external resemblance of a chemical superficial precipitate with the superficial secretion of living cells to a vital process, when the criterion of such, the regular and predetermined change of matter, is obviously wanting.—It seemed necessary to recall these important differences between the organic cell and the inorganic glue-cell in order to avert hasty conclusions, which might be drawn on the part of materialism from these in themselves extremely interesting experiments, although their contriver would certainly be least inclined to overlook, in their resemblance, the difference in principle of the two phenomena.

P. 328, l. 7.—Another distinguished botanist, N. Pringsheim, at the close of an examination of the connected series of forms of the Sphacelariæ, which leads from the simple Confervæ-like Ectocarpeæ through the genera Halopteris, Stypocaulon, &c., to the Cormophytes-like genus Cladostephus, expresses himself in the following manner (Transactions of the Physical Division of the Academy of Science of Berlin, 1873, extracted in the Naturf., 1874, No. 4): "Here a more favourable progressive adaptation of the variations to the life-conditions in which they have arisen is neither supposable nor demonstrable. The differences of form that arise nowhere exhibit distinct, physiologically advantageous peculiarities; they depend essentially on slight, gradual variations in anatomical structure, and in the position of the ramifying systems.—With these simple creatures this struggle (for existence) is limited to at the most a struggle for room. The only point that would here be of importance, the variety, the number, and the self-preserving power of the reproduced forms, speaks in no plain manner for the observance of the direction which the series has taken in its development. In contemplating these and other similar series among the lowest plants, we cannot fail to see that the first variations of form in these simplest organisms are of a *purely morphological* character, *i.e.*, that they have *no* demonstrable relation to any physiological functions whatever that are of *importance* for the maintenance of life. The existence of such purely morphological series appears to me decisive on the question as to the causes of the formation of species. Do not the series—not to go beyond the Algæ—of the Protococcaceæ, Palmellaceæ, Desmidiaceæ, Diatomeæ, Confervæ, Ulothritheæ, Ceramieæ, Polysphonieæ, &c., consist of such purely morphological species *in direct contradiction* to the Darwinian theory? Yet in all these series an *evolution* of the forms, proceeding from the simple to the complex, from the imperfect to the perfect, is unmistakable. Thus these lower purely morphological series decidedly tell in favour of the view, that the struggle for existence *does not of itself suffice* to explain the accumulation of the form-variations in a *constant direction* from the simple to the manifold through the whole created series. This struggle presupposes, indeed, of necessity, the physiologically more favourable nature of the arising variations, and the accumulation of these favourable qualities in the favoured direction. These conditions are, however, *wanting* in the development of the purely morphological series of species of the lowest plants. Here those *internal guiding forces* which urge on the development of the ever-accumulating variations in the favoured direction appear *in their purity*, unmixed with the effects of the struggle for existence, and do not allow a doubt of their existence."

P. 328, l. 19.—Another zoologist, Moritz Wagner, is, equally with Kölliker, an adherent of the theory of Descent, but at the same time regards the theory of Natural Selection as not merely of itself insufficient, but even false and wholly worthless. Now this is manifestly too extreme an opposition; but the arguments against the Darwinian over-estimate of the theory of Natural Selection which Wagner has marshalled in various treatises, and recently in "Ausland" (1875, May to July), are at all events well worthy of notice. His view is, that the local separation of several or a few individuals of an existing species is not only, as also Darwin admits, a favourable circumstance for the origin of a new species, but the indispensable condition, and at the same time forms the sufficient cause of this occurrence. If even his assumption were true, that the return of the novel variation into the stock by crossing is to be prevented by *no other* means than by local separation of one or several pairs (which at all events is still unproven), yet the separation could always only be condition, but never cause of the formation of a new species, and the question, which principle positively calls forth those important variations of separated individuals that are merely protected from destruction by separation, would still remain open after as before. The very examples cited by Wagner are such, that a recession to Geoffroy's principle of the influence of changed external circumstances on the organism must here appear still more insufficient than the Darwinian insistance on the principle of selection; and that Wagner too, when perfecting his "Seclusion Theory" on the *positive* side, must necessarily come to recognise "inner guiding forces" as an "indwelling tendency of development," *i.e.*, an organising principle determining the direction of the variation.

P. 329, l. 24.—The conjecture here thrown out by me has in the meantime been verified by a discovery of the marine apothecary, A. Bavay, in the volcanic rocky island Guadeloupe, according to which a species of small frogs (*Hylodes martiniecnsis*), found there in great abundance owing to the absence of marshes and fresh water for their life as tadpoles, simply pass through the tadpole-stage within the ovum, and emerge from the shell complete tailless little frogs ("Naturforscher," 1873, No. 17). In this particular case, the putting back of the metamorphosis into the embryonic life has certainly led to no further development-series of higher organisms; but the example offers us at least an analogy, according to which those reptiles also, from which the higher orders of the animal kingdom have sprung, may have developed from amphibia.

P. 331.—Comp. with this chapter my book "Wahrheit und Irrthum im Darwinismus; eine kritische Darstellung der organischen Entwickelungstheorie," Berlin, Carl Duncker, 1875.

P. 334, l. 14.—Comp. my "Erläuterungen zur Metaphysik d. Unbew.," p. 52–57.

P. 344, l. 29.—Comp. with this section my "Erläuterungen zur Metaphysik d. Unbew.," p. 57–74.

VOL. III.

P. 4, l. 16, and in A. Taubert, "Der Pessimismus und seine Gegner" (Berlin, C. Duncker, 1873), p. 70–76. That even Hegelianism is an evolutionism not hostile to, but inclusive of Pessimism; that it only views with a too hard and cold indifference the crushing of innumerable individual destinies by the iron wheel of historical progress, but at the same time recognises the tragic fate of everything finite to be consumed in the contradiction of its own existence, has been excellently shown by J. Volkelt ("Das Unbew. u. d. Pess.," p. 246–255).

P. 12, l. 3.—Comp. here Taubert, "Der Pessimismus und seine Gegner," No. 2, "The worth of life and its estimation."

P. 13, last l. but one.—Comp. Taubert's "Pessimismus," p. 27–28.

P. 15, l. 15.—Or if an unconscious will should actually exist, it is yet too weak to render itself observable by its non-satisfaction; and we may conclude *a fortiori* that *this* degree of will must be too weak to make itself perceptible by its satisfaction.

P. 27, l. 17.—Comp. with this section Taubert's "Pessimismus," No. 3, "The privative goods and work."

P. 41, l. 4.—Comp. also vol. i. p. 241, l. 20. Only unfortunately the point of view of the reconciliation of instinct with a consciousness enlightened by a philosophic monism still remains a *theoretical postulate*, that in *practical* reference must be realised by continuous conflict and ethical wrestling with an unbroken and persistent egoism. The reconciliation which philosophy offers, the ethicising of natural impulse, is no possession to be acquired once for all and then maintained without effort, but it is the enduring struggle of the reason of the All-one Unconscious arrived at consciousness with the necessarily given selfishness of natural individuality, which only when waged with energetic untiring zeal, and favoured by the bent of the original character, leads to the habitual harmony of virtue. This is, however, not to be supposed the ordinary point of view of human consciousness at the present time any more than is the naïve, still perfectly unbroken sway of natural instinct; rather is the discordancy of individual consciousness and its selfishness with the demands reaching beyond the individual of the instinctive and the philosophical reason to be regarded as the normal condition, whether this disharmony is only beginning to show itself in the innocence of native ingenuousness, whether it has developed to the bitter length of an apparently inextinguishable conflict; or, lastly, whether with the postulate of the subordination of the individual will to the All-Will a final solution and the method of reconciliation are revealed. And just because each fresh human being has always anew the destiny to give birth to and to conquer this discord in himself, because, however, the conquest is wont soonest to succeed when it has *behind* it the struggle of youth (which is the proper time of sexual love), I thought myself warranted in my examination in assuming the *discord* of the conscious individual will with the unconscious purpose as the empirically given normal condition (comp. vol. i. p. 232).

P. 41, l. 8.—Comp. on this section Taubert's "Pessimismus," No. 4, "Love."

P. 42, l. 2.—Comp. Taubert's "Pessimismus," No. 5, "Compassion."

P. 48, l. 34.—Thus the instinct to contract marriage

and found a family, and the desire to possess and to rear children, appears one of a number of connected instincts that mock egoism with delusive expectations, but are of the utmost importance for the maintenance of the world-machinery and the progress of the world-process. As love has the purpose of *producing* the most capable succeeding generation possible, so the instinct to conclude a marriage and found a family serves to *educate* the generation thus produced to the utmost excellence possible. As long as it is an irrefragable truth that no foundling-hospital nurture and orphan-house education can replace the maternal care and family education, so long will all the revolutionary plans directed against the existence of marriage and the family be dashed to pieces on the unconscious reason of history; for however much they may demonstrate that (what admits of no doubt) marriage brings with it the greatest inconveniences and that (what is very doubtful) people would be better off with the abolition of this social arrangement, yet the comfort of the spouses comes only in quite a secondary fashion into the question as to the value of marriage, since the family does not primarily exist for the sake of the married couples, but for the sake of the *children*. Hence there lies hidden in the belief subjectively so unreasonable of the lovers in the imperishability of their love so deep an objective reason. This illusion is only the bait to lead egoism to sacrifice its freedom, by imposing upon itself the legal bond of a permanent social fellowship, to which without this illusion it would at least with far more difficulty submit.

P. 60, l. 31.—Comp. hereon Taubert's "Pessimismus," No. 7, "Happiness as virtue."

P. 66, l. 26.—Comp. here Taubert's "Pessimismus," No. 7, "Happiness as æsthetic view of the world," and No. 6, "Enjoyment of Nature."

P. 88, l. 8.—The most complete and searching "Critique of the Idea of Immortality" in a small compass of a strictly scientific character is to be found in Biedermann's

"Christliche Dogmatik" (§ 949–973), where it is shown that a *religious* interest has been taken in immortality by historical Christianity only by reason of erroneous suppositions, but that in truth the question as to continued existence after death is *indifferent* for religion, and cannot be answered otherwise than in the negative on the part of anthropology and metaphysics.

P. 88, l. 27.—Comp. also Taubert's "Pessimismus," No. 9, "Happiness hereafter."

P. 115, l. 2.—Comp. with this Taubert's "Pessimismus," No. 10, "Happiness as realisable in the future of the world."

P. 129, l. 22.—We see from this that the individual negation of Will, even if it could lead to any result, would yet only concern the concrete phenomenon, without ever altering the essential being underlying this phenomenon. But if the assertion should be seriously maintained that the individual negation of will can affect and deny the essence of the will to live itself, it would immediately follow on monistic suppositions that then the first individual actually accomplishing in himself the negation of will must annihilate the All-Will, the will to live in its absolute totality, *i.e.*, the whole world at a blow. This consequence even Schopenhauer sees himself compelled occasionally to admit. He says (W. as W. a. I., trans. by Haldane and Kemp, i. p. 167), after showing that the unity of the will is unaffected by the plurality of the stages of objectification and the number of individuals at any stage, as follows:—"We may therefore say that if, *per impossible*, a single real existence, even the most insignificant were to be entirely annihilated, the whole world would necessarily perish with it. The great mystic Angelus Silesius feels this when he says—

'I know God cannot live an instant without me,
He must give up the ghost if I should cease to be.'"

From this passage it is evident to him himself that such an assumption can only be made *per impossibile*. In his individual theory of redemption he has obviously left this impossibility out of sight, when he endeavours to maintain a difference in effect between suicide and an ascetic mortification of the body and of the will to live.

P. 142.—Comp. my "Erl. z. Met. d. Unb.," p. 33-35 and p. 74-80.

P. 154, last l.—Comp. my "Erl. z. Met. d. Unb.," p. 12-22.

P. 173, l. 32.—Comp. on the preceding section my "Erl. z. Met. d. Unb.," p. 35-40. V. Kirchmann has protested against the application of the calculus of probabilities in the case before us ("Princip. des Realismus," p. 46-47), because the principles of the calculus of probabilities are only admissible on the assumption of a regularly acting causality, which supposition is here not satisfied. In opposition to this, it is to be remarked that a rigid uniform causality excludes, on the contrary, all computation of probabilities, which latter rather presupposes the assumption of non-causal *chance*, and is altogether dependent thereon. Now we certainly know that chance apart from causality has no place within the world-process, and therefore the whole calculus of probabilities is in strictness based on a mere fiction. This fiction is only possible on account of the insufficiency of our knowledge of the causes acting in the concrete case, since with perfect knowledge of these we should no longer talk of probability, but of certainty. On the other hand, however, this fiction is indispensable for our cognition, since probability offers us the *only compensation* for the certainty we are always desiderating. That now in spite of its fictitious basis the calculus of probability yields results relatively so exact lies in this, that with a more frequent recurrence of the same event for the most part only a part of the co-operant causes remains constant; another part, however, is so far variable that the effects compensate one another more completely, the more frequently the event is repeated. The constant causes, which are seen to be such, can now not be the basis of the calculus of probability, since their effects must be assumed to be necessary; the variable causes that compensate one another, however, do not afford an opening for the calculus of probabilities, *because* they act in each single case with regular causality, but *rather precisely because* in a larger series of cases their action is neutralised, *i.e.*, because the same result turns out *as if no causality had acted at all, but as if the variations of the several cases had been purely accidental.* What is here within the world-process a mere fiction (which certainly is not only practically harmless, but even a positively useful surrogate of the true state of the case), is in the instance of the uncaused resolve of the Will to will perfect truth; the calculus of probabilities, which is only *abusively* applied to the properly strictly necessary events within the world-process, is *rightly* applicable in this unique example.

P. 184, l. 22.—The "Idea" means in this passage not (as V. Kirchmann misunderstands it—"Princ. d. Real.," p. 36–37) "the *whole* unconscious *mass* of representations of the first attribute," but the IDEA as logical formal principle, as *matrix* of an infinite possible unfolding of unconscious intuitions; for of an actual mass of representations there can of course be no question at the commencement of the process, when the Will seizes the Idea.

P. 186, l. 10.—Comp. with this the inquiries on the nature of causality in my memoir, "J. H. v. Kirchmann's erkenntnisstheoretischer Realismus," No. 15–22 (Berlin, C. Duncker).

P. 187, l. 32.—Comp. on this section my "Erl. z. Met. d. Unb.," p. 28–35.

P. 194, l. 3.—Comp. my "Erl. z. Met. d. Unb.," p. 22–28.

PRINTED BY BALLANTYNE, HANSON, AND CO.
EDINBURGH AND LONDON.

www.ingramcontent.com/pod-product-compliance
Lightning Source LLC
Chambersburg PA
CBHW030916270326
41929CB00008B/718

* 9 7 8 3 3 3 7 0 7 8 1 2 6 *